Nationalism and Social Theory

BSA *New Horizons in Sociology*

The British Sociological Association is publishing a series of books to review the state of the discipline at the beginning of the millennium. *New Horizons in Sociology* also seeks to locate the contribution of British scholarship to the wider development of sociology. Sociology is taught in all the major institutions of higher education in the United Kingdom as well as throughout North America and the Europe of the former western bloc. Sociology is now establishing itself in the former eastern bloc. But it was only in the second half of the twentieth century that sociology moved from the fringes of UK academic life into the mainstream. British sociology has also provided a home for movements that have renewed and challenged the discipline; the revival of academic Marxism, the renaissance in feminist theory, the rise of cultural studies, for example. Some of these developments have become sub-disciplines whilst yet others have challenged the very basis of the sociological enterprise. Each has left their mark. Now therefore is a good time both to take stock and to scan the horizon, looking back and looking forward.

Nationalism and Social Theory

Modernity and the Recalcitrance of the Nation

Gerard Delanty *and* Patrick O'Mahony

SAGE Publications
London • Thousand Oaks • New Delhi

SAGE Publications Ltd
6 Bonhill Street
London EC2A 4PU

SAGE Publications Inc
2455 Teller Road
Thousand Oaks, California 91320

SAGE Publications India Pvt Ltd
32, M-Block Market
Greater Kailash - I
New Delhi 110 048

British Library Cataloguing in Publication data

A catalogue record for this book is available from
the British Library

ISBN 0 7619 5450 3
    0 7619 5451 1

Library of Congress control number available

Typeset by SIVA Math Setters, Chennai, India
Printed in Great Britain by The Cromwell Press Ltd,
Trowbridge, Wiltshire

Patriotism is the last refuge of scoundrels

Samuel Johnson [1775]

A nation is a group of persons united by a common error about their ancestry and a common dislike of their neighbours

Karl Deutsch [1969]

contents

introduction

It has often been repeated in recent scholarship that the study of nationalism had been neglected in the social sciences until the last 20 years or so. This viewpoint is coupled with the contention that the social sciences as theoretically oriented and practically applied to that point in time were not really equipped for the task of analysing nationalism. Perhaps, even more fundamentally, given their focus on other dimensions of social life assumed to have greater centrality to the study of social order, such as the differentiation of institutions or the interplay of social classes, it began to look in the eyes of many critics that the social sciences were not even equipped to notice such phenomena.

On the surface, this does indeed seem an extraordinary state of affairs. It could hardly be denied that the other objects of theory and research that social and political theorists did consider after World War Two were profoundly influenced by their embedding in national institutional orders and that these very orders themselves were susceptible to immense turbulence affecting every aspect of social life. A mere glance backwards at what were then very recent events, when the world was destroyed and reshaped by nationalism would have seemed to offer incontrovertible evidence of its centrality to social and political life.

Even though the circumstances of the First World War did make Emile Durkheim and Max Weber adopt patriotic stances on particular issues, they never incorporated nationalism into their respective theories of modernity. In the case of Weber, his concern with disenchantment as the central logic in European modernity led him to give only limited attention to forms of enchantment, like nationalism, that modernity itself creates. Aside from charisma there is little enchantment in the modern rationalization of life conduct. Durkheim, who was attentive to the powerful role of collective representations in modern society, did not address nationalism, believing that a civic morality based on citizenship would eventually become the dominant form of solidarity in modernity. He believed that the cosmopolitanism of Europe would override any narrow forms of collective identity, and that something like a European identity would emerge. To an extent, Parsons gave greater recognition to nationalism in the making of modernity. However, given the presuppositions of structural functionalism, he failed to recognize the tendency of nationalism to cause disintegration, seeing it as largely integrative and subordinate to what he called the 'societal community'. It remained a fundamental assumption of Parsonian structural functionalism that societal differentiation was held in check by integrative structures, such as culture. That culture might be anarchic rather than a force of stability was rarely questioned in modern social and political thought from Matthew Arnold through Durkheim and Weber to Parsons.

It would take a full length study in itself to understand how it was that social and political theory did not take its departure pessimistically from the twentieth-century experience of war but instead proceeded optimistically, at least in the mainstream version of modernization theory, from the apparent stability of the post-war order.[1] Without doubt this owed much to the fact that while the world wars of the twentieth century had been traumatic for all participants, and convulsed the entire world, there were, in the end, victors and losers. Not simply were there victors and losers but unprecedented moral blame could be attached to the losers for their actions of genocide. The victors, as theorized by modernization theory, saw the results of war as the triumph of their tolerant liberal and democratic civilization. This civilization was also organized into nations but these nations stood for greater civilizational values than those of nationality itself. The nation form could be seen as contingent, the values that some nations carried as enduring and fated to succeed on a global stage. The assumption, thus, was that nationalism was subordinated to the universalistic normative order of western civilization.

This standpoint was clearly reflected in the research programmes that came to prominence in the post-war United States, which in this period took over a certain leadership in social and political theory. These research programmes, whether in the form of research on political culture, research on media effects or in the progressive contribution of institutional differentiation, embodied a profound confidence in the values and social practices present in the civil society of the United States and other English-speaking countries. In the tradition of political culture research, for example, the values found to be present in the 'civic cultures' of the United States and other English-speaking countries were considered to account for the survival of democracy in those countries, in contrast to the findings from those countries in which liberal democracy had either failed or had not yet been instituted. In pivotal aspects of the social transitions created by the dislocations of war, structural disadvantage and revolution, the prescriptions of this optimistic reading of the cultural achievements of civil society and the structural differentiation which it supported could be applied. Examples include the post-war transitions to democracy in Germany, Italy and Japan, the modernization of the underdeveloped world and, most recently, the 'catching-up' processes unleashed by the fall of communism in Central and Eastern Europe.

In seeking to understand these developments, it may well be important that the theoretical frameworks and research programmes of this period 'solved' certain problem complexes of the social sciences in ways that were consistent with the professional aspiration of social scientists in the United States and, increasingly, in Europe. These frameworks and programmes were built, firstly, on the separation of the enduring organizational principles of a civilized society from the contingency of historical dynamics. The social sciences were concerned with the results of historical processes that could be teleologically reconstructed to tell the dominant western narrative of institutional differentiation, and the corresponding intermeshing of cultures and roles, within the framework of democratic regulation by the people. The social sciences could proceed to refine this standard, which was viewed as the historically confirmed outcome of modernization processes.

They were built, second, on the idea that the social sciences were not acting normatively, in the sense of partisans in arguments, but only normatively in the sense of demonstrating the 'functional' necessity of what had to be the case if all societies were to become both modern and democratic. Although this was a very strong normative – almost ideological – programme indeed, as its critics never ceased to point out, modernization theory could still convince itself that such a normative stance was not inconsistent with the aspiration to value neutrality by the social sciences. It could do this ultimately by recourse to an evolutionary account of modernization as the single correct way to get the desired result of a civilized society. The legitimacy of the modernization account of structural-functional theory was not attributed by its theorists to a normatively held conviction about the good life; it claimed to rest rather on the capacity to identify evolutionary trends and to explore their ramifications for social systems. Such a functionally cloaked normative stance attributed a role to culture as the binding glue of institutional stability rather than the contradictory, dynamic and malleable medium of conceptualizing change. This had the effect of inhibiting the exploration of cultural dynamics. Frameworks such as Parsons's pattern variables, documenting the transition from traditional to modern society, or Merton's fourfold account of the culture of modern science, appear as extremely strong idealizations that document a normatively desirable state of affairs rather than provide an account of actual practices. Even though such frameworks did contain substantial truth and orienting value, they normatively pre-decided issues that remained empirically open.

Finally, the frameworks and programmes of modernization theory that had diminished the significance of historical process, and normatively short-circuited culture, almost inevitably also diminished the potential of agency as a transforming or creative capacity. In functionalist theory, agency is on the whole reduced to the fulfillment of roles within a formal-rational institutional order. The institutional theoretic accomplishment of functionalism was used to delineate an almost stationary state theory of social order in which certain populations carry just those values and competencies required to maintain a complex and highly adapted institutional system that in turn incorporates just those preferences such a population would require. The assumptions about the stability of such a society render the question of action within systems of far greater relevance than actions that are intentionally or unintentionally oriented to changing them.

The chief academic rival of structural-functionalism from the late 1960s through to the early 1980s was a revitalized Marxism. In certain respects, the manifold theoretical currents of this academic movement did pose questions that lay beyond the framework of its rival. Its conception of class domination arising from control of the dominant form of structural differentiation, the division of labour, emphasized how the projects of collective actors mattered historically. The reciprocal concept of proletarian praxis also emphasized how system-transforming collective agency was possible and even explored how it worked or should work. Through its exploration of the relationship between ideology and social power, Marxism viewed norm building as a process of generalized deception and explored resistance to such assumed deception. In its theorization of historical change, the theory of the succession of modes of production, Marxism explored the dynamics of historical change, an exploration that could not assume some putative state of the 'end of history' since further transformation was required to reach the desired end state of a just, socialist order.

However much such Marxist theorizing normatively disagreed with the system-confirming assumptions of structural-functionalism, it shared with the latter theory tradition a set of assumptions that were highly restricting. Although it accorded more attention to the reciprocal dynamics of history and evolution, its account of historical processes could ultimately be led back to a theory of structural adaptation through the mode of production. Individual and collective agency were correspondingly subsumed within the functional roles required by this motor of historical development. The functional rendering of the categories of collective action – bourgeois elites and their proletarian opponents were alike derived from their position in the mode of production – did not lead, despite the dialectical ontology of Marxism, to an account of agency as a creative process.

The western Marxist tradition inherited the assumption of the 'withering away of the state', and this undertheorization of the state inevitably led to a neglect of national identity as well as of nationalism as a movement. For Marx, nationalism was the natural ally of socialism.[2] The events of the first half of the twentieth century were to show that nationalism was by no means a secondary force. The national question often overshadowed the social question, the rights of the nation, social rights and historical justice, and social justice. Although figures such as Lukacs and the Frankfurt School writers responded to the reification of class consciousness by national consciousness with a cultural critique of ideology, a theory of nationalism was not the result. Instead the focus for critical theory shifted to the study of political authoritarianism and fascism. With the emergence of new social movements in the 1970s and the subsequent redirection of critical theory by Habermas in this period, nationalism did not receive much attention.

The result of all this was that nationalism tended to be a marginal part of mainstream sociological theory and political science.[3] As we have noted, Marxist sociology proved unable to offer a convincing account, and within mainstream sociology there were few signs of the recognition of nationalism as a potent force. In this, Raymond Aron, writing in 1968, was an exception: 'During the final third of the 20th century, ethnic conflicts over social, political, or racial dominance – in turn or simultaneously – appear to be more likely than the continuation of the class struggle in the Marxist sense' (Aron, 1968, p. 46). It is true, of course, that a significant body of literature in social and political science was written on nationalism by such authors as Ernst Gellner, Eugene Kamenka, Hans Kohn, Kenneth Minogue, Elie Kedourie, George Mosse, Hugh Seton-Watson and Anthony Smith, but nationalism was never central to the conception of modernity in social and political theory.[4] As is best reflected in the seminal work of Ernst Gellner, the theory of nationalism was, at most, part of a broader theory of liberal modernity, but one that did not call into question some of the central assumptions of modernization theory that made nationalism appear derivative.

Thus when nationalism became a major international issue in the wake of the fall of communism from 1989 onwards, the dominant theoretical approaches were redundant. In any case, a whole range of new theoretical movements had arisen in the course of the 1980s, ranging from postmodernism, to globalization theory, new social movement theory, rational choice, systems theory, constructivism, postcolonialism and feminism. The result of these theoretical innovations – which were broadly products of a new cultural and historical turn in the social sciences – was a revitalization of social theory, which was not dominated by a narrow sociological theory but embraced wider theoretical developments in the social sciences, history and philosophy. It is in this tradition of the social theory of modernity that this book is written. However, it was apparent that most of the major social theories of the 1980s and 1990s did not fully address nationalism. Despite the salience of the topic, very few of the major works on modernity have given much attention to it, despite the relatively large literature on the subject. This may be in part explained by the fact that in classical social theory, nationalism was of secondary importance. Another explanation is that much of recent social and political theory has been heavily influenced by new social movement theory and does not address other anti-systemic movements. Nationalist movements have not been central to new social movement theory, which has mostly focused on the 'new' movements in western societies, such as the peace movements, civil society movements, the environmental and feminist movement. Nationalism, if it figured at all, tended to be regarded as a residue of the old regional nationalism.[5]

As we argue in Chapter 1, neither classical nor modern social theory paid a great deal of attention to the role of violence in modernity. Aside from the theory of fascism in the early Frankfurt School, most of the major social theorists saw modernity in terms of the progressive institutionalization of modern structures of consciousness. Even though Parsons gave attention to German fascism and was actively involved in trying to get the United States into the war, it was never central to his sociological edifice. Of course, the violence of World War Two figured in the work of such figures as C.W. Mills and Alvin Gouldner, but never became central to post-war sociological theory which moved to different concerns. Habermas's theory of modernity in his major work, published in 1981, *Theory of Communicative Action*, while making some interesting suggestions about the formation of nationalism as a 'second generation ideology' of bourgeois society, clearly saw nationalism as subordinate and irrelevant to the new cosmopolitanism of such movements as feminism and the environmental movement (Habermas, 1987a, pp. 353–4). A theory of nationalism did not fit easily into a view of rosy modernity as a progressive unfolding of communicative ratio-nalities. The central conflict in modernity was on the whole seen as one between instrumentalism and the defence of the life-world conducted by modern social movements. Nationalism thus did not figure in this con-struction of modernity, which tended not to question the nation-state as the geopolitical reference for the project of modernity.[6] It is of course clear that Habermas has modified his neglect of nationalism in recent works, such as the *Postnational Constellation* and the essays from the late 1980s on the historians' debate in Germany (Habermas, 1989c, 1994, 2001).

Anthony Giddens's writing on the nation-state and violence should also be mentioned in this context in an attempt to re-orientate sociology away from an exclusive concern with class power towards a focus on such issues as violence, militarism and surveillance in modernity (Giddens, 1985). However, Giddens's concern was more with the nation-state than with nationalism as such and cultural conceptions of nationhood did not figure. Nationalism in the more destructive sense of authoritarian communitarianism has also become more central to the later work of Alain Touraine (Touraine, 1995). It is the merit of S.N. Eisenstadt and Johann Arnason that they have attempted to redirect the study of nationalism as part of a wider and globally oriented conception of modernity (Arnason, 1990; Eisenstadt, 1999b).[7]

The analysis offered in this book follows Arnason and Eisenstadt's lead in theorizing nationalism as central to modernity, and not as an aberrant, inexplicable force. In many ways nationalism expressed some of the most powerful forces within the modern project, in particular it was an expression of the preoccupation with radical freedom in modernity. This received its most powerful expression in the Jacobin idea that modernity can endlessly transform itself through the actions of political elites, but it was also present in the republican vision of the self-determination of civil society. In one way or another these concepts of politics shaped the political project of modern nationalism in all its faces, liberal, romanticist and authoritarian. But the triumph of nationalism was ultimately not secured by the force of radical freedom and the triumph of the political, but by the ability of nationalism to combine the political and the cultural project of modernity in everyday life. Nationalism was the most successful major political discourse in modernity in this regard. Liberalism and other political ideologies – with the exception of communism – never set out to change the nature of everyday life. No modern political ideology has succeeded, to the extent nationalism has, in bringing the projects of political elites into everyday life, an expression of the intimate relationship between the appeal of nationalist ideology and the legitimation of political power in modernity.

Although nationalism has played a major role in modernity and has to be counted as one of the dominant forms of realizing collective identity, the idea of national identity is sometimes overextended. The identity marker of nationality is used to distinguish who should enjoy the privileges and responsibilities of belonging to a particular state. But the existential centrality of nationality in this fundamental sense does not mean, as is often suggested, that nationality is automatically the overarching identity of civil society. In this book we do not see national identity as the fundamental collective identity of modern society and therefore we disagree with the positions of writers on nationalism, such as Liah Greenfeld (1992) and Anthony Smith (1995). Neither do we see nationalism as a coherent ideology that has persisted because of its persuasive appeal. Nationalism is rather to be conceived as a semantic space, that expresses through manifold discourses the many kinds of projects, identities, interests and ideologies that make it up.[8] In fact the history of nationalism can be viewed as one of the constant recombination of ever-shifting modalities of thinking and feeling about society. What has made it a recalcitrant force in modernity is the persistence of certain key problems. The most enduring of these are those of conflicting expressions of nationhood and statehood. On the one side, the idea of the nation gave expression to the ideas of self-determination and of radical freedom while, on the other side, of the institutional reality of statehood frequently conflicted with the mobilizing thrust of nationhood. The first of these might be conceptualized in terms of Cornelius Castoriadis's notion of the 'radical imaginary' and the second in terms of the 'institutional imaginary', as outlined in his famous book, *The Imaginary Institution of Society* (Castoriadis, 1987). Nationhood gave expression to the open and radical idea of a society based on radical self-determination, while the institutional reality of the modern nation-state fostered a 'conservative' identification with the status quo. As a quintessentially modern form of dual collective identity based on radical and institutionalized imaginaries, we can thus see nationalism as having continued mobilizing appeal in the expression of nationhood as it also has institutional significance for statehood. This is an expression, continuing to the present day, of the most fundamental tension in modernity: the tension between the mobilizing power of collective agency and the quest for freedom and autonomy on the one side and, on the other, the institutional structures that modernity has created in which radical agency is tamed, although in the case of the recalcitrant phenomenon of nationalism, never entirely.

xvi

There are four aims in this book. Our most general aim is to situate nationalism in the context of the social transformations of modernity. Our second aim is to address nationalism from a comparative perspective. To achieve this the theorization of modernity must be capable of taking account of multiple modernities. Our third aim is to offer a critical synthesis of the existing literature on nationalism. The fourth aim is to relate nationalism to recent debates about cosmopolitanism. In this context, we ask the question whether nations without nationalism are possible. In Chapter 1 the basic ideas of a working social social theory of modernity are presented. The argument is that modernity can be best understood in terms of four dynamics, which we term: state formation, democratization, capitalism and the rationalization of culture. In Chapter 2, beginning from the logic of differentiation and integration contained in these four dynamics, we present nationalism as a form of dual collective identity, mobilizing and institutional. In the following three Chapters (3, 4 and 5), drawing from key texts on nationalism, structural, interpretive and mobilization theory, traditions and research are examined. In this exercise, the recalcitrance of nationalism as both a mobilizing and institutional force will be situated in the wider context of other movements and forces in modernity. In Chapter 6, a typology of nationalism is developed that leads into an account of the dominant eras of nationalism over the last two centuries. Chapter 7 deals with the rise of the new radical nationalisms, ranging from the new radical right in Western Europe and radical ethnic nationalisms in the former communist countries, to radical religious nationalism in Asia. Chapter 8 looks at the limits and possibilities of cosmopolitanism as a viable alternative. In this context the question of nations without nationalism is discussed.

NOTES

1 The recent work of Hans Joas marks a move in this direction (see Joas, 2000). See the special issue of the *European Journal of Social Theory* on war and social theory (Delanty et al., 2001).

2 For a critical account of nationalism Marxism and classical sociology, see James (1996).

3 The rise of postcolonial theory, which to an extent put nationalism back on the agenda, tended to confine the discussion of nationalism to cultural studies, having only a marginal impact on social science.

4 An interesting exception is Tiryakian and Nevitte (1985).

5 See, for an example, Johnston (1994) who takes this view, but Melucci and Diani (1983) for whom new social movement theory is applied to the new regionalist nationalism. In the work of Manuel Castells (1997), nationalism has become much more emphasized (see Chapter 8).

6 In recent times there is more questioning of nationally specific disciplinary traditions (Delanty, 2001a); Levine, 1996).

7 See also Chapter 5 of Poole (1995).

8 See Wodak et al. (1999) for a similar conception of nationalism as discursively constructed.

one

modernity, nationalism and social theory: a general outline

The aim of this chapter is to provide a working theory of modernity which will serve as a framework for locating nationalism in the modern world. For present purposes, a general conception of nationalism is used and the concept will be treated in a more differentiated manner in the following chapters. As noted in the introduction, despite the huge recent interest in both nationalism and modernity, the respective bodies of literature have not been brought together. The social theory of modernity has, on the whole, been blind to one of the most significant forces in modernity.

The idea of modernity has become one of the most discussed concepts in social and political theory over the last two decades, and it would appear to continue to have more contemporary relevance than postmodernism (which is now no longer seen as a major rupture but a moment within modernity).[1] While this has led to some important new insights about social change, in many accounts this has been at the cost of a loss in the explanatory power of theoretical analysis for social science, due perhaps in part to overtheorization resulting from the combination of sociology, philosophy and political theory that has been characteristic of social theory. The theory of modernity may be said to be one of the central debates in social theory in the specific sense of a combination of these three areas.[2] In our view this historically informed social theory of modernity can offer an important contribution to the analysis of some of the key features of modern society, such as nationalism.

The theory of modernity has been inspired by the historical and cultural turn in the social sciences over the last two decades. Modernity thus has a historical dimension to it but one that is conceived in terms of a 'history of the present'. Combining insights from philosophy, political theory and sociology, the social theory of modernity can be seen as an attempt to theorize the current situation in light of long-term social transformations. Such questions as the significance of globalization, postmodernity, multiple modernities and new social movements have dominated the agenda of the new social theory of modernity.

In the following, modernity is discussed, first, as a historical process driven by civilizational constellations; second, a more philosophical definition is offered by looking at some of the ideals of modernity as a cultural project; third, a sociological definition is given with a focus on some of the key institutional dynamics of modernity; and fourth, the problem of symbolic violence and radical freedom in modernity is discussed in relation to nationalism.

MODERNITY AND CIVILIZATIONAL PROCESSES

There is some advantage to be gained by beginning with a historical perspective, since modernity, while not being reducible to a particular historical epoch, is a historically constituted project. In order to avoid a crude reduction of modernity to something like 'modern history' that is counter-opposed to the 'medieval' or 'ancient' periods, we should see it as a developmental process that is driven by distinct processes, dynamics, conflicts and conceptions of the world. In this way we can avoid seeing modernity as a historical era that is defined by the categories of western history, which become absurd when applied to societies with very different histories. Thus Max Weber believed the roots of modernity lay in the process of rationalization that began with the overcoming of magic by organized religion and the emergence of intellectualized explanations of suffering. Other sociologists such as those in the functionalist tradition, from Spencer to Parsons, tended to emphasize modernity as the outcome of the process of differentiation. A more comprehensive interpretation might be that modernity emerged out of civilizational processes, in the sense of long-run historical logics of development that culminate in the condition of 'permanent revolution' that characterizes modernity. This presupposes an approach associated with that of Norbert Elias that stresses the formation of civilization in terms of process rather than structure (Elias, 1978, 1982). While Elias by and large did not go beyond western nation-states in his comparative account and was not primarily interested in the global context, other approaches ranging from the Annales school to the work of theorists such as S.N. Eisenstadt and Johann Arnason provide the foundations of a comparative civilizational analysis of the foundations of modernity.

Following Eisenstadt, the first major impetus of modernity arises from processes of augmented globalization that set in most parts of the world, from Europe to the Americas, to Asia and much of Africa, with the decline of the civilizations based on the universalistic religions of the world.[3] It is important to state that this is not a Eurocentric conception of modernity since modernity has impacted on all the universalistic civilizations of the world in ways that were endogenously, as well as externally induced.[4] In several cases the impact of modernity did not come until the twentieth century and in many other cases, of which contemporary China might be an example, modernity took at least two forms, one driven by communist reconstruction and a contemporary one involving the reconstruction of that earlier project in the response to globalization. In this view modernity is a radical transformation of the great civilizations of the world whose universalistic cultures it partly took over and transformed. In its most elemental form, modernity is nothing more than the permanent instutionalization of social change and cultural transformation by globalized communication. It is the nature of modernity that is a global force. By global means a more attenuated condition than merely universalism and, as has often been argued, globalization is as likely to lead to particularism as to homogenization.[5] Globalization is characterized by the diminishing significance of space and time as the world becomes more connected. The shrinking of time and space does not make the world more and more homogeneous. The result can equally well be fragmentation, the strengthening of the periphery and the appropriation of the global by the local. Globalization, so much discussed in recent times, is of course not particular to the current situation but has been a force in the world since the early civilizations. These civilizations integrated many social units under the aegis of imperial systems of statehood, formal law and universalistic religions based on written texts and a trained priesthood. However, despite the diffusion of the new systems of communication, the integration of peripheries by the centre and the emergence of new elites, globalization did not become a significant development until the last five centuries, when the pace of social change increased – due to developments in trade, technology, migrations of people, communications, warfare and science – and as a result many civilizations became more and more interconnected. The outcome of this upheaval was modernity. Modernity is global, not necessarily universal, in the sense that modernity is culturally appropriated in different ways. Aside from the globality of modernity, there is the fact of its multiple forms and different trajectories (Delanty, 2002c; Eisenstadt, 2000b; Featherstone et al., 1995; Wittrock, 1998). Indeed, as will be argued later in this book, the varieties of nationalism are partly a response to the different paces of modernity. As a historical condition, modernity is characterized primarily by global intercultural communication and the resulting pluralization of cultures.[6]

This conception of modernity presupposes a civilizational analysis, since the claim that is being made is that modernity in its first crystallization emerged out of the earlier civilizational constellations which gave it its basic impetus. Following Eisenstadt, Axial Age civilizations can be identified as emerging between 500BCE to the first century CE when innovative ontological and transcendental visions of the world were formulated and gradually institutionalized in the major world religions, in Judaism and Christianity, Ancient Greece, Zoroastrian Iran, early imperial China, Hinduism, Buddhism and Islam. In different ways and at different times these civilizations either collapsed or were greatly reconstituted by modernity, which formed out of the ruins of the earlier civilizations and was accordingly shaped by the different civilizational constellations. In line with the Weberian theory of modernity, it may be added that some of the civilizations were more conducive to modernity than others (Schluchter, 1985). By conceiving of modernity in this manner, the problem of reconciling tradition and modernity is largely solved, since modernity succeeds not tradition but civilizational constellations. Modernity in fact produces tradition and with it the conditions for nationalism.[7]

Although there is a tendency to conflate modernity with European developments, including westernization, modernity can be seen as a distinct condition, for globalization has not led to a single global order. While modernity is not to be reduced to a particular historical era, it is a historical condition and therefore there is little point in looking for modernity in, for example, ancient Rome or early imperial China. While traces of modernity, including components of its cultural models and geopolitical contours have clear origins in the Axial Age civilizations, modernity is a post-civilizational condition.

In Western Europe, modernity became a significant force with the gradual decline of Christendom in the wake of the Renaissance, the age of discovery and the scientific revolution. In the period from the sixteenth century to the nineteenth century modernity emerges out of the ruins of the Christian civilization of the Middle Ages, just as that civilization inherited the mantle of Greco-Roman civilization. Modernity was thus not a total break from the occidental European civilization; it inherited the universalistic mantle of Christendom and of science, which became detached from the Christian worldview. The concrete form that modernity took in Western Europe, expressed most seriously in developments arising from the Enlightenment onwards, represents one of its most pervasive forms. In other parts of the world modernity unfolded often as a result of the impact of western modernity but often too as a result of the internal dynamics of change inherent in the different civilizational constellations. However, even within Europe modernity took at least three major routes, which can be traced back to the principal civilizational constellations: Occidental Christendom, Eastern Orthodox Byzantine and the Ottoman Islamic tradition.

In sum, globalization can be seen as a civilizational process, in the sense of a long-run historical process whose origins lie deep in the civilizational complexes that preceded modernity. Other such processes are those of rationalization and differentiation, which while being intensified in modernity originate in pre-modern societies. Globalization, and the pluralization of cultures that it brings in its wake, while being older than modernity is one of the most important pace makers of social change leading to the formation of modernity.

THE CULTURAL MODELS OF MODERNITY

One of the main expressions of modernity is in its cultural model, that is its self-interpretation and vision of the world. This question of the consciousness of modernity has been the focus of many works of a largely philosophical nature on the idea of modernity, as in the writings of, for instance, Habermas, Castoriadis, Touraine and Arendt (Delanty, 2000b). The idea of modernity for many theorists refers less to 'modern society' or something more general such as 'the modern age' than to a particular spirit, consciousness, or ethos. Modernity in this sense is a 'discourse' or a 'consciouness', often denoting what for writers from Marx to Baudelaire was the permanent revolution of modern society. The spirit of radical modernism that 'all that is solid melts in air', as in the famous motif of the *Communist Manifesto*, suggests a conception of modernity as the self-consciousness of the dynamism of industrial society (Berman, 1982). The modernist movement in art and literature made this experience integral to the modernist aesthetic. Thus, for Baudelaire, modernity is expressed in the search after 'the fugitive, fleeting beauty of present-day life, the distinguishing character of that quality which, with the reader's kind permission, we have called "modernity"' (Baudelaire, 1964, p. 40). In these writings and others, such as Simmels's, modernity refers to particular kinds of experience, including, too, cognitive experiences, in the sense of the ways people gain knowledge of their society.[8]

Cultural interpretation systems mediate individuals' experience and wider social reality. Literature, art and philosophy can be seen as mediating discourses in this sense, operating on a higher and more reflective level than the discourse of everyday life. Nationalism is important in this respect, for it is discourse that mediates human experience in modernity in ways that are tuned into everyday life. Indeed, nationalism was possibly the first major discourse of modernity actually to penetrate everyday life. What is important to note for the moment is that modernity entails a reflexive moment. As Habermas has argued, whether in the high or in the low cultures, such reflexive moments are built into the cultural project of modernity from the Enlightenment onwards. The 'philosophical discourse of modernity', to take the title of one of Habermas's works, is a discourse produced by modernity about itself

5

(Habermas, 1987b). Although this approach to modernity – which combines sociology and philosophy – is primarily a reading of the history of intellectual constructions, it offers some important insights into the 'quasi-transcendental' structures that underlie modern societies. Thus in Habermas's social theory the cultural models of society actualized in communication draw from, and reconstitute, the basic structures of the modern, rationalized lifeworld. In the case of Touraine's social theory, cultural models are related to the capacity of society to act upon itself (Habermas, 1984, 1987a; Touraine, 1977). In the terms of Castoriadis's social theory, modernity concerns the struggle of the open horizon of the radical imaginary against the closed institutional imaginary (Castoriadis, 1987). In the present context it will suffice to state that the critical issue concerns the composition of the cultural models of modernity and how these relate to nationalism.

By cultural models is meant, then, the basic cognitive, normative, symbolic and aesthetic structures underlying the consciousness of modern societies. Drawing from a model developed elsewhere but refined for present purposes, the cultural model of modernity can be discussed under three categories: knowledge, power and the self (Delanty, 1999; Delanty, 2000a).[9] The thesis advanced here is that underlying all these dimensions of modernity lies a discourse of radical freedom, which can take authoritarian, romantic, liberal and collectivist forms. At the heart of the modern cultural model is the quintessentially liberal and post-Christian view that human societies are incomplete and that human nature is endlessly capable of perfectability. This was one of the central beliefs of all Enlightenment thought and led to the characteristically Jacobin ideology – decisive for modern nationalism – that through political action society can be transformed in the image of the political. This view was also present, albeit in a weaker sense, in the republican and historicist traditions. This, in a sense, expresses the key imaginary of the modern mind, the 'radical imaginary', to use Castoriadis's term, of a society based on perpetual self-creation and renewal through political action.

knowledge

One of the most discussed manifestations of modernity is in the sphere of knowledge. While modern structures of knowledge are a product of long-run historical trajectories, some key features of the cognitive models of modernity can be identified: autonomy, emancipation and universality. In modernity, secular intellectuals are the main repository of knowledge, as opposed to a priestly or political elite who have a monopoly over truth claims. Knowledge production in modernity becomes more and more autonomous of the state, church and other social institutions that are essentially extra-scientific. In the differentiated structures of modern society, knowledge production is professionalized, specialized and institutionalized in autonomous sites such as academies and universities where it is depersonalized. It is no longer a unified system of doctrines but is divided into specialized branches and disciplines. It is thus possible to speak of modernity in terms of the 'republic of science', for the autonomy of science was in many ways a mirror image of the autonomy of civil society. This feature of modernity was very important for the rise of nationalism, insofar as nationalism depends on the constitution of a body of historical and geographical knowledge that offers a basis for constructing a national culture. As we shall see in the next chapter, cultural innovation in the sense of constituting a body of knowledge suitable for nationalist utilization is a central feature of nationalism.

A second feature of modern knowledge is also significant for the formation of nationalism, namely the emancipatory nature of knowledge. Knowledge as emancipation was the motto of the Enlightenment, which may not have been the watershed it has often been held to be but certainly was a very important moment in shaping the state project. In modernity, knowledge is power: it can challenge the prevailing social and political order in the name of a normative ideal and in many cases in the name of science itself. Modernity can be seen in some measure as the progressive diffusion of intellectually formed knowledge in the wider society. In particular this dimension of modernity was important for shaping the Jacobin idea of radical freedom, which often gave a privileged position to an intelligentsia as the principal repository of a legislative model of modernity.[10] Through the Enlightenment, then, in a way fateful for the subsequent development of nationalism, knowledge became subject to political reproduction and contestation.

This leads to the third characteristic of knowledge in modernity: its universality. Knowledge is one of the main expressions of the universalistic spirit of modernity, for the truth claims of science, as a form of self-consciously fallibalistic knowledge, can be accepted or disputed by all. The very universality of the kind of knowledge claims made by science paradoxically had the effect of propelling modernity towards relativism, since it ultimately meant that everything could be challenged. Much of modernist knowledge was an attempt to reconcile the extremes of absolute universalism with particularism. The European Enlightenment was thus divided between the universalistic tenets of rationalism and positivism on the one side and, on the other, the quest for feeling and the emotions that was typical of historicism and romanticism and which tended to emphasize social context. This ambivalence at the heart of modernity would be of great significance for nationalism, which was the paradigmatic example of the use of universalistic ideas to justify particularism.

7

power

The second major expression of the cultural models of modernity that can be identified relates to power. It has been recognized by a whole range of theorists – Lefort, Castoriadis, Habermas, Foucault – that in modernity power takes a discursive form (Strydom, 2000). Modern society is characterized by ever-expanding spaces between the individual and the state. These spaces are never fully filled by social institutions, making social integration more than a matter of simply instituting the state project or of maintaining class power. Social classes or political, clerical and technocratic elites do not simply exercise power in an unmediated manner. Power is expressed in publicly constructed discourses where it may be legitimated or challenged but is always contingent and therefore indeterminate (Strydom, 1999). Even in totalitarian societies power is never total for the moment of closure is never entirely reached.[11] Such discourses may be expressed in ideologies, in identity projects, in debates about rights and social justice, for example. In this view, then, modernity can be seen in terms of democratization through civil society, citizenship and social movements. With respect to our theme of nationalism, the discursive nature of the doctrine of the nation becomes apparent: nationalism is a discourse that can never be entirely dominated by the state project; it is indeterminate, recalcitrant and can be codified by a whole range of social actors in many different ways. As Michael Mann has argued societies are not systems. 'There is no ultimately determining structure to human existence – at least none that social actors or sociological observers, situated in its midst, can discern. What we call societies are only loose aggregates of diverse, overlapping, intersecting power networks' (Mann, 1993: 506).

the self

Finally, one of the most important dimensions of the cultural models of modernity concerns the identity of the self. In the most general sense, modernity is a prolonged discourse about the self that originated in earlier movements, such as the Renaissance and developments in religion such as the Reformation where there was also a gradual turn to the subject as the measure of all things. However, the self in modernity is different from these earlier conceptions in that it is primarily shaped in the image of self-determination. In what would be of major significance for the genesis of nationalism as a psychological, social and political force in modern society, the emergence of modernity ultimately rested on a new conception of the self. Self-determination was to be the watchword of the political face of the modern project. Self-determination as an ideal gave a major justification to appeals for equality, universal human rights and popular sovereignty from the beginning of modernity.

It spoke in the name of a conception of the self that was self-legislating, sovereign and autonomous.

In sum, the main cultural models of modernity relate to developments in the understanding of knowledge, power and the self: knowledge as autonomous, emancipatory and universal; power as discursive and the self as self-determining. The key feature of modernity can be described as a search for an ethics of freedom, for what ultimately unites all these discourses that have shaped the cultural imagination of modernity is radical freedom, the view that power, knowledge and the self can be endlessly reshaped by human agency. This assumption of radical freedom was common to all the great ideologies opened up by Enlightenment and post-Enlightenment thinking, ranging from German idealism and romanticism to liberalism, socialism, anarchism and, of course, nationalism. We return to this later in this chapter.

THE DYNAMICS OF MODERNITY

So far in this chapter, we have considered modernity as a historical condition and a cultural project. In this section modernity is addressed through the more specific sociological question of the social and institutional forms that are the expression of its social project. Purely cultural approaches or ones formulated in terms of historical processes tend to be too general for sociological analysis. What needs clarification is exactly how these cultural models and the historical or civilizational process that carry them get translated into concrete institutional complexes by specific forms of social agency. In other words, a complete account of modernity must address the social project of modernity, as opposed to its cultural project or its historical evolution. The notion of institutional dynamics provide such a middle-range theorization.

In our view modernity as a social project is based on four main institutional dynamics:

- state formation
- democratization
- capitalism
- the intellectualization of culture.

It has already been outlined in this chapter how long-run processes – globalization, the pluralization of cultures, rationalization, societal differentiation – gave rise to modernity. These processes that began within the Axial Age civilizations and came to fruition with the emergence of modernity were ultimately institutionalized by the social project of modernity, which gave social form to the long-run cultural project of modernity as outlined earlier. The combination of the historical situation, cultural models, and geopolitical constellations interacting with the particular form of the organization of the social, especially within European modernity, created the conditions for nationalism to emerge in its modern form. The most significant forms of social organization shaping this conjuncture are now outlined.

state formation

In modernity, the state moves to the centre of social organization and impacts on every sphere of society. With the establishment of a particular structure of centre-periphery relations in early modern Europe, and with the increasing modern requirement for the state to legitimate itself before civil society, the cultural form of the nation became increasingly attractive as a means of constituting territorial units. While there is some evidence today that this framework is loosening if, indeed, not in decline, for some two centuries the nation-state has been one of the central forces in the shaping of the modern world. In Europe since 1648 the sovereign state has become the primary actor in international geopolitics and from 1918 the European territorial empires slowly crumbled and their remains were transformed into nation-states. The twentieth century was, on the whole, the century of the nation-state.[12] No account of modernity can ignore the role of the state in organizing modernity and in channeling global forces.[13]

Despite the different national trajectories and the varied paths to modernity, some suggestions can be made with respect to the role of nationalism in relation to state formation. Of central importance is the question of nationality. Nationalism is of course more than nationality and in many of its forms – for instance in nations without states – nationality is not central to it, but no account of nationalism can neglect the pivotal significance of nationality as the legal and normative basis of modern nationalism. To speak of nationality is to imply some relation to citizenship to which nationality is related in varying degrees. Virtually every model of statehood has been based on some kind of national citizenship (Bendix, 1964).

The modern state in one of its key projects has sought to make of its members full citizens with the rights and duties that this condition involves. In this respect the state project has been articulated through strategies of social regulation, for the control of population was one of the key functions of the state. Other functions were the defence or expansion of territory, the latter crucial for access to markets and, related to this, the permanent preparation for war. However, in the modern period the state has become more and more occupied with the control of populations. As described in Foucault's concept of governmentality, the state project is more than mere government; it is also about the regulation of populations through the control of key aspects of the social body, such as health, sanity, crime, education and poverty

(Foucault, 1979). But governmentality is still more than social regulation in this sense, it is also about the actual constitution of the subject as an individual and member of the national polity (Rose, 1989). In order to achieve this objective, the state project must set about creating citizens. One of the primary functions of citizenship is to distinguish between members of the polity and non-members (Hindess, 1998). Citizenship thus becomes coeval with nationality. However, it must be recognized that citizenship is more than social regulation and govermentality in the sense of social regulation for citizens themselves play a large hand in constructing the rules that regulate them, an idea at the very heart of democracy.

Citizenship has not simply been a passive condition but has been achieved through social struggles over a long period of time. As Foucault argued, power also entails resistance, for where there is power there is also resistance (Foucault, 1980). Govermentality is thus a project fraught with tensions of all kinds. In this sense citizenship can also be seen as a field of tensions where conflicts arise relating to rights and duties and more generally concerning the nature of participation in the polity.

With respect to nationalism, one area of contestation is the meaning of participation. In modernity the tendency has been for democracy to politicize citizenship by extending it beyond the passive condition of nationality. Participation thus becomes more than mere membership of the polity but can involve an active relation. This has inevitably led to conflicting notions of nationality. Nationality as membership of the national polity can thus be challenged by the very notion of national self-determination, when what is at stake is the nature of participation. The discourse of the nation is not easily controlled by the state project, and can easily be used against it as has been the case in the former Soviet Union (Brubaker, 1996). It is also in this sense that we can speak of the recalcitrance of nationalism, which even as an official state patriotism can be turned against the established state by various groups whose consciousness has been formed precisely out of those very structures. What we are saying, then, is that state formation and the concept of nationality that it entails can sometimes be in conflict with the forces of democracy.

democratization

Democratization, which cannot be subsumed under state formation, has also played a major role in the social project of modernity. With its origins in the popular revolts of the early modern period, in colonial liberation movements and in social movements of all kinds, democracy has been a potent force in linking and distinguishing society and the state. The birth of modernity coincided with the emergence of a wide spectrum of social actors, ranging from the early radical scientists, Protestant sects and Jacobin and socialist movements. Democratization

11

can be called a dynamic of modernity in its own right for this reason and also because of the link with agency that it suggests. Undoubtedly one reason why nationalism has been so successful is because of its association with democratization and the values that it has promoted: equality and self-determination.

Elie Kedourie, in one of the most cited books on nationalism, claims that it was a doctrine expressing a certain kind of collective belonging, invented in Europe at the beginning of the nineteenth century (Kedourie, [1960] 1994, p. 1). The tremendous popularity of nationalism must be understood in this light. It is not the inherent popularity of statehood or constructions of history that has played the primary role in the appeal of nationalism, but the notion of political community that lies behind it. This is the community of the *demos*, the essential belief in the basic equality of all people who are members of the polity. In the republican tradition of the Enlightenment, the nation is an idea of universalistic significance based on the principle of self-determination (Kamenka, 1976, 1993). Thus for Rousseau, writing in 1762, the nation was the expression of the general will that is civil society (Rousseau, 1968). In his later work, *The Government of Poland* [1770/01], he argued for a stronger kind of national loyalty based on citizenship (Rousseau, 1972). This republican idea of the nation was synonymous with civil society and was opposed to the state. A famous example of this republican kind of nationalism is the essay 'What is the Third Estate?', published in 1789 by the French revolutionary thinker, Emmanuel Joseph Sièyes. (Sièyes, 1963). The Third Estate was, in essence, the population defined as citizens rather than as subjects. It was also in this sense that the term 'patriot' was used. However, soon after the Revolution, the discourse of the nation became more important and overshadowed the notion of civil society. Yet, this radical Enlightenment notion of the nation continued to be subversive, as was evident in the patriot movement in England and France, and the radical reform movement which appealed to the idea of patriotism. The more radical Jacobin movement – with its stress on political leadership by a self-appointed elite – carried forward the subversive dimension of the republican idea of the nation. When Samuel Johnson said in 1775 'patriotism is the last refuge of the scoundrel' he was referring both to their kind of patriotism as well as to modern chauvinistic Nationalism (Johnson, 1934).

The American and French Revolutions promoted a view of the nation as the voice of civil society. The ideals of modern constitutional law and democracy, which stressed the formal equality of all individuals and their right to personal autonomy, provided the foundation for the idea of the civic nation, which perhaps explains why, historically, nationalism was so much a part of Western modernity. Modern republicanism was therefore the first nationalist movement in this universalistic sense. It has also been called patriotism and may be contrasted to the

12

particularism of late forms of nationalism which fostered strong identification with the state. The doctrine of self-determination that it led to – despite its close association with Jacobinism – was to become greatly influential in the second half of the nineteenth century, leading to a widespread acceptance of 'liberal nationalism'. In fact, it may be said it constituted the dominant ideology of modern nationalism and provided a widely accepted argument for the creation of new states, in particular in the period from the Congress of Berlin in 1878 to the Versailles Treaty in 1919.

The doctrine of self-determination was accepted by some of the most influential figures of the age, in particular Guiseppe Mazzini, William Gladstone and Woodrow Wilson. Mazzini was the apostle of modern republican nationalism and in a map of an 'ideal Europe' in 1857 claimed that nations of a certain size have a right to states of their own. In his conception the nation is essentially a large cultural community which has a historical right to be realized in a sovereign state. It is in a sense a natural unit. This doctrine of the inherent naturalness of nationalism, which derives from the Enlightenment's emphasis on self-determination and the romantic emphasis on the legitimacy of difference, was immensely influential in the second half of the nineteenth century, giving rise to many nationalist movements such as Young Italy, Young Poland and Young Ireland. Gladstone, the Liberal Prime Minister of Great Britain, accepted the principle and strongly supported the Irish Nationalist Movement in its successive demands for home rule and in 1876 supported the cause of Bulgarian nationalism, writing a widely read pamphlet 'The Bulgarian Horrors and the Question of the East' (Shannon, 1963). An influential statement of the basic ideas of liberal nationalism was J. S. Mill's *Considerations on Representative Government* in 1861. For Mill, nationalism and liberal government were perfectly compatible, for nationalism could provide government with the necessary loyalty (Mill, 1971). It may be suggested that the Jacobin tendency within nationalism finally lent itself to liberal democracy, given its tendency to separate elites from masses.

In the aftermath of the First World War the criteria for the formation of new states were laid down by the American President, Woodrow Wilson, whose famous Fourteen Point Plan included a commitment to the principle of self-determination, thus giving a powerful ideological legitimation to the idea that nations must be realized in states.[14] The principle was also strongly supported by V. I. Lenin, who played his role in shaping modern nationalism.[15] The point, then, is that much of modern liberal nationalism derives from the republican ideal of the Enlightenment that the nation is coeval with society and that this is somehow secured by a primordial state of nature. This led to the notion of self-determination, which in time came to be formulated as the doctrine that every nation must be allowed to govern itself. The ability

13

of nationalism to be able to claim the mantle of the *demos*, and with it the ideal of equality, has been crucial to its appeal. But because of the Jacobin thrust within it, that society can be eternally reconstructed by political action, nationalism remained a deeply subversive force in the post-Versailles order. This idea that appeal to nation categories involves a legitimate re-appropriation, reconstruction or transformation of governance has given consistent impetus to nationalist entrepreneurs and movements.

capitalism

While democratization and state formation are political projects, the dominant socio-economic project of modernity is that of capitalism. The difficulty with this claim is of course that it can lead to a too narrow focus since one of the major routes to modernity has been through state socialism (Arnason, 1993). Although this has vanished from Europe and Eurasia its consequences remain and capitalism has not been central to the formation of modernity in China. For this reason industrialism may be preferred as the principal dynamic that has shaped material life in modernity. It is indeed true that industrialism has been more prevalent in all routes to modernity, but the focus on capitalism has the disadvantage that capitalism has generally preceded industrialism in the West and has been one of the most consequential forces in the developing world. Therefore the material dynamic of modernity can be said to be capitalist in the general sense of the emergence of a global market society driven by technology and industrialism. In this sense the term includes state socialism or state capitalism.

The emergence of a modern market society organized around capitalism and industrialism has played an important role in creating the social and economic preconditions for the emergence of nationalism. There is no central or structural reason why nationalism is a product of capitalist society, for it has been present in precapitalist societies as well as in non-capitalist societies such as the Soviet Union and modern China. However, capitalism has been crucial in generating the conflicts in society that have nurtured nationalism. Capitalism by its nature generates social inequality and conflicting interests. A major impetus of nationalism is to offer an integrative response to problematic outcomes of capitalist dynamics. The nation-state has been the dominant model of social cohesion in the modern world and national identity has offered cohesive visions to communities threatened by capitalism and the related processes of industralization, population growth, urbanization and migration.

There are many examples of how capitalism, itself one of the most dynamic forces in modernity, created structural conditions that have given rise to profound social conflicts. Since the rise of the social question in the late nineteenth century, nationalism has been able to draw a great deal of ideological drive from popular struggles. While the categories of nationalism can never be fully translated into social issues, there has been in many instances common cause between popular struggles and nationalist mobilization. In late nineteenth-century Ireland, for example, the land question was the single most important factor in the momentum that led to nationalist revolution. The amplification of the land question reached a point that the national question eventually overshadowed the politics of agrarianism. It was also to absorb the socialist movement as well as all other social movements that emerged in late nineteenth-century Ireland. This has been the pattern in many countries, where the national question, initially marginal, becomes dominant as a result of the ability of nationalist elites to forge a coalition between the most important groups. This argument is not a reductionist account, since it is not being claimed that nationalist ideas always translate directly into other struggles.[16] In fact, the success of nationalism has often been due more to the divisions within the elites and the inherent divisions in other struggles such as class than to the intrinsic appeal of its message. The role of the public is also crucial in determining the fate of nationalist mobilization, since nationalist messages must have a resonance in general public discourse. In its ability to present itself as a hegemonic ideology it is often seen as the only alternative to an inadequate status quo.

15

There are many other examples of the impact of capitalism in the formation of modern nationalism. The rise of the middle classes and the emergence of the modern professions have been important factors in the formation of nationalism. Due to the disjuncture of expectations and experience that has been central to modernity, many groups, in particular the middle classes, have been alienated from the prevailing social order. From the mid-nineteenth century onwards, there are many instances of the professional middle classes turning to liberal nationalist movements, rather than to socialist movements or conservative parties for leadership. In many cases nationalist leadership was drawn from the urban middle class. The history of German liberalism since the *Vormärz* can be partly seen as increasingly determined by the close embrace of nationalism and conservatism.

Today, there is the phenomenon of 'welfare nationalism' by which the socially insecure have turned to extreme nationalist movements less out of conviction in their messages than because of the apparent absence of alternatives. Thus by playing the 'race card' and exploiting xenophobic fears about immigrants, many of these parties have gained support at the cost of the mainstream parties (see Chapter 7). Economic nationalism of a more official nature has been practised by many countries since the early twentieth century. Friedrich List's *National System of Political Economy*, published in 1831, was an important work in laying the foundations for protective economic nationalism (List, 1909). His ideas were adopted in Bismarkian Germany and were influential in many countries. Whether in the form of *Grossraum* expansion, economic protectionism, or trade wars many countries have adapted their national ideologies to protect capitalism. There is also the fact that national markets tend to homogenize the society. Economic nationalism has found more subtle cultural expressions in Japanese nationalism. The proliferation of the *nihonjineron* literature in the 1980s in the wake of massive economic growth was an important expression of Japanese nationalism.[17] With considerable support from the corporate culture, many Japanese social commentators sought to reinvent the myth of Japanese uniqueness (Yoshino, 1992, 1999).

It must not be forgotten that the penetration of capitalism into the sphere of cultural production has been very important for nationalism in recent times. For instance, sport which is self-evidently a major expression of national identity, is organized predominantly along capitalist lines. Without the driving force of capitalism and the rise of world arenas, such manifestations of nationalism would be relatively weak. Arguably the kind of 'banal nationalism' fostered by cultural institutions, sport, and tourism has been more significant in bringing nationalism into most people's lives today than the more jingoistic forms of political nationalism (Billig, 1995). In the recent past, but also going back to the late nineteenth century, world exhibitions, and other occasions where the great technological innovations of capitalism were displayed, played a major role in codifying national identity (Roche, 2000). This question of culture and its role in codifying nationalism leads to our next theme.

the intellectualization of culture

In addition to the political and economic dynamics of the social project of modernity, the final one to be specified is the cultural project, which can be described as the intellectualization of culture. As already discussed, the cultural model of modernity has given great salience to knowledge as an emancipatory and universal ideal. What needs to be stressed is that this ideal has greater significance than being what Lyotard has famously called a 'meta-narrative of legitimation' (Lyotard, 1984). The intellectualization of culture as institutionalized in the universities has been a dynamic of modernity in the very specific sense of being a formative feature of modern society (Delanty, 2001a). The full implications of this – already apparent in the creation of a national intelligentsia in the nineteenth century and in the emergence of professional society – have only become apparent today in the post-industrial and information society, which is coming to rest more and more on knowledge.

The role of intellectuals in shaping modernity cannot be stressed enough. Modern culture is an intellectualized one in that it is continuously constructed by knowledge producers whose growing autonomy is a feature of modernity. As a result power and culture are always in tension. In the context of nationalism this is very important since nationalism ultimately has historically rested on an intellectualized doctrine. It is based, first, on the fact of its largely secular nature. Even though nationalism has often made alliances with religion, it is an irreversibly secular force, and may be called a kind of civil religion.[18] Although nationalist ideas are often dogmatic and strive to be hegemonic, they are nevertheless discursively articulated and seek to convince. In general, then, secularization has been one of the strongest impetuses to the intellectualization of nationalism. A second strand to the intellectualization of nationalism is the role of popular education, for the existence of a reading public is a precondition for the reception of national ideas. While nationalism cannot be reduced to a set of ideas, compelling because of their ideological force, it does require a discursive medium. Finally, the abstract nature of nationalism might be mentioned, that is the fact that the idea of the nation must be imagined for it does not exist in a concrete form that can be immediately experienced.

This lends itself to intellectualization. Intellectuals, and in particular academics, have been pivotal in codifying the cognitive structures for imagining the nation (Giesen, 1998). In many countries the university has helped to define national identity by promoting national languages, collecting folklore and in codifying national literatures. University academics helped in the codification of national identity by collecting and defining ethnographic, geographical and cultural material without which national cultural narratives, consciousness and national memories would not have been possible.[19] Historians played a central role in writing the history of nation. Thus Heinrich von Treitschke's history of Germany reflected Bismarckian Germany and Trevelyan's history of England reflected the Whig intepretation of history. Archaeology has also played a significant role in codifying the national identity of many countries by furnishing the basic artifacts out of which historical narratives can be constructed.[20] In many countries major controversies occurred over the presevation of archaeological sites that did not affirm the official or dominant national identity.[21] Academics, in Germany in particular, emerged as the representatives of the nation and in this way made themselves indispensable to the state for whom they were the 'interpreters' of the nation. In Germany the university helped to shape German national identity. It served the cognitive function not only of providing the state with functionally useful knowledge but also was an important transmitter of national heritage. The autonomy of knowledge and the autonomy of the state were seen as inextricably connected. Thus the Prussian professors held the title of *Kulturträger* – the 'custodians of culture'. In many countries, the universities were supported by the state in order to secure training for the professions. The result was that academic research became more and more drawn into the state project, defining its goals but more importantly shaping its cognitive structures. Thus the disciplines of geography, history and statistics were important in laying the foundations of what may be called national cognitive structures. German national culture was spread through the creation of German-language universities in central Europe. In Sweden, Lund University was founded in 1688 as a step in the 'Swedification' of a region that formerly belonged to Denmark (Bertilsson, 2000, p. 164). Trinity College was founded in the reign of Elizabeth I to secure the survival of English culture and power in Ireland.

An important development in the intellectualization of culture was the new technologies of reproduction. It has by now become widely accepted that the printing press played a decisive role in the vernacularization of written texts, a process that gave major impetus to nationalism, as outlined by Calhoun (1997) and Anderson (1983) among others. Perhaps the most important technological innovation in relation to the diffusion of nationalist ideas in the nineteenth and twentieth centuries was photography. The camera introduced a new dimension into national consciousness: the eye. Previously the reproduction of experience depended on literary texts, speeches or the evocative tunes of national music. The photograph made possible the reproduction of experience on a far greater scale. It also allowed the present to be reinvented as the past.[22] With the rise of internal tourism that came with the steam engine, increased national holidays and vacations, the nation became more available to ordinary people. The commericalization of photography and national tourism were crucial steps in the shaping of modern nationalism. In more recent times technology has shaped nationalism in different ways, ranging from the famous tapes the Ayatollah Khomeini used to disseminate Islamic nationalism from his exile in Paris to Iran in the late 1970s to the use of the internet by neo-fascist nationalisms of today.

This suggests that nationalism is a form of knowledge by which members of society come to 'know' their society. As a form of knowledge, nationalism allows people to imagine their society as a community, as Benedict Anderson has argued (Anderson, 1983). Nationalism in this sense is based on basic codes, such as those that Eisenstadt and Giesen describe: primordial, sacred and civic (Eisenstadt and Giesen, 1995). An important part of the cognitive codes of nationalism is the construction of boundaries, both territorial and symbolic. These boundaries can be expressed in, for example, maps, pictures and souvenirs, which are important cognitive structures for the imagining of the nation. Language, too, has a cognitive function in providing basic structures for the construction of the codes of nationhood. Many countries have a national language that is distinctive to that country and most countries have a national press and television. Linguistic nationalism is by no means the most important kind of nationalism and language is only one of many possible markers of national identity. Where it is a minority language, as in the case of Wales, it can be deeply divisive. However, in many cases it has played a very important role in defining nationhood. More immediate and visible codes of nationhood are symbols, such as flags, icons such as uniforms, stamps and a coinage, national flora and fauna, national colours, national holidays and ceremonies, exemplary figures, national anthems, heritage sites, monuments and buildings, national cuisine and national memories based on selective historical experiences. The symbolic and cognitive level is important in tying national identity to the psychological level of the individual. The symbols of nationalism are often unacknowledged, being embedded in language, personality and the taken-for-granted assumptions of everyday life.[23]

Finally, the aesthetic component of nationalism is very important. Many of the symbols of nationhood have an aesthetic function, in addition to their function in creating meaning. Such aesthetic codes are frequently to be found in national literatures and music. Composers have themselves been important in shaping national identity. Some famous examples are Sibelius who shaped Finnish national identity and the struggle against Russia, Verdi who symbolized Italian national resistance to Austria and Grieg who embodied the Norwegian cause against Danish rule. Other examples might be Dvořák as the champion of Czech national identity, Smetana's celebration of Hungarian identity and Elgar's glorification of English national identity. The aestheticization of politics has been a very important means of popular mobilization in modern times and has given nationalism a highly charged emotional animus akin to religious devotion (Mosse, 1975). At certain times the nation takes on the character of a sacred and enchanted essence that is beyond human will and requiring great acts of sacrifice. This is often related to the feminization of the nation (Mosse, 1985). Persuasive national myths – for instance Joan of Arc, Britannia, Marianne – have been created by giving the national a feminine form. Such aesthetic codes can give the nation a transcendental status, even a divine mission and its representatives a charismatic appeal. Fascism was the ultimate expression of the aesthetization of the nation, but the tendency for nationalism to aesthetize politics is always present insofar as the nation is a glorification of a national essence. Thus many liberal nationalists who came under the influence of aesthetic politics embraced fascism, for instance D'Annunzio in Italy or W. B. Yeats in Ireland.

19

SYMBOLIC VIOLENCE, RADICAL FREEDOM AND NATIONALISM

The idea that conflict is central to the constitution of the social was a basic assumption of much of classical sociology. For Simmel, 'conflict is a form of sociation' and a society that does not have conflict is devoid of process and dynamic (Simmel, 1955). Emile Durkheim (1915) also saw conflict as central to, what he called, the organic forms of social integration in modern societies where there are wide and empty spaces between the state and the lives of individuals. The existence of such forms of conflict gave rise to the need for citizenship as a form of cooperation between different groups. In the tradition of conflict sociology, for instance the work of Lewis Coser (1956), the normality of conflict remained a central assumption, as it did in the sociology of knowledge, as reflected in Karl Mannheim's seminal essay 'Competition as a cultural phenomenon' (Mannheim, 1952). Only the functionalist theory of Parsons remained convinced that conflict was a symptom of dysfunctionality.

This way of looking at conflict as *social* was of course related to one of the main questions of modern sociology, namely the question of how social order is possible under the condition of conflicting values and interests (Wrong, 1994). The answer that was in general acceptable to the classical tradition was through two related frameworks: the legal order of the state and a shared normative order. By means of the political community of the state and a wider cultural community, the conflict that is latent in all social action would not endanger social order and could even be essential to social integration and cultural cohesion. In this way the line between disorder and social order was preserved and the existence of conflict remained, on the whole, a sign of a healthy society. Of course, for Marx classes constituted themselves through conflict which was linked to social revolution and for Sorel (1950) violence rather than conflict was the essence of politics. But on the whole the mainstream sociological tradition saw modernity as a process of pacification and of civilization. Even in the Marxist tradition, the dominant theme was that of the institutionalization of class conflict.

Violence and conflict were thus two quite separate phenomena. Violence has generally been conceived as primordialism, as in Girard (1981) following Freud, or as in Levinas as non-recognition of the other. From Hobbes to Carl Schmitt and Max Weber, violence was prior to the state. According to Weber,

> today the use of force is regarded as legitimate only insofar as it is either permitted by the state or prescribed by it. Thus, the right of a father to discipline his children is recognized – a survival of the former independent authority of the head of a household, which in the right to use force has sometimes extended to a power of life and death over children and slaves. The claim of the modern state to monopolize the use of force is as

essential to it as its character of compulsory jurisdiction and of continuous operation (Weber, 1998, p. 56).

The Weberian image is thus of a political and social order that has progressively eradicated violence.

That violence is the antithesis of the social is also expressed in Elias's theory of civilization as the taming of violence which is externalized and transformed into culture or relegated to the margins of society (Elias, 1982). For Hannah Arendt (1969), too, violence is pure instrumentality, quite different from power. The tradition of the 'just war' can also be seen as an expression of the view that war can be justified so long as it is conducted by states in the name of an overriding principle of justice (Elshtain, 1992; Walzer, 1977). In sum, modern sociology and much of modern social and political thought was based on the myth that violence had been overcome by civil society and that while a state of nature may exist in the normative vacuum between states, the state had, in effect, tamed society. It may be speculated that this is due to the fact the sociology emerged in relatively peaceful times as a science of social order – the end of the nineteenth century and the post-Second World War period.

Recent social and political thought has revised this view of violence as the antithesis of conflict. In several works on modernity, violence is now being seen as deeply constitutive of the social, a view that recalls Rousseau's suspicion that the state cannot solve the problem of war since this is rooted in the condition of the social. In an essay published in 1921, Walter Benjamin questioned the relationship between violence and just ends and dismissed the notion that violence can be justified by positive or natural law (Benjamin, 1978). Works such as this and others, for instance Freud's exchange with Einstein on war (Freud, 1985) lay outside the classical canon in modern social thought. The late modern mind has given a more central role to violence. Violence and the social are seen as more closely bound up with each other (Campbell and Dillon, 1993; Keane, 1996; Mestrovic, 1994). Franz Fanon (1966), in *The Wretched of the Earth*, gave a vivid account of violence in decolonization. Zygmunt Bauman (1989), following Horkheimer and Adorno (1979), writes of violence as central to modernity. This view that sees the holocaust as the paradigmatic event of modernity is also reflected in the early work of Foucault on the proliferation of discourses of violence in modernity. Derrida (1990), too, in 'The force of law', wrote of violence as deeply implicated in the foundation of any society based on a legal order. From a different point of view, Bourdieu has written of symbolic violence as the violence of power and is part of the constitution of the social order (Bourdieu and Passeron, 1977). Violence also figures in the social theory of Jürgen Habermas (1987a) but it is seen as coming from the 'system' which intrudes upon the 'life-world' colonizing and fragmenting it. The penetration of violence into the wider social has

21

also been discussed by Enzensberger (1994) who paints a picture of the return of the state of nature. It may finally be observed that feminist writing has drawn attention to the violence that is central to the construction of gender and much of the private realm lying behind the public domain.

Modernity was a discourse about the emancipation of the self. Democracy, as a form of institutionalized conflict resolution based on citizenship, the rule of law and representation was justified as an expression of the self, in the sense of self-legislation. For this reason democracy and nationalism developed alongside one another, and in many parts of the world nationalism was the principal path through which democratic reform unfolded. But today the question of self-determination is more complex and the self is not the measure of all things – the politics of postmodernity can be seen at least in part as the emancipation of the other from the self. In many parts of the world democracy is providing a legitimation of triumphalist kinds of nationalism, with demands for self-determination being the other face of the determination of the other by the self (de Vries and Weber, 1997). Eric Hobsbawm also writes about the descent into barbarism which he sees as 'a response to a double collapse: the collapse of the political order as represented by functioning states – any effective state which stands watch against the descent into Hobbesian anarchy – and the crumbling of the old frameworks of social relations over a large part of the world – *any* effective state which stands guard against Durkheimean *anomie*' (Hobsbawm, 1994, pp. 46–7).

Michael Mann has criticized the view that democracies are essentially pacific and almost never go to war with one another. He has argued that many democracies have conducted genocidal acts and that these genocides have been justified 'in the name of the people':

> By claiming legitimacy in the name of 'the people', genocidal regimes claim kinship to movements which are usually recognized as the bearers of a true modernity, like liberalism or social democracy. Indeed, modern genocide can be regarded as 'the dark side of democracy. (Mann, 1999, p. 19)

Mann goes on to argue that it was class struggle and its institutionalization that has restrained liberal democracies from cleansing atrocities and genocides. There is much truth to this, since it has been states that have been the greatest perpetrators of violence. But when this has happened it has been because the civic order of the state has collapsed and in the absence of an international normative order, violence has often been the only possible result. Mann's analysis reduces democracy too much to self-determination or simple majoritarianism, neglecting the dimensions of citizenship, representation and constitutionalism that are constitutive of democracy. Yet, it is clear that democracy and nationalism have been closely linked because of the underlying assumption of 'the people'.

This precarious relation of elites and masses has been central to political violence in modernity. Standing at the critical juncture of modernity was the Jacobin ideology which encapsulated the spirit of modernity.[24] Jacobinism reflected some of the central elements in modernity by establishing the absolute superiority of political leadership and political goals as shaped by a political elite who could represent the popular will. According to Eisenstadt, Jacobinism has been the source of many political movements in modernity, ranging from communism, nationalism, fascism to fundamentalism (Eisenstadt, 1999b).

It is reasonable to suggest, then, that violence has been a neglected dimension of modernity. The centrality of violence to modernity resides in modernity's ethic of freedom. The Jacobin notion of radical freedom that lies at the root of all modernity's major cultural narratives cannot be separated from symbolic violence. Thus, for instance, the concern with a founding event has always been deeply implicated in violence, both direct and symbolic. Such quests for a clean slate have been closely related to purges or forcible assimilation. As discussed earlier, the very notion of the people as an undifferentiated *Volk* can be a legitimation of violence. Because of the obvious fact that the people can never be embodied in a single political form, the question of the necessity for their rebirth never goes away. The idea of birth, or rebirth, has been a major motif of modernity – as is reflected in the Renaissance, the French Revolution, modern nationalism and fascism – and has given a cultural legitimation to violence, justified in the name of historical meaning or a transcendental principle that asserts the subordination of the social to a non-social principle. This principle has generally been held to be nature.

That society springs from nature has been an old idea, going back to the liberal myth of the state of nature in the early modern thinkers. Although modern thought abandoned some of the cruder notions of natural man and, since Kant, the idea of natural law went into decline, the conviction that society was constrained by a non-social principle remained. The German idealists and much of Enlightenment romanticist thought believed nature was the domain of radical freedom.[25] Rousseau, for instance, believed that modern human beings longed to escape from oppressive social institutions into a natural condition. The suggestion then is that modernity has been haunted by the belief that the social derives from a non-social principle and which might be constitutive of a greater kind of freedom. This fundamental discord between the social and natural has given animus to modernity's ethic of radical freedom which has been driven by the belief that nature is a domain of freedom. With regard to nationalism, this connection is very striking, since nationalism has been an ideology of rebirth, in the sense of a quest for a primordial natural condition.[26]

This tendency for modernity to revert to primordial violence is illustrated in the purges of the Reformation and in the terror that followed

23

in the wake of the French Revolution and most of the major revolutions of the twentieth century: the October Revolution, the Islamic Revolution in 1979 and Mao's Cultural Revolution. To achieve a new beginning, a clean slate from which the past would be wiped away, has been central to these movements. Nationalism, too, inherited the desire to create a founding event which would be the recovery of a primordial past. Thus the French Revolution and the Jacobin Terror sought to emulate the Roman Republic. As with the European Reformation and the Wars of Religion in the seventeenth century a new beginning necessarily requires the destruction of the present in order to recover the primordial past. Cultural memory and historical amnesia elucidate each other, for every memory is in part a forgetting of that which distorts the dream, as Renan argued in a famous essay published in 1882 (Renan, 1990). The other side of amnesia is animosity, for collective self is very often shaped in relations of adversity. As Karl Deutsch wrote: 'A nation is a group of persons united by a common error about their ancestry and a common dislike of the neighbors' (Deutsch, 1969, p. 3).

Many modern nations came into existence as a result of violent struggles. The memory of these struggles does not easily go away, despite a great many discursive techniques, such as the construction of a scapegoat whose function is to externalize otherness and to bear responsibility for primordial violence. The foundation of the Irish state in the 1920s was marked by a bloody civil war which continued to shape the major political cleavages until the present day. In other cases the foundational act required genocide, such as the genocide of Armenians by Turkish nationalism, or partition, as in the cases of Ireland, Korea and Cyprus. Nationalism in these cases has been able to provide a model of integration only by separation. One of the paradoxes of nationalism is its combination of the new and the old. On the one side, it is obsessed with the new but, on the other, the birth of the new must be based on the old. This tension within nationalism has been the source of many violent conflicts.

The meaning of the very idea of the nation is *natio*, or birth. Nationalist movements have often understood themselves to be seeking the rebirth of the nation, an act that is frequently connected with primordial violence. The religious and aesthetic connotations of birth and violence have remained with nationalism. Although a secular force in the modern world, nationalism inherited many of the tenets of religion, such as the assumption that the social is founded on a non-social principle, such as an original act of creation or the sanctity of death or loyalty to an absolute principle. Secularization in modernity has been primarily achieved through differentiation rather than through rationalization, that is through the institutional separation of church and state rather than the decline of religious belief as such. However, the separation of church and state never prevented many interconnections, as well as more formal connections as in the case of those countries that established state churches. What is significant is less the institutional role of religion than its subliminal role in shaping the primordial and mythic ingredients of nationalist consciousness. In the present context what is important is the presence of symbolic violence. By postulating a non-social principle – the radical freedom in the state of nature – modern nationalism has been haunted by violence since social arrangement must always be denied. Jack Goody has remarked:

> It is no accident that the two defining genocides of the twentieth century, though each was committed by a supposedly secular political force, both engaged ancient religious hatreds: Muslims against Christians in the Young Turk slaughter of the Armenians, Christians against the Jews in the Nazi extermination of the Jews. (Goody, 2001, p. 15)

In his view, to believe in one god is to exclude the many. The cognitive structures of monotheism have been very powerful in the creation of enduring forms of symbolic violence which have survived in the secular political forms of modernity.

Important as religion has been in shaping the modern notion of the nation, the idea of nature has been even more central. Many of the founders of modern nationalism, such as Mazzini, believed the nation was a natural unit. It is for this reason that the nation has often been imagined in terms of geography, with reference to rivers, seas, mountain ranges for evidence of natural frontiers (Hooson, 1994). The belief that the territory of the state must correspond to an ethically defined nation has been held to be natural, despite the obvious fact that few states are based on a single sense of nationhood in this sense (Tilly, 1994).

25

CONCLUSION

Modernity is a complex field of many forces, ranging from long-run historical processes, which we have termed civilizational processes, to cultural and social projects. The analysis in this chapter has placed an emphasis on the latter, which we have conceptualized in terms of institutional dynamics. Of these, four in particular have been stressed:

- state formation
- democracy
- capitalism
- the intellectualization of culture.

The conditions for nationalism as a central force of modernity is produced by the interactions of these different dynamics of modernity as their projects complement and contradict one another. Only in this way can we understand the diversity of nationalism which is a reflection of the diversity of the different paths to modernity and of its different political forms. Moreover, nationalism is more specifically a product of modernity's preoccupation with radical freedom, which it inherited from the Enlightenment. In taking over the mantle of radical freedom from the Enlightenment, nationalism internalized the symbolic violence of modernity.

NOTES

1 For an assessment of the modernity and postmodernity debate see Delanty (2000b), Turner (1990).

2 On the theory of modernity in social theory see Delanty (1999), Dodd (1999), Wagner (1994, 2001).

3 See Eisenstadt (1986, 1995b, 1998, 2000a).

4 We follow some points made by Johann Arnason, who criticizes Eisenstadt for ignoring the diversity of civilizational break-throughs (Arnason, 1997, pp. 61–71). However, Eisenstadt in his recent work has made a more explicit statement on the nature of multiple modernities, as in his book of that title, *Die Vielfalt der Moderne* (Eisenstadt, 2000b). See also Eisenstadt (1999a, 1999b) and Eisenstadt et al. (2000).

5 This has been argued by Roland Robertson. See Robertson (1992).

6 This is not to deny the role of rationalization and differentiation in the formation of modernity.

7 For examples of the wide-ranging literature on this subject, see Hobsbawn and Ranger (1983) and Vlastos (1998).

8 On Simmel and modernity see Frisby (1986).

9 In formulating some of these points concerning cultural models, I am grateful to Piet Strydom.

10 This has been argued by Bauman (1987).

11 This has been argued by Claude Lefort (1986).

12 On the rise and decline of the state see Van Creveld, (1999).

13 On organized modernity see Law (1994) and Wagner (1994).

14 Point ten was autonomous development for the peoples of the Austro-Hungarian Empire and point twelve was the principle of self-development for the non-Turkish peoples of the Ottoman Empire.

15 On Lenin's conception of nationalism see Lenin (1970).

16 On nationalism and socialism see Szporluk (1988).

17 *Nihonjineron* means 'debates on Japanese identity', which were common in the 1980s.

18 Several authors have stressed the origins of national festivities in religion. Mosse (1975, p. 74) argues the public cults and festivities of modern nationalism were not so different from those of the Christian rites.

19 The role of the university and modernity is discussed in more detail in Delanty (1998, 2001a, 2002b, 2002e).

20 Diaz-Andreu and Champion (1996) offers a good overview of the impact of archaeology on national identity in Europe. See also Kohl and Fawcett (1995).

21 For example the debate over the preservation of the very significant Viking site in Woodquay in Dublin in the 1970s. The implication of the discovery challenged the nationalist view that the Celts were the founders of the national capital. Nationalists including archaeologists and prominent public figures thus opposed demands for the preservation of the site which suggest the national capital was founded by foreigners.

22 The past thus becomes a foreign country. See Lowenthal (1985).

23 See Reicher and Hopkins (2001) for an account of nationalism from a social/psychological perspective.

24 The term originally refers to the revolutionary movement led by Robespierre in 1793–4, which established the Reign of Terror on France following the French Revolution.

25 This was clearly expressed by Schelling, who was also a pivotal figure in communicating idealist thought to the romantic movement. He argued, largely against Fichte, that nature was not a domain of necessity or an inaminate object but one of creativity and process. While Fichte radicalized Kant's principle of freedom, he did not extend it into the domain of nature. With Schelling and Hegel, idealist philosophy reconciled freedom and nature.

26 Oleg Kharkhordin has noted the connection with natality and the idea of the nation (Kharkhordin, 2002).

two

modernity and nationalism: transformation and integration

This chapter sets up a relational framework for understanding the different theoretical accounts of nationalism. The idea lying behind it is that the various approaches to nationalism could benefit from understanding their own place in the overall field of nationalism as well as by greater interaction with one another. A first step towards advancing such understanding and interaction is to show that, at least in some respects, the various theories can be complementary to one another in covering various parts of the interdependent overall field. But this requires demonstrating that such a field exists, a task for which we employ certain traditions of social and, to a lesser extent, political theory.

The key insight that animates our selection of social theory is that nationalism is a collective identity that can be constructed through mobilization or institutionalized as a form of social integration. Nationalism is therefore conceived, on the one hand, as a cultural form that gives rise to mobilization and is elaborated and reshaped in that process. On the other hand, it is also a collective identity that offers a societal basis for identification with political orders, hence a main contributor to social integration. The latter, of course, does not imply that social integration is necessarily consensual and does not deny that the integration of some is often at the expense of the exclusion of others. Neither does it imply that the nationalist basis of such social integration is always stable for nationalism can be a volatile phenomenon. Nonetheless, the full scope of nationalism can only be represented if both its dynamic and structural qualities are recognized and related to one another.

In this chapter, therefore, we explore how nationalism has a particular status within the social order of modernity as an integrative counter-movement to the differentiating, disembedding processes that characterize that order. In this process, nationalism establishes itself not as a transfiguring aesthetic discourse somehow outside the normative order of society but one on which modern society in part rests. Nationalism could not endure if it did not have such structural significance. However, as we have learned with declining satisfaction with purely structuralist accounts of nationalism, nationalism is not only a structural category fulfilling a social function in the organization of society. It is also a way of seeing the world and of finding elusive meaning within it in the conditions of a disenchanted modernity. Moreover, it is a way of seeing beyond the world as it is and making a new one through forms of creative collective action. In the chapters that follow, we show how nationalism studies have reflected the relatively recent drive of the social sciences to examine the significance of semantic patterns and constitutive collective action that contradict the teleology of structure. Scholarship on nationalism, as we shall see, sits squarely at the heart of this endeavour.

THE CONDITION OF MODERNITY: PERMANENT REVOLUTION

Several theories of modernity have stressed an underlying central conflict in modernity (Delanty, 1999). In classical sociology this was conceived as a perpetual crisis emanating from a contradiction at its heart. Thus for Marx modernity was shaped by the conflict between labour and capital; in Weber's sociology of modernity the fundamental clash is between instrumental rationality and value rationality; for Durkheim it was the tension between mechanical and organic forms of solidarity that defined the modern situation; for Tönnies modernity involved the conflict of community and society; for Simmel modernity was expressed in the conflict between objective and subjective culture. Contemporary social theory also sees modernity in terms of a central conflict. Thus for Castoriadis (1987), there is the conflict between the radical imaginary and the institutional imaginary; Habermas (1984) has made the conflict between lifeworld and system central to his conception of modernity; Touraine (1995) sees modernity as a struggle between instrumental reason and subjective reason. An interpretation of these views on modernity might be that modernity is the condition of 'permanent revolution'.[1] This seems a plausible characterization of modernity, whose condition has often been discussed in terms of its dynamism, a capacity for perpetual change, subversion and the unleashing of creative cultural and social forces.

The permanent revolution of modernity is due to contradictions between the various dynamics, such as those discussed in Chapter 1: state formation, democracy, capitalism and the crystallization of new cultural forms as a result of intellectualization and rationalization. As these dynamics become more and more intensified, spheres of contradiction, conflict and reconciliation emerge As a shorthand, we shall term these last processes described as contradictions. The contradictions can sometimes lead to outright conflict, sometimes lead to reconciliation of differences and sometimes just subsist, latent in the social order. We

29

propose the view in this chapter that the dominant such contradiction affecting modern nationalism is that between differentiation and integration.[2] Nationalism should be understood in substantial part as an integrative counter-movement to differentiation processes. The qualifier 'substantial part' is used to indicate that nationalism is, of course, more than this integrative counter-movement. It is also a cultural discourse of collective identity based upon cultural criteria of membership and rules for what membership means. Hence, nationalism is more than a means of social integration as this understanding alone could not make sense of why nationalism occurs in certain places and times and the forms it takes. Nonetheless, if nationalism is to be understood as intrinsic to modernity, if that is it has a critical role in to play in our understanding of the kinds of societies produced by modernity, then its general standing as an integrative movement has to be properly grasped. It is the central role it plays as a critical contributor to the cultural integration of modern societies that enables nationalism to endure. The view that nationalism is often an expression of dissatisfaction with the nature of social integration from the standpoint of certain groups, rather than a consensual basis of such integration, does not contradict this insight. It merely makes it more salient in that secessionist movements might wish to make *their* nationalism the basis of another kind of social integration, or at least one with different ethnically defined elites in dominant positions, or that ethnic movements within multi-ethnic states would wish to make the mechanisms of social integration reflect their specific values and experiences.

Alexander (1982, 1992) describes differentiation as the process whereby institutions gradually become more specialized. In this process, familial control over social organization decreases, political processes become less directed by the obligations and rewards of patriarchy, the division of labour is organized more by economic criteria than by reference simply to age and sex, community membership reaches beyond ethnicity to territorial and political criteria and religion become increasingly abstract and generalized and begins to become disentangled from its involvement in other social spheres. Integration, contrariwise, has to do with those belief systems, norms and institutional mechanisms that enable such modern societies, in the face of general differentiation, to realize the necessary cohesion to secure the aspirations contained in their cultural models, for example, identity, security, health, prosperity, justice, responsibility, egalitarianism and knowledge. Such aspirations emerge from discourses of the common good. The degree of differentiation attained in modern societies makes these kinds of discourse more difficult and yet more necessary. It is not obvious in the face of complexity and competing interests what the common good is and hence its specification requires intensified communication. Nationalism is one of the most influential, but far from the only, cultural form of this communication. What has made nationalism so attractive a discourse is that it has achieved cultural resonance among modern publics and far-reaching potential for institutional change. Nationalist discourse often holds the distinct prospect of greater levels of political power and cultural influence for its proponents, which in turn heightens the prospects of nationalist mobilization.

In some versions of classical sociology integration and differentiation were regarded as compatible in that the more differentiated a society was, the more stable it would be. This was a basic tenet of the socio-logical theory of Spencer, Durkheim and Parsons for whom differentia-tion would not contradict wider societal convergence in industrial society and the possibility of social order. In the Parsonian framework even the most differentiated social systems are anchored in the 'societal community'. With some few exceptions, the existence of the nation-state was never seriously questioned as the basis of integration. However, others among the classical sociologists diagnosed greater tensions between differentiation and integration such as the Marxist theory of class contradiction and Weber's identification of a tension between modern forms of rationality, especially the instrumental rationality that drove on differentiation as opposed to the more reflective, intentional and integrative form of value rationality. The course of social change today is making the basic insights of these last mentioned theorists once more relevant, albeit highly adapted and transformed by application to contemporary circumstances. According to Touraine, the four main components of modernity (politics, social relations, economy and culture) are being torn apart from each other and the possibility of unity being re-established is much diminished. The social theory of Luhmann represents the most extreme version of the view that differentiation no longer obeys the kinds of integrative value generalization at the heart of structural functionalism, and the ultimate guarantor of social order in that understanding of modernity (Luhmann, 1995, 1998). Luhmann's theory advocates an understanding of modernity as a society without a centre in which differentiation takes the form of autonomous social systems such as the economy, law, education, science and politics, which are integrated only by their own operational codes. One implication of Luhmann's theory is that such social systems, less and less burdened by their embedding in specific societal communities, have greater poten-tial to become global systems, driven by the force of spatially indiffer-ent techno-economic processes. These theories, although extreme in their formulation, do draw attention to the inescapable fact that the nation-state has diminished as a guarantor of social integration as the forces of differentiation have become unfettered. This differentiation, which can also be understood with Max Weber as giving rise to charac-teristic types of rationalization within the newly created differentiated systems, is, of course, still following Weber and also Habermas (1984),

31

a selective release of rationalization potentials, above all one in which techno-economic processes increasingly overwhelm the integrative restraints imposed by national states. The integrative function of the nation-state has been seriously weakened by global production systems and markets and the implications of modern communication systems. Consequently, social fragmentation is becoming more a feature of the current situation and even the very coherence of the social is being called into question.[3]

The last remarks are a late modern expression of one of the key dynamics of differentiation and integration in modernity, the relationship between capitalism and democracy. In the social theory of modernity, capitalism is presented as a Leviathan that tears asunder established ways of doing things, imposing interests and quantities on values and qualities. It a main contributor to the pluralization of life forms generated by a complex division of labour, a process that sets in train the possibility of realizing higher levels of individuation. By the same token, democracy presupposes the existence of socially differentiated units while at the same time expressing the sovereignty of the *demos*, acting in the general good of society, as an integrating power. Democracy is not simply a set of procedures rooted in the assent of all, it is also made and remade through social projects demanding rights, justice and responsibility (Strydom, 2000). These projects include the Puritan movement in Britain, the movement for democratic republicanism in the eighteenth century, the nineteenth- and twentieth-century liberal, suffragist, labour and anti-slavery movements and the contemporary environmental movement. As against these movements, fundamentalist movements can also be counted as resisting at least some of the implications of capitalist modernization, including some Islamic movements and, in a more total way, fascist movements in various parts of the world.

One set of implications of capitalism has, therefore, undoubtedly been differentiating, creating social differentiation through the division of labour, producing a differentiated economic system and giving a powerful impetus to individuation processes in modernity. Capitalism also played a pivotal role in the separation of state and society by creating the conditions for a modern civil society, of vital importance to the creation of the early bourgeois public sphere (Habermas, 1989a). It helped to create the social structure for a new form of public opinion formation that in time took on a democratic, political function – a new form of publicity – and through the communications revolution, released by the printing press, it provided these new social strata, located in their own civil societal milieux beyond the oppressive intimacy of courtly society, with the means of literary and news production, distribution and consumptions. Both Anderson (1983) and Gellner (1983), among others, have emphasized how important this process was to the development of modern nationalism. But with this insight, it can already be seen how initially a differentiation process in turn led to an innovative kind of integration process as the newly formed civil society first developed its own forms of communicative integration and then increasingly came to challenge the absolutism of the early modern state through the development of a public sphere with a political function. The model of accountable government guaranteed at bottom by new ideas of democratic publicity led on to the model of representative governance. But the question remained: representative of whom? The answer was, of course, representative of the people, but the idea of the people as an abstract category holding to an ethical idea of democratic publicity required more than numerical, procedural representation; it also required metaphorical representation. As part of the solution to this problem, a solution that also underpined the preservation of sovereign boundaries, came the idea that the people were in fact the national community. A fateful conjunction was made that has been at the heart of modernity ever since.

It would be wrong, however, to pass over from this idea of the conjuction established between people and nation to the corollary that from the French Revolution onwards, the people were only seen in terms of the nation. Apart from the important distinction between the public, charged with a specific democratic role as the holders of a kind of secular, democratic reason, and the people, the equation of nation and people also had to meet the challenge of cosmopolitan ideas. Cosmopolitanism was driven by the process of globalization that hastened the emergence of modernity and consisted of a belief in universal values. It was deeply embedded especially in European modernity, in its literature and arts and, particularly, in science. The cosmopolitan idea was above all the expression of the universalistic heart of the democratic project of modernity. In its various precepts, which include that all are equal before the law, all have certain basic human rights, all should enjoy democratic freedom, all deserve a certain material minimum to live, the universalistic idea was anchored in this democratic project.

The collective identity that in the first instance is based on such universalistic ideas had an ambivalent relationship to the particularism of national identity from the romantic response to the Enlightenment onwards. On the one hand, nationalism was often the carrier of cosmopolitanism.[4] Many of the leading European nations competed with each other to be the embodiment of European civilization and to shape Europe in their own image (Delanty, 1995a). Many cosmopolitan designs, for instance those that sought a federal Europe, were hegemonic aspirations by national elites for the mastery of Europe.

On the other hand, this cosmopolitanism with a national tincture was often still based upon a convinced cultural commitment of an elite that had more affinities with other trans-border elites – often located in any

33

case within the same imperial civilization or linguistic-cultural zone – than with the uneducated masses. The cosmopolitan idea, however, was weakened by the growing internal reference of the democratic *demos* with dramatic social mobilization and the intrastate implications of the communicative revolution. Universalistic ideas had the paradoxical consequence in a gradual transition through the nineteenth and twentieth centuries that even the poor and ill educated, in social or geographical peripheries, counted for as much, in formal demcratic terms, as the rich and educated elites. A set of cultural ideas was needed to include these peripheries in the *demos*. Here lies the origins of the fateful reworking of the idea of the '*Volk*', the common community of descent, and more generally of the discourse of inclusion in the nation that in time became anchored in all political ideologies. Here also was the relative demise of cosmopolitanism for much of the last two centuries. However, in the context of contemporary globalization, the question of democracy is no longer confined to the nation-state and new ideas of democratization are becoming significant forces in the rapidly forming transnational civil society (Held, 1995). In this scenario new elites are emerging, ranging from the the leaders of INGOs, fundamentalist movements, and a vast range of global mini-nationalisms and other anti-systemic movements. In these movements, the central Jacobin spirit of modernity is fully present and is strengthened, not diminished, by the erosion of the sovereignty of the national state.

34

This inclusion process before the nation, both rhetorical and real, also embodied the final tension between differentiation and integration that we wish to consider, that between disenchantment and enchantment. According to Max Weber, the process of rationalization can be described as disenchantment. Disenchantment is the progressive loss of substantive forms of meaning in the face of growing formalization of reason in all social spheres and the retreat of religion from society. In this Enlightenment view, modernity represented the decline of tradition and above of all religion. Much of classical sociology assumed that modernity and tradition were in opposition to each other and that secularism was therefore the inescapable fate of modernity. Three concepts of secularization were presupposed: the separation of church from state, the decline of religion as a belief system, and the growing intellectualization of religious belief. However, the movement towards secularization in modernity is far from a one-way street that departs from the disjunction of modernity and tradition. In fact, modernity recreates traditions, including religious traditions that are often animated by modern anti-modernism, modern in their organizational form, anti-modern or ambivalent in their values. As has been pointed out by several studies, the survival of Islam in modernity was not in spite of modernity but because of it (Kaya, 2000; Turner, 2000). Post-Enlightenment cultural change that, on the one hand, has undoubtedly led to a growth in secularization but, on the other, has given impetus to continuing religious survivals, revivals and reinventions, has benefited nationalism both ways. In the first case, nationalism gains credence as a meaning-generating response to a world that has lost its cosmological anchorage. However, it can also often profit from the rise of cultural forms of modern traditionalism which are frequently also revolts of the cultural or geographical periphery against cultural and political centres.

The dialectic of differentiation and integration, disenchantment and re-enchantment is pivotal also to the relation between nationalism and the state. For Max Weber, it was the instrumental formalism of the calculative spirit, manifested in both the bureaucratic organization and capitalist enterprise, that was the most characteristic expression and main driving force of rationalization as disenchantment. The relationship between the state and nationalism at one level, therefore, can be seen as one more manifestation of the dialectic of dis- and re-enchantment. Instrumental reason cannot by itself generate the kind of normative and affective meaning that are intrinsic to the collective identities of modern civil society. The ideologies of civil society such as nationalism have to do so. Nationalism inculcates feelings of collective belonging out of the sense of being part of a community of common experience and common destiny and plays an important part in gener-ating non-rational feelings of horizontal identification with national peers in civil society. But nationalism is not only a form of re-enchantment that generates meaning in civil society. It is also is an important part of the legitimation of the state. In this respect it is important on the normative level. State power is not something antithetical to the idea of nationalism. Nationalism is also generated in a rational, objective even instrumental way by the activities of the state and national movements which understand the importance of state power, often for the well-defined material and ideal interests of particular groups that will benefit from such power. In the latter scenario, re-enchantment and ideology become difficult to distinguish.

35

NATIONALISM AND SOCIOLOGICAL THEORY

To this point in the current chapter, we have sought to place nationalism in a framework of differentiation and integration showing the various ways it fashions and refashions this key dialectic of modernity. Building from the preliminary connections established in pursuit of this task, we now begin the task of placing nationalist theory into some kind of framework that bears relation to wider social-theoretical frameworks. This task is a prelude to the task of interpreting writing on nationalism according to the categories of the framework over the next three chapters of this book. Placing accounts of nationalism in a broader theoretical context is designed to advance productive interchange and mutual learning across and between accounts of nationalism and other areas of social, political and historical scholarship. In general, the idea is advanced that contemporary writing on nationalism is increasingly drawing from wider theory and research traditions as part of a relatively rapid progression towards the 'mainstreaming' of the study of nationalism. Such a development is not only occurring because of the conscious efforts of writers on nationalism to draw from theory and research in other areas, although this is an important development. It is also occurring because of a more indirect 'paradigmatic' diffusion of theoretically formed ideas that have become preconditions of scholarship in the field.

In pursuit of this task we return briefly to the question of differentiation and integration in relation to how they have been formulated within sociological theory. We explore how the idea of differentiation has undergone significant change within sociology as the imagination of sociology – and indeed much political science and the new discipline of cultural studies – has turned away from structural explanation of social phenomena. New ideas about differentiation processes have been developed that attempt to make the structural-realist backdrop more amenable to cultural analysis and the constructivist challenge of approaches focused on agency. At the same time, developments in the analysis of culture and agency also imply that long-run structural accounts are not always needed. Nationalism appears as a critical testing ground for these investigations because its presence was largely elided and its centrality to modernity under-recognized before the interpretive turn in the social sciences of the late 1960s and afterwards.

In the remainder of this chapter, therefore, major sociological theory developments are outlined, spanning structure, culture and agency, and the implications of these developments for the theory of nationalism outlined. This task provides the basis of a theoretical framework for addressing theories of nationalism that will find application in the following three chapters, where a review of the literature is conducted from these standpoints.

differentiation and de-differentiation

Within the discipline of sociology, the immediate post-war period saw a sustained attempt to identify secure foundations for modern society that would overcome the apparent contingency of the world and create an evolutionary highroad for sociological theory. Within functionalism, and to some extent also within Marxism, the idea of structural differentiation played this role. Earlier functionalist theory such as Parsons saw such differentiation processes, allied to the construction of institution-specific and general cultural value patterns, as emergent orders immanent in the telos of modernity. They were emergent in the sense of actor-less processes of structural evolution.

However, in recent neo-functionalist theory there has been a sea change. While certain kinds of differentiation, making possible institutional structures such as law, markets and democracy, are functional requisites of social advancement they should not be seen as historically inevitable or the outcomes of linear processes. Rather, as emphasized in Alexander (1995), the form and extent of differentiation hinges upon the normative aspirations, strategic position, history and powers of particular social groups. Alexander (1992) distinguishes between differentiation and various historical situations or contexts such as revolution, reform, and reaction that open up potentials for the rapid incorporation of processes of change. In the same article, Alexander also draws attention to the need for 'a more phase-specific model of general differentiation and of social process alike'. For Alexander, therefore, certain kinds of differentiation are intrinsic and necessary for core dimensions of modern society to be realized. However, whether they occur and how they occur depends on the balance of social forces in given historical situations. For example, the differentiation of state and society associated with the rise of the French model of democratic republicanism requires the presence of regime crisis, the existence of social actors capable of conceiving, desiring and bringing about democratic innovation and a cultural model of democratic republicanism itself (Hunt, 1986). Eisenstadt (1990) also distinguishes between levels of structural differentiation and elite activity, especially as regards the formation of the boundaries of collectivities, the regulation of power and the creation of meaning and trust.

37

The addition of actors, situations and models of interpretation to differentiation theory adds a definite fluidity to the understanding of these processes. As Alexander emphasizes, differentiation cannot be simply assumed to follow a linear pattern. In principle, as we have seen already, non-differentiation or de-differentiation are also possible outcomes of historical processes. Dominguez (1999) draws attention to the way in which de-differentiation acts as a counter-process to differentiation in neo-functionalist writers such as Eisenstadt, Alexander and Colomy. Tiryakian (1992) develops this theme, speaking of a dialectics of modernity in which the twin processes of differentiation and rationalisation are counterbalanced by the 'counter-processes' of de-differentiation and re-enchantment. As an example, Dominguez emphasizes how democracy itself could be regarded as what he calls a process of 'disdifferentiating equalisation of individuals' that could be counterposed to social differentiation through stratification. Tiryakian, very pertinently, instances the 'great nationalist movements' of the nineteenth and twentieth centuries in which the actors and groups of actors, seeking to emancipate themselves from a differentiated system, call on the modern values of egalitarianism, freedom and autonomy. Both of these examples put a positive slant on de-differentiation. However, de-differentiation can be linked to negative consequences also as, for example, in O'Mahony and Delanty (1998) who identify regressive de-differentiation in the re-establishment of religious values in other social spheres after Irish Independence in 1922. Other examples of fundamentalism are also open to such a reading.

It is the possibility that differentiation or de-differentiation can be ascribed negative or positive implications that underlies Eder's insistence that 'the path of development leading into modernity lies in the learning processes and the symbolic practices in the sphere of culture' (Eder, 1993, p. 36). These determine not only whether rationalization leads to enchantment or disenchantment but this in turn determines whether and what kind of structural differentiation will occur. This perspective reverses the temporal priority normally ascribed to differentiation over culture and hence requires that analysis focus far more centrally on cultural innovation. A further reversal effected by Eder is to oppose the idea that 'normality' can be associated with differentiation and rational-ization. He emphasizes instead that it is the blocking or realization of collective learning processes and symbolic struggles that enables explana-tion of 'pathogenic forms of differentiation or de-differentiation, of disenchantment or re-enchantment'. Eder's remarks already bring us to consider the extent to which the reconsideration of structural differenti-ation is intrinsically bound up with a re-evaluation of culture and, since learning processes in Eder's schema are primarily initiated by movements, to the relation between action and structure. These themes are taken forward in the next section.

What is already clear from these brief remarks on differentiation theory is that this theory has undergone significant changes in recent decades. These changes, emphasizing the role of actors in mediating between differentiation and disenchantment on one side and de-differentiation and re-enchantment on the other, are intrinsic to under-standing the relationship between modernity and nationalism. This is the case because nationalism cannot be understood as an actor-less process of modernization and is better grasped as part of a dialectic of differentiation and de-differentiation than from within the parameters of differentiation viewed as the master process of modernity. The issue that arises therefore is how nationalism and nationalist actors play a part in this dialectic of differentiation and de-differentiation at the heart of modernity.

the transformation of the study of culture

Eisenstadt (1995a) distinguishes between the order-maintaining and order-transforming dimensions of culture. He identifies some structuralists and extreme Marxists as emphasising the former dimension, seeing cultural orders as relatively uniform and unchanging within a state of society. By contrast, theorists such as Swidler see culture as a set of resources that can be activated more dynamically according to the 'material' or 'ideal' interests of social actors. In considering political culture, Brint (1994) similarly notes a movement away from thinking about sources and influence of public mores in the direction of thinking about the generation, meaning and uses of expressive and classificatory symbolism in political life. He claims that the functionalism of the older work has given way to the spirit of text analysis characteristic of the present self-conscious age. He calls this turn the 'new textualism' and links it to the interpretive turn in social theory, where the generation, circulation and implications of meaning systems become the centrepiece of social analysis, while the old realist conceptual backdrop of classes, institutions, organisations and forms of relationship are themselves considered through the lens of meaning construction.

Citing the work of Geertz and Lynn Hunt as paradigmatic of the tradition of explanation-oriented structural analysis, Brint finds that, on the whole, the new cultural writers are actually more concerned to establish the autonomy of culture from social structure than to connect the two levels of analysis. Their approach to culture has the virtue of emphasizing culture as a dynamic element within the overall openness and contingency of the outcomes of social or political episodes. However, as Brint is concerned with the role of the social sciences in providing generalising explanations, he prefers to turn the elements of cultural analysis into variables and to analyse their incidence and effects across multiple cases. In his view, Gellner's work on nationalism is a good example of this kind of cultural analysis because of the parsimony of his account. A small number of variables linked to industrialization and literacy are invoked to explain the incidence of nationalism across a wide variety of cases.

This programme would be quite at variance with the theoretical and methodological premises of much cultural analysis, where singular crystallizations of cultural forms in all their richness are the object of analysis. This idea of the autonomy of culture is lent much strength by the growing realization that the formation of structures is still characterized by wide-ranging differences that can be attributed to quite different ways of making sense of the social and political world, while at the same time in spite of this variation there often are common structural outcomes in countries which are at an advanced state of development or exhibit similar patterns of disadvantage. Brint's desire to sustain and advance sociological generalization by annexing cultural considerations to case and variable analysis may have its value, but such a strategy will by no means exhaust all the ways in which cultural analysis could contribute to theory and research in the social sciences. Much insight will

39

continue to be gained from research with no strong univocal technological procedure, but rather which is given direction by the semantic exploration of ideas and their social realization.

Brint's desire for a cultural analysis that connects with structural analysis does elicit some wider sympathy, however, when consideration is taken of how little progress has been made within cultural analysis towards building the methodological capacity to generalize from singular cases. One of the principal reasons for this is that cultural analysis is often addressed in periods of social upheaval or institutional transformation whose interpretation leads to emphasis on unique configurations of events, meaning, and actions. Brint's citing of Lynn Hunt's analysis of the role of democratic republicanism in the French Revolution is a case in point. Hunt distinguished between the conditions of possibility of the ideology of democratic republicanism in the contradictions inherent in the political culture of the old regime and the actual definitive shape it took in the midst of revolution by a new political class, who themselves were moulded by their responses to new ideas and symbols. In periods of social upheaval, the connection between social structures and cultural interpretations can become loosened and the power of culture, tied to the capacity for action of situated actors, becomes more apparent.

The emphasis on the affinity of culture and social change draws attention to the creative role of culture in constituting possible futures that depart from existing social arrangements. In instances such as nationalist agitation, social revolution or protest movements, actors develop programmes that project alternative futures and seek to build wider constituencies for the declared imperatives contained in such scenarios. In more technical language, actors seek to build sustained 'resonance' among a wider public for their messages. Brint (1994) sees the social constructionist approach as applied within the political field to be most promising when directed at the analysis of public discourse. However, his view that such analysis concentrates on the role of politicians and the media in shaping the mentality of citizens, who are reduced to the status of a residual, is too restrictive. Movements for social change, including nationalist movements, have to develop a collective identity that first binds the movement together and then succeed in binding a sufficient section of the wider public to a diffused variation on this identity. This theme is taken up again in the next section.

Many large questions to do with the areas of concentration, strengths and weaknesses of cultural analysis have to be left to one side in a short commentary of this nature. From the foregoing consideration, there is, however, one essential point to be noted for our present concerns. This has to do with the idea of nationalism as a meaning system that for many interpretive writers on nationalism, as we shall see in Chapter 4, acquires a constitutive capacity to bring about social change.

40

Nationalism is a set of ideas whose potency may be related to wider social change but which may also buck the trend of such change. For example, people may choose relative poverty in the name of ethnic or national dignity. It is an expression of the power of ideas, even of ideologies, a text rather than a structure. As a text, the logic lying behind its dynamics may have more to do with cultural ideas generated and used by collectivities, as opposed to impetus to action derived predominantly from their social situations. This is not to deny, of course, that nationalism is often powerfully shaped by the social situations experienced by collectivities. But one cannot derive nationalism from social situations alone. To understand nationalism, one must fundamentally understand it as a cultural form making sense of social situations and generating particular kinds of response (Brand, 1992).

agency and the micro-macro link

A third significant change in social theory relevant to nationalism may be summed up as the new respect attached to the capacity of agents to make social change. Sztompka (1994) distinguishes between system and field theories of social change. The system account of change, historically the dominant one, analysed state changes in populations, structures, the functions of systems, the erection and maintenance of boundaries, the arrangement of subsystems and the role of the extra-societal environment. More recently, this view of social reality, ultimately rooted as we saw in the account of differentiation theory earlier as a meta-stable entity, has come to be challenged by what Sztompka calls the dynamic social field model. He notes that two intellectual trends appear to have grown in importance to make way for this model. The first is the emphasis on the pervasive dynamic qualities of social reality, perceiving society in motion, or what he describes as a 'processual image'. The second is the avoidance of treating society, group, and organization as an object, which he calls the 'field image'. Sociology moves, according to this perspective, to considering society not as a 'rigid quasi-object' but as a stream of events that exists only insofar as something happens inside it. He ascribes the methodological consequence as rejecting the validity of purely synchronic studies and the affirmation of a diachronic perspective, often described as the historical turn in the social sciences.

The assumption underlying this approach is that society is in constant flux. While stable elements can be identified as in the organic-system model, they are endlessly subject to small or large changes driven by events and sequences of intentional or unintentional action. The field metaphor explores not how stable elements constrain processes but rather the other way round, how processes underpin stable elements within different fields of action. Sztompka speaks of micro, mezzo and macro fields of action,

41

which are not isolated from one another but interact in a complex manner. The field model envisages a co-determination of levels, whether the shift from micro to macro is conceived with Sztompka in relation to spatial elements, global, regional, local and personal or in relation to the levels of action, respectively the actions of individuals or legal individuals, the action of collective actors and the level of action systems.

A key idea that could be associated with the field model is that of constitution. The idea of constitution suggests a society that is substantially given form by individual or collective action, as much or more than the emergent properties of social structures. This implies therefore a re-emphasis in the social sciences towards a theory of constitutive action, which inevitably amounts to a renewed emphasis on the structure-forming role of individual and collective action. Joas (1996) speaks of the creativity of action and Dominguez (1999) talks of collective subjectivity. This renewed emphasis on the constitutive role of action, and its attendant emphasis on micro to macro links, as opposed to the more traditional emphasis on the other way round, results in a substantial enlargement in the types of action to be considered. The move from conceiving social change in terms of changes in macro-societal organization of populations, structures, functions and systems to modalities of change located at levels other than the macro involves a significant increase in the analytic and empirical scope of the social sciences. The field of nationalism is an object domain par excellence of such increased scope for which the older accounts of social change appear hopelessly insufficient.

Of considerable theoretical interest is one dimension of recent scholarship that reflects this expansion in levels and scope, the relationship between collective action and changes in social structures. This is notably the case in relation to nationalism where the mediation between differentiation and de-differentiation is given form by collective actors. Joas (1996) correctly sees much of the animus among social scientists for addressing the question of collective action as lying in the emergence of the new social movements. He follows Tilly et al. (1975) in identifying two historical-theoretical interpretations of the emergence of modern collective action. The first tradition derives from the impetus given by enhanced individualization to specific kinds of collective action that often lead to the constitution of new kinds of authority. The work of Michel Foucault is prototypical for the process of the replacement of models of solidarity with models of a specific kind of individuation that is both produced and monitored as an intra-psychic and bodily set of disciplines, 'technologies of the self'. Disciplinary regimes of this kind are the product of the *collective action* of new professions emerging in the nineteenth century – for example, psychology, penology, pedagogy – working together with the advancing authority of the state, itself gaining power by organizing and supervising the process. The other historical-theoretical model emphasizes, to the contrary, the building of solidarity for which the Marxist emphasis on the working class as the architects of a new social order or that of the Chicago School on oppositional ghetto cultures is prototypical. Both historical-theoretical interpretations, which need not exclude one another and can indeed be highly complementary in specific analysis, draw attention to the distinction between the macro order and a kind of collective actor that is sizeable enough to have an organizational form and collective identity of its own and whose efforts may just as likely be directed at structural innovation as structural maintenance. This distinction can be linked to two related concepts of collective identity that will be described shortly.

Dominguez (1999) speaks of 'collective subjectivities' rather than movements. These possess what he calls a variable level of 'centring', i.e. organization and identity, and 'intentionality', coordinated action and common direction on the part of their members. The idea of collective subjectivity in this sense is extended beyond highly articulated classes and organizations but extends to 'more dispersed group, more amorphous classes, varied elites, the state, the economic system, several sorts of social movements, parties and many other social systems' (Dominguez, 1999, 28–9). This comment offers interesting possibilities for making sense of the fact that it is often difficult to identity the boundaries of movements. Most movements exhibit at some points in their lifecycle a wide range of support that can be difficult to distinguish from the movement proper. Is a political party that supports a nationalist claim part of the movement or not? Is an economic association that converges on some points with the programme of such a movement, but not on others, part of the movement or not? Whether one uses the term collective subjectivity or, our preference, collective identity, the idea of a cultural programme that spans various organizational forms and clarifies how movements interweave with their nearer and wider contexts at various periods in their lifecycle remains important.

Movement research has had considerable success in explaining the origins and dynamics of mobilization. McAdam, McCarthy and Zald (1996) speak of a gathering synthesis that encompasses the hitherto separate worlds of a resource mobilization school that emphasizes the activities of organizing in its structural context and a cultural approach that emphasizes how movements depend on forming identities and winning wider cultural support for their arguments. The new synthesis, according to the authors, involves a three-level consideration of, respectively, the structural conditions that create opportunities for movement action, the organization of that collective action itself, and the cultural interpretation patterns that mediate between structure and action. However, while representing a significant step forward, some limitations can be identified in relation to this synthesis. The first is that the idea of structure is predominantly understood as political, drawing from Kitschelt's (1986) work on political opportunity structures such as, for example, the openness or closedness of political systems, and not social or cultural opportunity structures such as blocked mobility as a source of recruitment or shifts in the political cultural climate (Brand, 1992). The second limitation is the failure to theorize adequately the role of movement contexts such as public support, sympathizers in administrations, or other actors who share part of their aims. The third is the relative neglect of the outcomes of movement activities, especially movements that aspire to far-reaching social change such as nationalist, environmentalist or feminist movements. The predominant focus on movements as forms of organization militates against consideration of the long-run *socio-cultural* as distinct from political outcomes of movement activity. We shall see in Chapter 5 how the application of movement theory to nationalism, while highly innovative, has in one of its variants at least a tendency to replicate these problems. Nevertheless, the application of movement theory in its various forms to the study of nationalism is highly promising. It will have a significant effect on perceptions and evaluations of the origins, cultures, and consequences of nationalism, both in general and in particular cases or constellations of cases.

44

nationalism and collective identity

Nationalism is at root a collective phenomenon. It is collective both as a form of identification and as an orientation to collective action. In spite of the variety of individual interpretations the idea of a private nationalism, as opposed to a private spiritual life, for example, makes no sense. Most fundamentally of all, nationalism is a phenomenon of culture, a kind of collective identity. The idea of nationalism as at base a form of collective identity is sustained because the manifestations of nationalism such as cultural production, the nationalization of the state, nationalist mobilization, all depend on the existence of, or the attempt to constitute, a strong collective identity. No other dimension is so intrinsic.

The collective identity of nationalism has formed, somewhat ambivalently, as a product of and response to, the historical process within modernity of the differentiation of spheres of action and the corresponding rationalization of culture. Most fundamentally, nationalism was a response to such differentiation; it has often been a form of modern re-enchantment in the sense of building the forms of identification that overcome the psychological emptiness that follows differentiation. The relationship vital for nationalism, between differentiation and the building of re-enchanted collective identities admits of two clear possibilities. The re-enchantment undertaken by nationalism has no significant effect on differentiation processes that proceed in much the same way in spite of nationalist mobilization, even when such mobilization is successful. In this case, nationalism merely replaces one elite with another while the underlying logic of modernization continues apace. Alternatively, and perhaps most commonly, nationalist movements may be seen in the sense of Tiryakian as movements of de-differentiation in which the institutional order is redirected to serve new kinds of integrative goals. In this case, there is an intimate relationship between nationalism and social mobilization. What lurks within both possibilities is the role of ideology in modern societies through which representations of situations may not equate with the situations themselves. Hence, nationalist movements and post-mobilization institutions may claim great strides towards equality, and may be believed by their fellow nationals to be achieving such goals, even where this is manifestly not the case. This question of belief is intrinsic to nationalist collective identity and may bear no or only highly indirect relationship to actual social change. This attests to the degree to which cultural perceptions of integrative changes towards for example rights, justice, gender equality and multicultural tolerance may not square with the extent of change itself. The rider, of course, needs to be added that nationalist mobilization can sometimes manifestly serve the goals of particular social mobilizations and create a consonance between fact and perception. In the latter case, whether particular groups stand to gain or lose is at least evident to all, although not necessarily to the good of all.

45

As a collective identity that seeks to bind the population of a territory to a specific cultural framework, nationalism has immense historical credentials. This collective identity has evolved in conjunction with modern structural arrangements, above all else the simultaneous differentiation and integration achieved through the modern state in its relation to modern society. Over time, nationalism has also become 'inter-textually' securely anchored within other collective identities such as 'social' collective identities based on class, democratic collective identity based upon the *demos*, 'spatial' collective identities built upon place, 'material' collective identities built around the production and circulation of goods and services, and sometimes even the cultural identities based on 'new' movements, such as the environmental or feminist movements. These other modern collective identities fuse with nationalist collective identities and assist it in maintaining its prominent place within the field of collective identity. This assertion, of course, merely documents in a broad, unspecific way the historical success of national identities in becoming institutionalized. It cannot be taken as a universal prescription to describe the inevitability of such success. Empirically, there are many cases in which the state is forced to become more 'identity neutral' as it balances precariously between alternative and opposing ethnic identities in civil society. Furthermore, at periods in history, for example the post-Second World War era in the western world, other collective identities gained in potency relative to national identity and reduced its centrality.

In line with ideas developed in the previous chapter to do with the non-social fundament of the social, Melucci (1995) speaks of the transfer of identification processes from outside society to its inside through the loss of such 'meta-social' guarantees as god, history or the invisible hand. Contemporary identification processes depend on the reflexive, intra-societal processes of identity construction. As identity is recognized as a process of social production, he claims that notions like 'coherence, boundary maintenance, and recognition' can only describe it in static terms. By contrast, in its dynamic connotation collective identity 'increasingly becomes a process of construction and autonomization' (1995, p. 50). Melucci persuasively makes the case for regarding the collective identity of meso-level collective actors such as social movements as a dynamic process of continuous construction out of the underlying texture of social relationships. It is not to be regarded as something univocal and stable but as something always dynamic and often contradictory. However, there is a need also for a more 'static' analysis, using his phrase, such as that developed by Münch (1987) and other neo-functional theorists. In this approach, identity is not as in Melucci a product of change so much as an expression of stability. Identity is secured by its correspondence to routinized structures and processes. From this standpoint, only those identities that are 'functionally' adapted to the appropriate generalisation of capacities for action will survive. In this reading, identity is the expression of the institutional mediation of social processes. It is true, and Münch partly recognizes this by placing identity-forming processes in relation to the dynamics of argumentation and discourse production, that such identity is also subject to change. However, its rate of change is much slower than that identified by Melucci. As we shall see later, much theorizing on nationalism, even professed accounts of cultural dynamics, depends more on the Münch version of collective identity than on that of Melucci. Such theories depend on quasi-functional assumptions about the necessity of national identity to the structural reproduction of modernity. In our view, while there can be problems with the way such arguments are adduced, the theorization of national identity does require a focus on the conditions of stability, however relative, as well as those of change. This can be seen, for example, in relation to cases in the nationalist typology in Chapter 6, where state patriotism is more likely to be institutionally stabilized and other nationalist forms such as extreme nationalism more likely to be institutionally destabilizing.

Melucci's account of collective identity, applicable to both dimensions of the phenomenon just discussed, describes three intrinsic aspects of collective identity. The first is the coherence of the relevant collectivity's own identity, the second is its delimitation from other collectivity's and non-belonging individuals, and the third is its capacity for either self-recognition or to have recognition accorded to it by others. Relatively long-run forms of institutionalized collective identity such as nation-states and classes have particular strengths in each of these dimensions, nascent ones, such as the origins of a national or ecology movement much less so. In the neo-functionalist version, learning takes places formally in what is described as the field of 'adaptivity'. Such learning is conceived as a somewhat diffuse 'emergent' process in the conditions of late modern society. For Melucci, learning is actually expressed in the process that leads to the formation of a social movement and, by extension, carried forward in the challenge such an actor presents to societal institutions in either a political or social plane, or sometimes both. But in order to understand the societal consequences of movements as learning forms it is necessary to examine their effects, including transformations, on the institutional order. A movement becomes transformative in both social and political dimensions, when it involves transformation not just in the associative and cultural practices of the lifeworld, but also succeeds in generalizing its identity and programme by shaping social systems as well.

It is hard to see why Melucci's point about the contemporary nature of reflexive, 'post-meta-social' movements does not historically apply to nationalist movements. It may well be that one of the principal reasons why nationalism has been historically neglected in the social sciences is its status as a highly modern cultural phenomenon, as something, following ideas already developed in the previous chapter, marking in a curious paradoxical way the end of socially applicable transcendental ideas carried by religions and philosophies of history and yet carrying within its manifold forms competing claims to transcendence. Modern nationalism can be seen therefore as something constructed and reconstructable, however much out of pre-existing cultural forms, as a horizontal response to the social and functional differentiations of modernity, often innovative and unstable but fuelled always – here the neo-functionalist perspective has its moment – by the model of a stable institutional and cultural order shaped in the likeness of its collective identity.

47

The recognition of the separate existence and yet interaction of dynamic and static types of collective identity is paralled by the way in which action and structure are related to one another in some of the most influential approaches in modern social theory, such as the work of Bourdieu, Elias and Giddens, who have in their different ways laid the foundations of a non-dualist conception of agency and structure. In these theories, agency has a certain autonomy and social structures are conceived of in a way that does not undermine the autonomy of the social actor. Hence Bourdieu's preference for a notion of practice which suggests a view of social action as strategic and guided by what he calls a 'practical sense' (Bourdieu, 1977, 1990). This is not too distant from

Giddens's notion of the 'duality of structure' by which social actors act upon structures as well as being shaped by them, for on the one side the social actor is primarily a knowledgeable agent and, on the other, social institutions are never so constraining that agency cannot exercise a transformative role (Giddens, 1984).

These reflections can be combined to form a sense of two complementary forces shaping nationalist collective identity. The first is the historical, agential and diachronic dimension of the constitutive power of nationalist action. The question that arises here is whether nationalism is innovative or reproductive, whether agency is respectively characterized by extra-institutional movements or by institutionally embedded associations. The second is the contemporary, synchronic dimension of how different facets of national identity are simultaneously institutionalized in both everyday life and in the institutional order[5] and how these dimensions of national identity are related to one another. We further develop these complementary distinctions in the next section in constructing a relational field of nationalist activity.

TOWARDS A THEORETICAL FRAMEWORK: FIELDS OF NATIONALIST ACTIVITY

48

The theoretical field encompassed by studies of nationalism, as it historically emerged and is currently situated, is not easy to summarize. Nationalism appears to elude easy categorization. One of the principal reasons for this is that it never received extensive theorization within functionalist theory, whose version of modernization theory when applied to disadvantaged countries was focused on development not the nation. The relative neglect of culture and agency, separately or combined in the social sciences, as outlined above, all but rendered the often diffusely rendered effects of nationalism and the nation invisible. Nationalism distracted from the search within the social sciences for secure, temporally well-ordered social and cultural foundations that had strong meta-theoretical status. It has only been with the widespread questioning of the linearity, extent and even desirability of the Western idea of progress that new theoretical ideas, more usable for the study of nationalism have become available. Nationalism studies, as we shall see in the following chapters, have not neglected to use such ideas but this in its turn, perhaps unavoidably, has generated a further set of problems to do with the disorienting effect of a profusion of temporal ranges, types of cultural interpretation, transfers across disciplines, borrowing between different theory traditions. The question that arises in light of this is not one of whether a single comprehensive meta-framework could be envisaged – of the types attempted by the stronger versions of structuralism and Marxism, so much as can the field somehow gain 'interchange coherence' between its different parts. It is in order to make some modest beginnings towards this goal that, drawing from the above theoretical reflections, various fields of nationalist activity are outlined in this chapter and applied, somewhat loosely, in the subsequent chapters.

In the preceding pages, a distinction was drawn between the agential processes involved in constituting new nationalist collective identities and the institutionalization that occurs once such identities accquire a sufficient degree of power within the overall organization of society. A further distinction can be drawn within this basic distinction between the constitutive and institutional moments of collective identity. This has to do with the process of innovation and stabilization of cultural interpretation systems and the process of innovation and transformation of social systems. The respective processes of change and stabilization in these two dimensions allow for the identification of four distinct but highly inter-related fields. The fields are, firstly, the generation of new knowledge, values and sentiments, and cognitive frameworks through cultural innovation. A second field involves the stabilization of cultural interpretation systems and identities within socio-cultural lifeworlds, e.g., nations and ethnic groups. A third field has to do with organized socio-political mobilization more or less consciously directed to particular episodes of social change. Finally, a fourth consists of the institutional and systemic organization of society.

A strong assumption that we bring to our understanding of nationalism is that each of these four fields separately and in various combinations are critical to its different manifestations. They are therefore described in more detail in what follows. An additional consideration in constituting these fields is to relate them to key dynamics that explain their interplay in producing social change. Two dynamics appear as absolutely pivotal. These are, firstly, the dynamic identified by Giddens and Bourdieu, among others, which emphasizes the relationship between agency and structure. Secondly is the dynamic identified by a wide variety of authors including Habermas, and various kinds of functionalism between culture or life-world and social systems. The first of these dynamics, already traced in this chapter, is understood here as the long-run dynamic generated by movements for cultural re-interpretation or social change that can lead to the constitution of new kinds of structure or the re-orientation of existing structures. These structures are dove-tailing structures of action and knowledge that endure over time such as those represented by parties, classes, occupational groups, intellectuals, cultural and political associations. Political and cultural movements are not socially, politically and culturally embedded at the outset but they can become so over time, resulting in a transformation in their organizational forms towards other more stable forms such as parties, associations, or learned societies. They also aspire to change the orientations of other already embedded groups such as classes and occupational groups (professionals, industrial or agricultural workers,

49

armies) and, of course, ethnies. These more stable forms reciprocally condition the possibilities for cultural or political mobilization and at various points and in various ways react back upon forms of agency, the so-called duality of structure.

The second dynamic is that between life-world and system. This dynamic is one that is institutionally patterned, specifying basic relations between levels of differentiation, integration and cultural orders, which allow for a relatively stable reproduction of basic social processes organized in the form of institutions. The basic idea is that this synchronic, less temporally dynamic relationship between system and life-world allows for 'necessary' levels of organizational and cultural co-evolution.

These two dynamics can be analytically distinguished from one another but in actual practice they interpenetrate. Actors concerned with cultural innovation seek to change life-world beliefs. Contradictions built into the life-world reciprocally result in the formation of innovative ideas giving rise to cultural movements, which may in turn generate political movements for the transformation of social systems. Schematic distinctions of this kind are useful for analytic purposes, for drawing distinctions and ensuring that different dimensions of a phenomenon bearing on a situation are kept in sight, but descriptions of real situations are required to be considerably richer. However, somewhat paradoxically, distinctions of this kind can be used to heighten rather than diminish richness of description and certainly give structure to descriptive – and evaluative – activities.

Figure 1 opposite, diagrammatically summarizes the fields of nationalist activity that follow the above distinctions and dynamics.[6] The diagram is constructed around two poles that follow the two dynamics of agency/structure and life-world/system. The first, on the vertical axis, is the agency-structure pole that emphasizes the active creation of cultures and institutional orders through nationalist agency. This pole emphasizes the historical-temporal dimension of nationalism as an agent of social change. The other, on the horizontal axis, is the system/life-world pole, which emphasizes the role of nationalism as an institutionally stabilized culture in the life-world that establishes cultural parameters for the operation of social systems. This pole, therefore, emphasizes the institutional presence of nationalism in relatively stable societal value systems and institutions. These two axes mirror the distinction drawn by Sztompka, as already described, between field and system theories of social change. In Figure 1, the two axes, action-structure and life-world-system allow the identification of four fields of nationalist activity, the fields respectively of socio-political mobilization, cultural innovation, the socio-cultural life-world and the institutional core. These fields are next described and related to characteristic types of nationalist activity.

Beginning top right, we have identified the field of socio-political innovation carried by 'movements', where that term is relatively

50

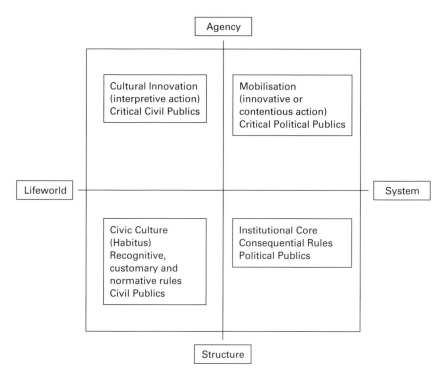

Figure 1 *Fields of Nationalist Acitivity*

loosely applied to a variety of forms of collective political agency. This field, corresponding to the quadrant between agency and system, is entitled *mobilization*. It is concerned with bringing about innovation in the political system or principles of social organization by transformation of the political order. This is the classic field of goal-directed collective political action for which we use the generic term *mobilization*. Mobilization depends upon the creation, expansion and maintenance *of critical political publics* who consume the messages or support the actions of mobilized actors. Nationalism has proven to be perhaps the most potent source of political mobilization in the modern world and the relationship between the messages produced by nationalist actors and receptive publics critical of the status quo has been pivotal.

The top left-hand quadrant of Figure 1, between agency and lifeworld, represents the field of *cultural innovation*. This cultural innovation is also carried by movements, in this case cultural movements. These movements tend to be less clearly organizationally specified than more overtly political movements from which they may also be hard to distinguish as they often work hand in hand. This field of cultural innovation, however, produces a wider kind of cultural production, typically by intellectuals of various kinds, that is oriented to the construction of a new nationalist identity but not necessarily operating with clear political objectives, at least in the early stages of nationalist agitation where it tends to precede political movements proper (Hutchinson, 1987). Cultural production about the nation also characterizes 'everyday' nationalism in the socio-cultural life-world – the bottom left-hand quadrant – in which the texture of national identity is interpreted and subtly re-ordered. However, the field of cultural innovation involves more radical shifts and the creation of innovation bodies of argumentation in support of nationalist aims. Often, it constructs categories of 'nationness' that had not before existed at all or were not extensively diffused in the population. Cultural production of this kind is very commonly antagonistic to the established cultural or political order or to other ethnic groups. The interpretative theorists of nationalism, whom we shall examine in Chapter 4, tend to be concerned more with this field, involving the creation of cultural idea systems and their resonance in the socio-cultural life-world, and not with the phenomenon of political mobilisation *per se*. The interpretative activity characteristic of this field once more depends upon the creation, extension and maintenance of *critical civil publics*, that is to say, publics seeking an innovative expression of their individual and collective identities that speaks to their deep-most needs for cultural belonging (Brand, 1992).

52

The third quadrant, between life-world and structure poles, is the lower left-hand field of the socio-cultural life-world or *civic culture*. This field is composed of relatively stable cultural rules of a customary, recognition-related (rules of collective belonging) and normative kind. It is characterised by a general set of cultural beliefs and rules that offer a sufficient basis for the inter-subjective and co-operative requirements of social order. However, it almost goes without saying that one group's co-operation and mutual understanding may be at the price of another group's exclusion. Therefore, identities anchored in rules of custom or recognition may also exhibit a most uncooperative form of ethnocentric exclusion or foreigner hatred, as documented in Chapter 8. Apart from recognitive and customary rules that underpin community, ethnic and national identities, this field is also characterized by those normative rules that provide foundations for social institutions. This field is normally characterized by stable civil publics who culturally legitimate an existing social and political order. A critical threshold of nationalist cultural and/or political mobilization occurs when this civil public switches to support of the nationalist case. In that instance, the abnormal case occurs of a certain co-incidence of radical cultural ideas and a culturally inflamed national habitus that may of course exclude substantial sections of the population placed outside the national or ethnic community. Another manifestation of the interplay of identities in this field is the case of ethnically divided societies, in which ethnic groups either reach some form of consociational arrangement for the sharing of political power or are characterized by a dominant ethnic identity and one or more suppressed ethnic identities.

The final quadrant in Figure 1, the bottom right-hand quadrant between system and structure, is the *institutional core*. Following Habermas (1984, 1987a), institutional orders can be characterized in relation to the extent to which they are media-steered or are more loosely co-ordinated by cultural meaning systems to a greater or lesser extent anchored in the life-world. The economy (money) or the public bureaucracy (power and information) are predominantly media-steered systems. The legal system stands somewhere between the two while education and the family are substantially anchored in the values of the life-world. The institutional core in Figure 1 is taken to be composed of institutionalized organizational rules and the operational and legitimating cultures that allow such institutions to function. The relevant public in this case is the institutionalized political public who participate in various ways in political deliberation processes in general or within institutional areas such as education, health, the economy and so on. This representation of the political system could of course be made much more complex, detailing kinds of agency and their interaction with structures within the contexts of circuits of power and the relational fields of politics (Habermas, 1996).

In the chapters which follow we will explore three major kinds of nationalist theory traditions, those that emphasize structural factors, the dynamics of cultural meaning creation, and the conditions and forms of nationalist agency. The first, covered in Chapter 3, primarily emphasizes the historical constitution of social structures, cultures and institutions on the diachronic-vertical axis and, on the synchronic-horizontal axis, the implications of these social structures for nationalist activity in modern societies. This approach primarily emphasizes how certain kinds of structural configuration explain the incidence, forms and implications of nationalism. It is therefore concentrated on macro-structures of the kind represented in the bottom two quadrants, though it also considers the historical genesis of these structures. Secondly, cultural dynamics is covered in Chapter 4, and is mainly concerned with the interplay between cultural innovation and institutionalization; the concerns of the top and bottom left-hand quadrants. Thirdly, Chapter 5 focuses on agency, and is concerned with the conditions and dynamics of cultural innovation and political mobilization, and hence is concerned with the top two quadrants in the broader context of the structural framework conditions illustrated by the bottom two.

53

CONCLUSION

In this chapter, we have explored how social theoretical insights can be used to understand nationalism in a manner that is alive both to its dynamic, change-oriented aspects and its role as a relatively stable part of social reproduction. In the three chapters that follow, we show how different accounts of nationalism can be related to this understanding, how they place emphasis on different dimensions and how they might profit from co-operation. The essential idea lying behind our explorations so far is that nationalism does have a structural role in modern societies, but its dependence on a volatile and conflictual cultural order complicates the relationship between nationalism and social integration. Nationalist world perceptions often extend beyond structural realities to imaginary constructs and these imaginary constructs are capable of radically transforming existing structural arrangements. This process makes the elucidation of nationalist discourse intrinsic to an overall understanding of the phenomenon. Nationalism is a particular kind of collective identity held by a social group or by an entire 'nation' that ultimately derives from the prior 'discursive' constitution of such a collective identity in a long- or short-run time frame. While structural stages of differentiation and integration set limits to the creative powers of nationalist discourse, they do not by any means circumscribe them fully. The social sciences have not been sufficiently alive to the cultural dynamics of modern society but nationalism forces attention to it. Further, it draws attention to the intrinsic relationship between power and cultural interpretation.

Nationalism is also par excellence a theatre of agency generated by the manner in which the social and cultural projects of the carriers of nationalism, nationalist movements, states, parties and others, situate themselves, sometimes with the grain of structure, for example, in the conjunction of nationalism and class, but also sometimes in the interstices of its disjunctions, for example in the phenomenon of nationalism as an apparent but unrealized remedy for inequality. Nationalist agency has acquired two enormous advantages over the course of late modernity. It has acquired a clear social project as a model, control of the institutional order through control of the state by a culturally defined collectivity, and it has good prospects for resonance amongst affected publics. Together, these opportunities make nationalism not just a fertile site of cultural and socio-political movements but also offer clear institutional and cultural models for the socio-political embodiment of actual or potential movement success.

NOTES

1 The term permanent revolution is suggested by the title of Leon Trotsky's *The Permanent Revolution* but is obviously used in a different sense here (Trotsky, 1931).

2 See Delanty (1999) on differentiation and integration as the underlying dynamic of modernity.

3 For some discussion on this see Delanty (2000b), Urry (2000).

4 See Meinecke (1970).

5 One of the central achievements of nationalism in modernity, as pointed out in the introduction, is this double reference of nationalism to everyday life and political reality.

6 This approach takes a lead from Strydom (1987) who develops a parametric framework for the positioning of social theorists. Following Strydom, the action-structure axis follows the work of theorists such as Bourdieu and Giddens and the system/life-world axis follows Habermas.

three
nationalism and structure

In the previous chapter, we outlined the centrality of structural differentiation processes to the historical development of sociology as well as the increasing questioning of the presumed independence of these differentiation processes from the dynamics of culture and agency. In the current chapter, this question is taken up afresh and related to those accounts of nationalism that in their theory and methodology can be said to belong to structural traditions in sociology and politics. An overview of the literature on nationalism today, albeit one largely confined to the English-speaking world, reveals this to be a less prominent tradition than the interpretative approaches that we will discuss in the next chapter. The work of Ernest Gellner, for example, is noticeable because it is often treated in isolation as representative of structural approaches. Gellner's popularity, apart from the intrinsic interest of the work itself, perhaps also owes something to the fact that he combines a strong structural hypothesis, the intrinsic 'causal' connection between industrialization and nationalism, with a cultural inflection, that this causality expresses itself in the need of industrialized societies for a literate 'high' culture that facilitates nationalism.[1] Even Gellner's structuralist credentials are sometimes under emphasized by the way his work is contrasted with 'primordialists' such as Anthony Smith who sees modern nationalism as having early modern roots. In this debate, Gellner is represented as a 'modernist' who by contrast to writers such as Smith sees nationalism as a product of 'construction processes' in modern society.

Two sets of distinctions can be made in relation to our approach to the structural issues in the study of nationalism. The first lies between the reconstruction of historically long-run macro structures that are woven into explanatory accounts of nationalism, and it might be added into cultural-interpretive accounts also, and structural factors that are identified as significant to concrete episodes of nationalist mobilization and which have a less encompassing, more 'middle-range' scope. The first include structural outcomes of historical processes such as capitalism, democratization and print technology, as outlined in Chapters 1 and 2, and the second involves the sedimentation of a certain range of structural forces that throw light on nationalist mobilization, such as factors giving rise to competition between ethnic groups or a cultural division of labour. Only the first of these accounts of structure will be considered in this chapter with the second being regarded from the standpoint of the structural factors shaping nationalist mobilization and hence treated in Chapter 5. The second set of distinctions arises between different understandings of structure as between social structures, political structures and cultural structures. The distinction is normally drawn between emphasis on the first two, often taken together, dealing with phenomena such as the formation of classes and political institutions, on the one hand, and cultural structures as embodied in systems of ideas such as social order, rationalization, legitimacy, justice and responsibility and, of course, nationalist collective identity itself on the other. Some aspects of cultural structures in this sense are taken up in this chapter by considering the relationship between nationalism and the public sphere.

The chapter will begin with an account of the work of Stein Rokkan in relation to European nation building. Rokkan is counted as being a major figure in developmental accounts of nationalism that presume that geographically and culturally articulated ethnic cleavages will be superseded by functional cleavages based on class interests (Lipset and Rokkan, 1967; Ragin, 1979). In this sense, he is counted among those modernization theorists who are increasingly represented as not theoretically useful for the study of nationalism and ethnicity since they are taken to view the historical process as involving their long-run supersession. However, Rokkan cannot be regarded as a scholar with marginal interest in nationalism and ethnicity; in fact, his historical reconstruction of the economic, cultural and institutional dimensions of European nation building was acutely sensitive to questions of nationalism. In addition, Rokkan exemplifies the continuing value of the historical macrostructural orientation of the developmental approach, even if its explanatory accounts must be highly qualified by more particular and dynamic considerations. Notwithstanding this desire for qualification, the fact remains that nationalism continues to be regarded as connected with structural phenomena that vary in their temporal and spatial scope and endurance but at least some of which such as democracy and capitalism are seen as relatively long standing. At a minimum, some elucidation of these structural phenomena and their relevance to nationalism continues to be required for making general sense of nationalism beyond particular cases. For example, the claim is often made that nationalism is a movement of integration, a kind of balm for the tearing apart of social spheres that accompanied the dominant logic of differentiation processes in modernity.[2] Such a view requires that treatment of differentiation and its counter-moment of integration must be considered as part of the general theory of nationalism, out of which a specific set of questions can be generated in particular cases.[3]

57

Our treatment of these issues builds on their treatment in the previous chapter. In this first section of the chapter, therefore, we will present some historical-theoretical insights provided by Rokkan and supplement it with some other reflections on relatively long-run structures of modernity that he does not cover at all or does not cover in depth, drawing centrally from the work of Norbert Elias, and, to a lesser extent, Ernest Gellner for this task. We then proceed to consider the relationship between nationalism and the public sphere.

ROKKAN'S HISTORICAL DIACHRONICS AND THE STUDY OF NATIONALISM

The work of Stein Rokkan[4] is pivotal to any attempt to establish a relationship between structural persistence and change in modern societies and the many particular episodes of nationalism. The work is pivotal in an interdisciplinary sense also. Although his work has been primarily claimed by political science, Rokkan wove together history, sociology and political science as need demanded. In the introduction to his collection of Rokkan's writings, Flora et al. (1999) identify four key dimensions of Rokkan's approach:

58

- the attempt to bridge the gap between sociological generalization and historical context specification by means of region and period specific models
- the aim of elaborating a unified macro model of political development in Europe in the form of *configurations* rather than hierarchies of *factors*
- the use of *retrospective diachronics* in the analysis of long-term development, in order to explain variations at one point in time by combinations of earlier variations
- the concentration on a *comparison of structures* which, although in principle not incompatible with an actor perspective, in practice does not consider actors.

A number of consequences of this approach as identified by Flora et al., are important for our consideration. First Rokkan, along with Tilly (1984), breaks with the idea of nation-states as isolated units to be compared. Rather the very genesis of these nation-states is examined within the context of a larger interdependent system. This system is constituted by the interrelation of territorial, economic and culture variables in the historical action space of the European continent. The approach is configurational rather than hierarchical in that the combinations of variables are geared to explain variation and differences of nation-building outcomes in relation to common structural contexts rather than sameness of outcomes. This emphasis owed much to the fact that Rokkan was a historical-comparative scholar of the origins of nation-states, not a predominantly synchronic theorist of modern societal structures. For this reason, Rokkan's work offers vital insight into how broad structural contexts *are related to* differences of outcomes generated by a variety of factors. As Flora et al., argued, Rokkan's work accords a high degree of autonomy to various structural processes and developmental dynamics and hence his approach remains open to various possibilities of their combination in producing particular outcomes.

The second dimension identified by Flora et al., is that while Rokkan describes his own work as historical diachronics, it had, in fact, both a synchronic (spatial) and diachronic (temporal) moment. From a synchronic standpoint, Rokkan speaks of packages of programmes, commitments, outlooks and worldviews from which citizen actors 'choose'. The diachronic dimension accords a central emphasis to the timing in which temporal sequences occur. According to Flora et al., timing is expressed in the model building of Rokkan's work in which he distinguishes between: 'Four developmental processes of territorial political systems; state formation in the narrower sense, nation-building, democratisation and the establishment of welfare states. Taken together, the features of these individual processes and the ways in which they combine over time make up national *developmental paths or trajectories'*. (Flora et al., 1999).

In relation to the parameters of the framework outlined in Chapter 2, Rokkan is well spread across the various axes and quadrants. He accords considerable significance to the force of historical agency, but the historical agents he theorizes are not so much human agents as historical forces. His work is therefore open to history but at the same time highly structured as regards the agency axis. There is, within Rokkan, a certain teleology in the treatment of elites who manifest a kind of ontological permanence in an ongoing attempt virtuously to shape historical dynamics towards the appropriate outcomes of the modern, democratic nation-state. His treatment of action is therefore a highly reductive one. A most interesting feature of Rokkan is that while his work, by his own description, is of a 'retrospective diachronic' nature, he attempts to link this diachronic reconstruction to a fully textured synchronic account of these historical forces. It is therefore quite developed towards the system pole, especially in relation to the institutional mediation of the late modern state-society relationship, and also towards the lifeworld pole where certain key variables, especially around the theme of mass loyalty to state and nation, are explored. But Rokkan's treatment of culture does not go so far as to embrace the hermeneutically encrypted peculiarity of different collective identities. Since his object of explanation is ultimately territorial patterns of nation building and state formation, his synchronic orientation is somewhat more towards economic and governance considerations, while by no means excluding culture or not taking it seriously.

59

The next section follows Rokkan's work in three steps, moving from his treatment of *territory formation* to how he conceptualizes variations generated by *identity* to the stabilization of the form of the European *nation-state*.

territory formation, identity variation and nation building

Rokkan builds on Parson's theory of differentiation by presenting the differentiation of primordial local communities, characterized by minimal functional differentiation, on four lines. These are, first, economic-technological differentiation whose main expression is the formation of cities and with them cross-local commercial-industrial organizations. The second is military-administrative differentiation whose main early modern expression is organization for control of external conflicts. Third, he identifies judicial-legislative differentiation, which is expressed in the organization for internal conflicts. Finally, there is religious-symbolic differentiation whose main expression is in the formation of cross-local script religions. From the standpoint of the formation of territory Rokkan is focused on only three of these points, economic, cultural-religious and military-administrative, since these are pivotal for boundary transactions and boundary control measures between emerging territorial centres. Rokkan places these mechanisms of differentiation and territory formation in the context of a theory of centre-periphery relations on the basis that territories as the expression of variations in political systems cannot be understood without looking into the structure of the space over which they exert some control. Rokkan therefore proposes to analyse centres, the places where major decisions are made and the site of the political and social networks of decision makers; peripheries or those areas controlled by centres in which are located populations in one way or another dependent on decisions made in the centres; and transactions between centres and other centres and between centres and peripheries.[5] For each of the three focal points of differentiation and boundary drawing, Rokkan identifies the key resource holders. So, for the boundary-spanning and boundary-control dimension of the production and exchange of commodities and services the commercial/industrial bourgeoisie in the cities are pivotal; similarly, for the circulation of messages and codes, is the educated elite in the churches, universities and schools; finally, for the control of populations the alliances of landowners and military personnel is central.

Rokkan derives three key dynamics of the extension and resistance to the power of centres over peripheries from these axes of differentiation. First, military-administrative system building leads to the dynamics of, on the one hand, territorial integration generated by elite alliances and administrative subordination and, on the other, to territorial separation created by resistance and counter-mobilization on the periphery.

Second, in the case of economic system building there are the twin processes of, on the one hand, the extension of monetization and the incorporation of the periphery in exchange networks, hence increasing economic dependence and on the other, attempts on the periphery to maintain a distinct economy by strategies of autarky or the seeking of alternative markets. Third, in the case of cultural system building there is, on the one hand, a process of linguistic, religious and ideological standardization and the maintenance of distinct identities expressed in the retention of separate languages, literatures, churches and schools on the other. What is important to remember is that this model of integration and resistance is specified to apply to large-scale territorial systems.[6] This has the implication that broad structural forces such as monetization or cultural standardization happen at roughly the same time across the territory, although with highly uneven patterns of diffusion. Diffusion lags are created by resistance but also simply by the capacity of centres to exert themselves or by brute geographic facts such as remoteness. This, of course, has the further implication that processes of resistance also follow a distinctive temporal and spatial logic.

This framework on its own is already of some importance for situating two kinds of nationalism. Already here in the model of centre-periphery relations are two basic ideological options for the pursuance of nationalism that represent a super set of the basic types of nationalism (see Chapter 6). These are the ideological promulgation of integrative codes from a state-building alliance of elites that extend not just to distant peripheries but also over the territorial centre itself and, conversely, the rejection of such ideological forms by peripheries which, for a variety of reasons, are determined to follow their own paths. However, both options are constrained not just by the balances of forces within it but by the basic historically sedimented experiences of organization and ideology that condition types of sovereignty over territory. In Europe the model of the nation-state became more dominant than in other parts of the world because of a variety of complex factors to do with the relative strengths of peripheries over centres and the consequent formation of multiple centre-periphery relations. However, as we shall see later, the model of the nation-state emerging from such centre-periphery relations was conditioned by the model of state building and later had to accommodate itself to social mobilization associated with democratization and the building of welfare states. What is already clear is that the linking of differentiation processes to the constitution of centres and peripheries offers an important framework for exploring the relationship between nationalism and the institutional development of modernity.

Turning to the application of the framework to the real dynamics of state formation in Europe, Rokkan notes that all attempts at military-administrative centre building fails in Europe until the nineteenth century. Although the centre belt was institutionally, technologically and culturally highly advanced, it was unable to extend its power to peripheral regions. Pivotal events here were of course the unification of Germany and Italy that created a new and unstable consolidation of territories in Europe. Prior to this in Rokkan's view the decisive early developments towards a restructuring of territory took place in the periphery of the heartland. Europe therefore experienced a fragmented modernization in which developments such as the growth of literate bureaucracies, the emergence of national scripts, the growth of trade and emergence of new industries led to the consolidation of peripheries and created the basis for the multiple nation-state model.

However, this process of territory formation cannot be understood without taking centrally into account the construction and diffusion of territorial, later national, identity patterns. Flora et al. (1999) note that for Rokkan identity was a central concept, though he nowhere defines it. He sees such identity as competing with other forms of collective identity such as class or emergent forms of ethnicity. For Rokkan, territorial identity has a number of distinctive features such as geographic extensiveness, a two-dimensional 'spatial' reference to whom shall be accorded membership and to territory, a dependency on culture and a monopolistic tendency either towards other collective identities or towards other national identities. In the case of national identity, identity-building processes involve the setting of cultural boundaries, an activity whose reconstruction is prone to great uncertainty and imprecision. This is why:

> It is so difficult to determine when the process of nation-building began in Europe: its origins were bound up with the crystallisation of ethnic structure, the emergence of ethnic/linguistic centres, and the development of different written languages and literatures – all processes that took centuries to evolve and combined in very different ways with the consolidation of military-administrative centres and territorial states. (Flora et al., 1999, p. 67)

The interpretation of Rokkan by Flora et al., accords to nation building also a normative significance. Early processes of identity formation from the combination of ethnic, linguistic and religious elements 'created conditions for democratization in the form of communication, trust, identity, solidarity across communities, and in close connection with the territorial consolidation of the state and the strengthening of central authority' (Flora et al., 1999, p. 67). Conversely also, democratization was an essential element of nation building, merging the concept of citizenship with territorial identity. Problematic forms of national-identity formation such as that of Germany, which indicate that national we-feeling may just as easily end up as a social pathology and not in egalitarian social mobilization, are addressed by Rokkan as part of his framework but only as qualifications to the generally positive normative outcomes of nation building. Rokkan refers in this connection to the greater difficulties of late comers to the nation-building process such as Germany, because the national elites did not have time to solve the problems of state formation before the attempt at nation building and the related incorporation of mass political participation. Territories with longer histories of continuous state building such as Britain and France were better positioned to build stable nation-states.

The variables used by Rokkan as central to nation building were religious traditions and linguistic diversity. The first is used in order to specify potentials of nation building in the first place, while the second defines the capacity of peripheries to resist cultural standardization emanating from centres. In Rokkan's view it was distance from the territorial sway of the supra-territorial Catholic church that created the conditions for the formation of distinct cultural identities in Europe's northern and western peripheries, Spain, Portugal, Britain, Sweden, France. However, it is language that receives most analytical attention in Rokkan's attempt to chart the survival of peripheral identities across the territories of Western Europe. He claims that while peripheries can retain an identity without a language of their own – Ireland and Scotland are prominent examples – the likelihood of erosion of other forms of distinctive identity is greater once the language is lost. Rokkan uses language, therefore, as the central variable for defining which peripheries survive with a distinctive identity and adds to it various exception rules such as tensions between the church and state affecting Catholic peripheries to explain cases where territorial identity survives without it.

A further dimension of Rokkan's work we wish to consider is his treatment of the ideal-typical temporal path to European modernity, most typically fulfilled by the older nation-states of France and Britain. For this, Rokkan proposes a scheme of four stages. The first covers the initial state-building process from the high Middle Ages to the French Revolution which he describes as a process of political, cultural and economic unification at the elite level. This can be characterized as a period of network formation, identity building and institution building. The second moves outwards from elites to masses who are increasingly brought into the system through conscript armies, compulsory schools and the emerging mass media that create communication channels between elites and parochial populations on the periphery and lead to the development of common feelings of identification. The third phase brings these subject populations on the periphery into active participation in the workings of the territorial political system through the extension of privileges of opposition, the extension of electorates, the formation of parties and the articulation and aggregation of demands. Finally, in the fourth phase, there is an expansion of the administrative apparatus of the territorial state through the growth of agencies of redistribution and the building of welfare services so as create more egalitarian life chances. As already observed, in the older countries of Western Europe this ideal type model approximates the real most closely. The fit is not as close for the later European states and even less so for processes of secession from metropolis and empire outside of Europe. This is due to the fact that in the last cases the four phases are often confronted together, regularly leading to an over loading of complex problems in different dimensions. In relation to the centre-periphery model, the first two phases involve the extension of the political, economic, legal and cultural power of the centre, and the second two are associated with the response of the periphery as part of the transition to democratic, mass political systems. The latter association goes some way towards explaining why nationalism is often accorded a generally positive normative status, although as Hobsbawm (1990) and others make clear, nationalism has an ambivalent relationship to democratization and social inclusion, especially from the late nineteenth century onwards.

Rokkan does also not neglect to schematize movements of opposition and protest in territorial political systems. In this case, he identifies four thresholds to full-scale involvement. These are, first, the stage of legitimate organization with the expression of the rights of expression, assembly and other forms of collective action against incumbent power holders; the second, the threshold of incorporation, involves the extension of certain political rights to under privileged strata; the third is the threshold of representation giving minorities representation in local and national assemblies; and the fourth is the threshold of executive access, the opening up of channels of control from the assembly to the executive organs of the state. Clearly, these thresholds are also conceived from a temporal perspective in relation to the emergence on the historical stage of major territorial national movements and the civil societal movement of labour that have had the most significant effect on the constitutions of political systems and the dominant cleavages within them. Any subsequent protest movements in democratic societies would from the outset, at least in principle, enjoy the necessary rights *potentially* to cross the final threshold; whether in fact they do so is dependent on mobilization success in the context of a shifting structure of political opportunities. In the context of the emergence of strong national identities, it is interesting to note that Rokkan sees the opening of electoral-plebiscitarian channels, presumably also executive channels, as accentuating territorial identity and helping to nationalize the citizenry.

In a short treatment of this nature, we cannot follow the extraordinary depth and range of Rokkan's empirical and synthetic treatment of how the key variables he identifies combine to produce a set of national outcomes in Europe. What is important is that it represents the most sustained attempt to apply a variant on modernization theory to the development of national identities in a territorial political system. The question that arises is not the apparent one of whether it succeeds. This is a question of such huge empirical range that it would require an entire book to address. The central question for a study such as this is whether the attempt to provide historically informed comparative-theoretical foundations for the exploration of nation-state formation in a single territorial system is plausible? Our answer to this question would be positive for a number of reasons:

- Rokkan works at the level of interlinked cases within a territorial system and does not try to aggregate from the individual cases themselves as happens with much literature on nationalism. Only from such a perspective can a meaningful macro-theoretical framework be produced that necessarily must move between generalization and particular cases in a flexible or configurational manner. By this stratagem the twin problems of the abstract domination of individual cases by big structures or the positing of structures by the aggregation of separately conceived individual cases can be avoided.
- Rokkan is prepared 'inter-textually' to link issues of national identity with other forms of identity and, more centrally in his work, with economic and political factors. He is further prepared to place this inter-textual matrix on an extended temporal plane. Even if the range of variables considered by him is narrow – deliberately and perhaps necessarily for the success of his endeavour – the number of possible relationships charted is vast. Rokkan demonstrates simultaneously the benefits of a multi-factorial conceptual framework that can do justice to a complex reality and the extreme difficulty of applying it.
- Not alone does Rokkan's work provide foundations for the repeated use within accounts of nationalism – in relation to Europe and elsewhere – of concepts such as differentiation, integration, religious rationalization, democratization, periphery, territory and others, he also provides new insights into a central debate on theories of nationalism. This is the debate centring on the pre-modern longevity or nearer-run constructedness of national identity, the debate between the so-called primordialists and modernists. Basic empirically grounded distinctions used by Rokkan offer some qualifications on the extent of the modernity of the construction of national identity, while leaving open the possibility that it may be substantially or in some cases completely so constructed. In effect if territorial political boundary markers, and even territorial identity, is substituted for national identity it is plausible to believe that these in certain cases are based on variables of historically long-run provenance that may survive to later times and influence the form taken

65

by modern national identities. Examples include the experience of peripheralization, control over the levers of welfare satisfaction, religious orientation, linguistic affiliation, and experience of democratic participation. At the same time, Rokkan's theory of stages, as we have outlined, shows his awareness of the immense difference in relation to the function of national identity that is present between pre-democratic and democratic societies. The reason why Rokkan's framework can be used to suggest a 'compromise position' of this kind is down to his attempt to provide temporally gradated macro-societal theory constructs that allow such connections and distinctions to be made.

In wider profile, Rokkan's work exhibits significant limitations. It is not our remit here to consider empirical-theoretical criticisms of his conceptual framework (Allum, 1995; Badie and Birnbaum, 1981). More immediately relevant to our concerns is the criticism levelled at Rokkan by Tilly (1990). Tilly criticizes Rokkan and other 'statist' proponents of an orderly path of European political development for basing their work on the model of successful unified nation-states. These nation-states such as France or England appear as normative models towards which the rest of Europe was teleologically oriented by state-building elites, who would choose the nation-state and democracy if events did not make this impossible. This intentional framework is quite apparent in Rokkan where state- and nation-building processes appear as elites battling with circumstances towards a desired democratic nation-state outcome rather than, as in Germany for example, significant sections of the elite being hostile to or indifferent to democracy (Eder, 1985; Elias, 1992). More specifically, Tilly criticizes Rokkan for leaving a 'muddled idea' of the social processes connecting socio-political changes in relations between rulers, neighbouring powers, dominant classes and religious institutions to state trajectories. In other words, Rokkan's approach left too few variables spread too thinly over too many cases to the neglect of a whole range of factors – Tilly singles out the impact of accumulation of capital and means of coercion – to capture the rich dynamics of multiple interlocking actors and contexts.

Turning back to the theoretical framework outlined in Chapter 2, we can follow this criticism by suggesting that Rokkan's limitations lie in the way he conceived, following Parsons, a progressive normative and empirical teleology built into the dynamics of differentiation and integration. The role left even for elites is circumscribed by the logic inscribed in these larger historical forces. The logics of collective action, and of collective learning as and through action, are left out of the picture. Also left out of the picture are cultural processes other than ecclesiastical organization and linguistic structures. The latter is the substance of one of Allum's criticisms of Rokkan. He contrasts Rokkan's approach with Elias's identification of three models of the formation and propagation of national cultural norms and the more extended treatment of the dynamics of cultural formation contained therein (Allum, 1995; Elias, 1978, 1982). We propose at this point first of all to follow Allum's useful synthetic account of Elias and then add some general remarks with respect to Elias's work. This will have the purpose of extending the range of consideration of structural factors relevant to nationalism to a fuller treatment of the long-run relationship between political development and cultural structures. With Elias, we certainly do not leave the realm of differentiation theory, but we do also enter the sphere of the theory of cultural rationalization.

THE CONSTRUCTION OF NATIONAL CULTURES

Following Allum, Elias distinguished between three types of national cultural norms:

- the English model of an aristocratic-bourgeois culture
- the French model of a national culture as a product of state power (aristocratic before the revolution, bourgeois after it)
- the German model of a bourgeois and academic culture.

67

These cultures were formed from different experiences of state formation. These ranged from the French experience of the early stabilization of a centralized monarchy and the consequent imposition of a courtly culture from Versailles, to the English monarchy's failure to impose such a courtly culture and the consequent survival of aristocratic conceptions of freedom and authority, to the German case, where the absence of a single central authority led to the development of a bourgeois and academic culture as a reaction to the cosmopolitanism of the small courts too weak to impose a national culture. Elias progresses from such bases to the specifics of these national cultures within a European civilizational framework. He identified freedom and authority, tolerance and inequality, self-discipline and pragmatism in England; ideological intolerance and instrumentalism, authoritarianism and formalism in France; authoritarianism, bureaucratism, discipline and conformism in the German case. The mechanisms he examined in detail included the loss of military role of the English aristocracy and consequent commercial alliance with the bourgeoisie, the replacement of the court of Versailles by a bourgeois-representative state in France and the role of the *Volkgeist* and the aristocratic military-bourgeois bureaucratic alliance in Germany. These mechanisms helped to consolidate the cultural traits of the elite among the people. Finally, to conclude Allum's account, he notes how Elias claims that these elite cultural traits have endured in distinctive cultural features of these societies to the present day.

It is striking how similar the questions posed by Rokkan and Elias are, though the empirical-theoretical organization and evidence and the mode of analysis are quite different. Alhough Rokkan's approach covers many more cases, a central feature of his work, as with Elias, is the contrast between the construction of early nation-states in France and England in contrast to the German experience of fragmentation. Elias's approach is markedly different from Rokkan's and could be described as detailed comparative case studies of how the dynamics of territorial consolidation and state formation in three originally loosely defined territorial spaces help understanding of key dimensions of the organizational and affective cultures of later nation-states. Elias speaks of the incomprehensibility of the later monopoly organization of the nation-state until 'the special character of the preceding social phase of "private initiative" has been understood' (Elias, 1982, p. 125). By private initiative, Elias means the centuries-long struggles in all three proto-territories under consideration between centralizing monarchies and warring magnates. The nature of the outcome of this battle for feudal supremacy together with certain patterns of capital accumulation and functional differentiation led to specific proto-national experiences in the period of absolutism. The balance of forces established in the latter period, and the later conflict and alliance-building process between monarchical, aristocratic and bourgeois elements, established foundations for mass national cultures.

Elias's empirical-theoretical investigations, seen from one vantage point, are consistent with the modernization theory of Rokkan and others. Functional differentiation is accompanied by mechanisms of monopoly formation, at first military and violent, later civil and more sophisticated and hence more deeply intrusive in the literal sense of that word. This intrusive quality is realized by subjects who experience it as a progressive increase in intra-psychic instinctual control. This renunciation of instinct in favour of civility as individuals confront the multiplicity of roles is at the heart of Elias's celebrated account of the formation of conscience, 'conscientization', in the civilization of western modernity. The account is completed, and made relevant to nationalism, by the manner in which he charts the different national paths that canalize this intrinsically modern experience and give it a distinctive national form. This national form often has historically deep roots such as the German sense of inferiority and frustration in the first half of the twentieth century by the inability to live up to a presumed Golden Age in the past or, another example, the differences in national cultures between peoples of similar ethnic composition, the Germans as opposed to the Dutch and Danes (Elias, 1992).

However, in terms of the conceptual distinctions made in Chapter 2 between disenchantment and enchantment, the approach of Elias is far more revealing than Rokkan about the dark, not necessarily the same thing, irrational side of national culture formation. His exploration of such basic concepts as monopoly formation, differentiation and rationalization within nation-states is balanced by his earlier and later treatment of the mechanisms of the production and reproduction of socially potent sentiments of shame, guilt, resentment, inferiority and embarrassment. Although the basic motif running through his theory is that of differentiation and disenchantment, there are good grounds also for seeing Elias as a theorist of de-differentiation and enchantment. On both sides, he is a theorist of institutionalized national collective identity, although his treatment of the mechanisms of formation of this collective identity is theoretically more centred on the differentiation tradition.

When considering Elias as a theorist of nationalism the most striking factor, as with Rokkan, is how little cited he is in the literature on nationalism. Extensive treatment is to be found of the question of how modern is the nation with no reference to a celebrated sociologist whose life's work was dedicated to a line of inquiry that illuminates this question. What explains this apparent lacuna? Our attempts at explanation reveal a number of central preferences in the theory formation of nationalism. The first has to do with the type of countries normally subject to the attention of scholars of nationalism. Elias was a theorist almost exclusively concerned with big countries, England, France and Germany and while the last is central to the imaginary of nationalism, the former two are not often considered as examples of nationalism, perhaps owing to the longevity and quasi-natural appearance of the nation-state in these cases. There are, of course, exceptions to this (Greenfeld, 1992).

If this is not entirely satisfactory as an explanation in itself, then the fact that Elias was simultaneously a theorist of the mechanisms of boundary drawing towards outsiders *and* of internal rationalization of national cultures may also be relevant. Theories of nationalism are not on the whole directed towards the internal dynamics of societies. The significance of Elias for a wider approach to nationalism is the way in which he conceives of nationalism as an integrative ideology within states and as a set of boundaries with other nation-states generated in the interstate arena. In the first case, a particular national ethos and sensibility is constructed out of the dynamics of social forces within the nation but, even though it varies in each case, it happens everywhere in the nineteenth and twentieth centuries. This process of formation of what Elias calls a 'canon' is profoundly related to the learning processes generated within and diffused out of the milieux of particular social classes. In the countries Elias gave most consideration to, the ethos and sensibility of the *national culture* was powerfully shaped in a normative direction by the egalitarian canon of the Third Estate. This was first carried by preponderant influences emanating first from the bourgeoisie and later the working class.

This normative-egalitarian influence on the national habitus is counter-posed by an inegalitarian *nationalist* canon deriving from the Machiavellian tradition that the land, the state, the nation belongs to a single individual. This is modernized into inegalitarian feelings of attachment to one's own nation to the exclusion of all outside non-members from the moral community. It can also lead to a willingness to accept inequality within the nation in the context of the sacred quality of the *transcendental-we* created by the sense of belonging to the nation. In the second case, the inegalitarian canon is extended to the international arena as a constitutive condition of the 'amoral realism' that has historically tended to guide relations in this sphere. The acceptance of inequality is often also a condition of the exercise of nationalism in multiethnic societies in which a dominant official nationalism leads to the suppression of equality to excluded or disadvantaged ethnic groups. All this implies that the presumption of an intrinsic connection between nationalism and egalitarian norms of modernity is only true in some cases.

The detailed consideration of the internal analysis of national culture and the distinction between normative learning processes that influence this culture and identification with the nation per se may have placed Elias before his time. Today political theory is giving increasing attention to the role of identification with the nation on normative orders (Canovan, 1996; Habermas, 1998; Miller, 1995, see Chapter 8). Divisions in this area of scholarship reflect wider divisions in the treatment of nationalism in the social sciences, where it is not too difficult in many instances to spot opposing positions on the benefits and disbenefits of nationalism, even where not explicitly stated. In another sense, however, this consideration of the moral-normative implication of nationalism makes it all the more surprising that there is not more attention paid to Elias's path-breaking treatment of both normative and affective aspects of national culture building, especially given the gradually increasing recognition of the importance of emotional factors in accounts of nationalism.[7]

If these reasons excluded Elias from serious consideration by theorists of nationalism who see it as a relatively long-run and enduring phenomenon, then the recent turn to constructivist analysis that we will encounter later perhaps excludes him in another sense. In our view Elias's account of cultural traditions can certainly enrich the constructivist analysis of spatio-temporally local reality constructions by situated actors in the crucial, and academically very scarce, dimension of foundations for such analysis. For various reasons, including limitations of resources to 'construct' from first principles all relevant aspects of the culturally given situation, constructivist analysis depends on interpretations of such traditions. However, insofar as constructivist ideas have sought to legitimate themselves in the field of nationalism by emphasizing how relatively short-run interactive dynamics 'creates' new cultural orders, there has been a tendency to claim that this cultural creation process is entirely comprehensible from categorial attributes of late modernity itself (Brubaker, 1996). But this position, and indeed the opposing position of the longevity of national identity, only focuses on the manifest form of national identity itself, not the anchoring of this mutable identity complex in wider *national cultures*. Few constructivists would deny that outside the field of national identity proper there has not existed longer run traditions of rationalization that form part of the repertoire out of which national identities can be formed. The crucial point here is that this need not originally have the form of a territorial collective identity *in the first place* but offers the potential to be so constructed under different circumstances. Hence, the longer run rationalization traditions built into state and civil society, with their stabilization of instrumental, normative and emotional rule systems, can be relevant to later national identity formation but in the first instance may not be equivalent to it. This, above all, applies to the national ethos or habitus that lies at the heart of the culture of the modern nation-state and which Elias sees as underpinning all identity-constructing efforts.

We may conclude on Elias by observing that the combination within his empirical-theoretical framework of attention to rationalization and openness to the dynamics of identity construction makes him an important theorist of the relation between nationalism and modernity. Elias is not altogether dissimilar to Rokkan in that his work has a diachronic cast oriented to the historical processes of differentiation, integration and rationalization, but with concentrated attention to specific situations and the role of agency in giving shape to these processes. Attention to the structure-forming impact of these latter processes also enables Elias to be positioned quite far towards the structure pole. Agency never entirely disappears from Elias's work but he is a modernization theorist to the extent that in later modernity historically formed institutions and structures set strong preconditions for the possibilities of action. On the synchronic axis, Elias is the theorist par excellence of the national habitus, a position that insofar as nationalism is increasingly seen as intrinsic to modernity, places his work at the core of the theorisation of modernity itself. Elias's empirical-theoretical span also extends on the synchronic axis to consideration of the development of the state, a process that for him goes hand in hand with the civilizing process itself. The state is the institutional complex that gives integrative cohesion to functional differentiation and whose cultural environment is provided by both modern culture itself and a specific variant of this culture, the national habitus. In this dimension, his work has quite a strong functionalist orientation in that the relationship between the semantic forms of culture and the system of institutions are taken to be mutually constitutive. Elias's work is without doubt more developed, at least for later modernity; his field of consideration is neither cultural nor political movements but his work, as we suggested earlier, can be attuned to these more dynamic elements of the nationalist field.

Another prominent theorist whose emphasis lay primarily on structural explanations of nationalism is Ernest Gellner.[8] Gellner's treatment of nationalism puts him at the centre of nationalism studies, partly because of the breadth and, to many, the provocative nature of his hypotheses, and partly because of the generality of his claims. Gellner had the further advantage over Rokkan and Elias of being identified as for long explicitly concerned with questions of nationalism, even when as a field of scholarly activity it was far less in vogue than currently. Gellner, unlike Rokkan and Elias, manifests *one* central claim about the structural derivation of nationalism that unites his work: nationalism is a product of industrialization.

There are two elements to this assertion. The first has to do with the social and cultural implications of industrialization in that industrialization creates a complex division of labour which in turn leads to an increase in knowledge work and crucially for nationalism this in turn requires the creation of a high culture. Such a high culture involves the establishment of standardized, literacy- and education-based systems of communication. Nationalism for Gellner is the general imposition of a high culture on society, which previously exhibited only low cultures for the mass of the population.

Nationalism involves the 'generalized diffusion of a school-mediated, academically supervised idiom, codified for the requirements of reasonably precise bureaucratic and technological communication. It is the establishment of an anonymous, impersonal society with mutually substitutable atomized individuals, held together above all by shared culture of this kind' (Gellner, 1983, p. 57). As Gellner provocatively formulates it, this is what nationalism *really* is, although it is understood by the world and by itself as something else. This other account of nationalism presents it as a putative folk culture 'whose symbolism is drawn from the healthy, pristine, vigorous life of the peasants, of the *Volk,* the *narod*' (Gellner, 1983, p. 57). What Gellner calls the deception and self-deception of nationalism marks him out as a curious kind of structural constructivist. He declares nationalism often to be an inventor of cultures, which have no commensurate contemporary or historical existence. Both the real and imagined nature of nationalism means for Gellner that it engenders nations and not the other way around, an index of the transformative power of modern culture even as it misrecognizes itself.

The second element to Gellner's claim is that nationalism is a product of uneven modernization (Ragin, 1979). The uneven spread of industrialization creates more and less advanced collectivities. When these collectivities reside in a common territory as in the multiethnic empires, cultural differences may coincide with developmental ones leading to inconsistencies in the allocation of roles, rewards and resources. According to Ragin, in Gellner's account 'ethnic political mobilization should be seen as the product of exclusionary practices that accompany the uneven spread of industrialization' (Ragin, 1979, p. 621). Taking the two elements of Gellner's claim together, nationalism *is* the homogenizing culture of modernity but the very premise of homogeneity built into this culture in an unequal world creates the conditions for the expression of difference. On this basis, Gellner constructs typologies of the spread of nationalism based on different experiences of the rewards of modernity.

Although Gellner's work is much more cited in the theory of nationalism than that of Rokkan and Elias, its central contention and its theoretical implications are problematic. True, Gellner makes an important point when he speaks of the role of nationalism in engendering nations. The understanding revealed therein attests to a conception of the volatility of modern culture and above all nationalist collective identity that strongly qualifies the development gradualism of the other authors. However, to understand nationalism as the instrumental culture of modernity overextends its range. To couple this contention with the fact that apparently everyone conceives of nationalism as something other than what it really is contains a kind of essentialist ideology critique of modernity that is built on too slender foundations. Even if we are to accept the contention that nationalism is something other than what the nationalized masses think it is, then this other is nonetheless real in its effects as Gellner himself would recognize. Are the real consequences of such 'mistaken' beliefs not to be considered as nationalism at all? Would it not be simpler and more comprehensible to say that nationalism is, among other things, a response to the wider cultural rationalization of modernity and the unequal allocations of the fruits of development across territories and peoples, often based on invented reality and spurious distinctions but for real and present goals? Argument could certainly be enjoined about how far nationalism is a response to cultural rationalization and to what extent it is constitutive of it. But the really important point is that nationalism is overextended and rendered a vague and even erroneous term when it is considered *as* the high culture of modernity as opposed to a component of it or, as in Elias, a mechanism for canalizing it.

NATIONALISM AND THE PUBLIC SPHERE

In addressing the question of structures of modernity and nationalism, we have thus far concentrated on work that is already identified in the social sciences as structural in emphasis. The thrust of this work is that nationalism is 'inter-textually' constructed in relation to other social and cultural structures such as democratization, the formation of the national habitus, industrialization, social mobilization and divisions of social interest, the construction of high or intellectual cultures, industrialization and urbanization. What becomes clear from this account is that nationalism, as at root a form of cultural identity, is connected with all these phenomena, although not necessarily all of them together in a given case. Hence, we can readily accept that nationalism is in some measure an integrative response to differentiation, a product of urban forms of life arising from economic expansion, a result of social mobilization for improved citizenship rights, and a movement of enchantment to compensate for the disenchantment of modern rationalization.

The strength of the structural accounts of nationalism in modernity, sketched earlier, is that if we eschew the strong evolutionary assumption that there is one right path to 'true' modernity, then this theoretical tradition can be employed to provide a context for more particular accounts of nationalism. It offers the possibility that distinctive types and incidences of nationalism at different places and times can be connected to broader structural forces that help us make sense of them. Such structures cannot be separated from dynamics, however, as in the classic modernization account.

74 They can only be understood in relation to the manifest forms that nationalist collective identity and nationalist practices actually take. Contrariwise, these forms are more amenable to theoretical conceptualization if it is not possible to progress from a multiplicity of cases to some generalities and back again to cases. The work of Rokkan and Elias in particular allows scholars of nationalism to ask certain pertinent questions and to explore the presence of certain connections between manifest appearances and structural generalizations.

Such work, of course, needs to continue to investigate the long-run relationship between structures of modernity and the dynamics of nationalism, filling in along the way what are the key manifestations of structure that matter in various periods of nationalist activity. By periods of nationalist activity we mean the early nations, early modern nationalism, the belated nations such as Italy, Germany and Ireland, the late nineteenth- and early twentieth-century emphasis on self-determination, colonial and postcolonial nationalism, the transition nationalism of Eastern Europe, the contemporary wave of ethnocentric nationalism.[9] Different kinds and degrees of structural forces matter in relation to these and other waves of nationalism. The paradox of such an employment of structures is that they take analysis quite far but never far enough. It is obvious, for example, that the rise of ethnocentrism in both East and West Europe is connected to the dissolution or erosion of previous institutional forms of collective choice making – the communist order, the welfare state – and it is important to explore the dynamics of action to test the presence and extent of the implications of such a shift in context, especially in the less obvious case of the decline of western welfarist solidarity. But as research and analysis penetrates deeper into contexts it encounters either the need for more situated kinds of structural interpretation – for example, the structure of discourse or the logics of contentious activity – as the peculiarities of individual cases need to be documented in respect of their unique configurations of elements. The structural context can only set up the questions that need to be taken up in specific cases or comparative sets of cases.

Up to now, we have documented forms of structural analysis that directly address dimensions of the structural origins of nation-states and nationalism. Even in this exercise it is apparent that those theories that seem most useful for developmental context building are not prominently considered in much of the literature. This is also the case for what might be described as cultural structures, i.e. institutionally enduring cultural interpretation systems. The most prominent example in the literature on nationalism of this kind is the significance attached to the transformation in the technology of the production and reproduction of culture, most centrally associated with the printing press. This point is now widely addressed in accounts of nationalism.[10] A picture emerges of how the discourse of nationalism interfaced with the emergent print culture and how this complex was affected by the economic transformations wrought by trade, capitalism and industrialization, the political transformations wrought by a literate bureaucracy and mass-media informed political public, and the cultural transformations wrought by the reproduction and consumption of academic cultural goods, meant primarily for a specialized readership, and literary cultural goods for a consuming public.

On the whole, it is probably fair to say that there has been no sustained treatment of how phases in the transformation of print culture are linked to transformations of nationalism beyond the drawing of some general theoretical connections, and preliminary empirical indications. There has certainly been no sustained movement within sociological and political studies of nationalism that builds on Habermas's path-breaking study on the structural transformation of the originally bourgeois public sphere or later academic treatment of this important category of modern society (Calhoun, 1992; Habermas, 1989a). The original account of the transformation of the public sphere by Habermas moved from optimism to pessimism. The initially bourgeois public sphere emerged at different speeds in different countries (England, France and Germany) in the period from the seventeenth to the early nineteenth centuries, depending centrally on the strength of the bourgeois stratum and on relations between it and the nobility. While in all cases the call for accountability of government and various liberal political freedoms met with much success, the political power of publicity ultimately depended on the formation of parliamentary constitutional states. This progressive account is coupled with a regressive one in the late modern conditions of the political public sphere of the welfare state. This latter-day public sphere is marked by two competing tendencies:

> Insofar as it represents the collapse of the public sphere of civil society, it makes room for a *staged* and *manipulative* publicity displayed by organizations over the heads of a mediatized public. On the other hand, to the degree to which it preserves the continuity with the liberal constitutional state, the social-welfare state clings to the mandate of a political public sphere according to which the public is to set in motion a *critical* process of public communication through the very organizations that mediatize it. (Habermas, 1989a, p. 232)

Habermas's early work centres on the paradox presented by the transition to mass society. In this transition, there are greater opportunities for participation for more of the population, coupled with such organizational and cultural constraints that these expanded opportunities can only be accessed in degenerated conditions. The early Habermas exhibited a progressive-regressive normative interpretation built on the claimed historical achievements of the bourgeois public sphere and its later degeneration, while the later Habermas offers a more consistently optimistic account of the continuing critical function of the public sphere (Habermas, 1996). In certain respects at least it is the historical foundations of the earlier work that potentially offers most to the structural analysis of nationalism.

Two research questions arise in respect of the relationship between the public sphere and nationalism. The first has to do with the relation between nationalism and the public sphere from the standpoint of how nationalism is connected to the structural conditions conducive to the effective and appropriate functioning of a democratic public sphere. This question has to do with whether, to what extent, and in which circumstances over the long haul of modernity the discourse of nationalism has become an intrinsic part of a civic culture able to provide minimally consensual foundations for the interplay of differentiated and competitive political publics. It therefore has to do with the bottom quadrants of the framework outlined in Chapter 2, *civic culture* and the *institutional core*. The second is how nationalist claims-making activity actually operates within the public sphere. This second question has to do with the content and public resonance of nationalist discourse in the context of the broader set of available political and cultural opportunities. It addresses nationalism as an identity in formation that is not or not yet institutionalized and therefore is connected to dynamics, often interrelated, of a cultural and socio-political kind addressed in the top half of the framework, *cultural innovation* and *political mobilization*. Only the first question interests us in the current chapter, which has to do with the structural status of the public sphere for nationalism.

In relation to the issues raised by the first question, Craig Calhoun (1995) distinguishes between three different but interrelated modes of claiming a political community outside the state that became influential in the transition to democracy. The first is the republican idea that public discourse should set and monitor the government agenda in the name of the public. The second is the secularization of the Reformation idea that the people should serve as the source of legitimacy for the state. And the third is the invocation of ethnic, cultural and local solidarities in the name of the nation. Calhoun allocates each of these a categorial status in the legitimate democratic order when he says that the idea of the public entailed the idea of a differentiated citizenry, people emphasized the unity of the ruled within a difference between rulers and ruled, and nation implied a unity of the whole (Calhoun, 1995, p. 238).

As with Habermas's account of the public sphere, Calhoun empha- sizes that the growth of ideas about political community depended on the emergence of civil society as a sphere of non-political social organi- zation or, as Habermas describes it, a locus of initially non-public opin- ion that only through a filtering process actually becomes public opinion (Habermas, 1989a). Calhoun accords ideas of the nation an important role in shaping the civil society out of which the notion of democratic accountability emerges. An accountability that is to be achieved through the mechanisms of rational, critical deliberation in a public sphere. He opposes the view that nationalism is a 'fading inheri- tance from primordial history' and asserts its 'centrality to our modern ideas of publics and more generally of politically salient identities' (Calhoun, 1995, p. 240). This is the case for Calhoun even though he recognizes that 'nationalist rhetoric commonly employs certain tropes' in which the nation is presented as pre-political, as prior to political deliberation, as 'the basis for recognizing a public rather than as subject to constitution or re-definition in public' (Calhoun, 1995, p. 238).

At the heart of Calhoun's position on nationalism is the idea that 'politically salient identities' do not simply arise out of public deliberation, although such deliberation certainly influences them. They are, above all, products of the *interaction between* the identity-forming capacities of civil society and rational critical public discourse, whether orderly or unruly. In his view, the sharp distinction drawn by Habermas between private and public spheres with clear translation rules between them is too restricted to the institutionally dominant issues associated with organized interests, fair procedure and justice that arose with bourgeois society as part of its 'normal' politics. Calhoun actually claims that the clear dis- tinction between the private realm and the single authoritative public sphere in liberal theory *depends on* pre-political criteria for the drawing of boundaries and the subsuming of difference into a discourse of the whole that ultimately emanates from identification with the nation.

Calhoun is right to stress both the dependence of political identity on the cultural self-interpretations of civil society, a point not dissimilar to that raised by Klaus Eder in his analysis of the degeneration of nineteenth-century German political culture (Eder, 1985) and also the significance of nationalism for delineating the extent of the territory in which such collective identities should operate. However, along with others such as Greenfeld (1992) and Miller (1995), he overstates the case when conceiving of the nation as the overarching basis for a discourse of the whole. A distinction must be drawn between expressive discourses of the whole and normative discourses of the whole or common good discourses, most critically between the cultural solidarity of the nation and the democratic solidarity of the category public. The discourse of the nation is too mutable, too capable of acting as a normative cloak for authoritarianism, inequality and exclusion to be seen as the dominant foundation for social integration. The discourse of national identity can in the same society over a relatively short time period, or even at the same time, be used in the service of authoritarianism or democracy, as a principle supporting ideas of equality or difference or as an ideological cloak for the denial of equality and difference to certain groups.

In addition, using ideas of Elias, adherence to certain principles in respect of the treatment of fellow nationals but not of non-nationals can contradict some of the universalistic precepts of modernity. These reflections imply that unlike republican ideas of popular sovereignty the idea of the nation should not be seen as a set of normative principles underlying modern democracy. The nation instead provides criteria of membership and cultural identity that *sometimes* allow for democratic practices and are *sometimes* inimical to them. The paradox is that it is precisely when national identity reduces to a pure cultural form or, put differently, as it separates itself from normative discourses and practices – democracy, equality, responsibility, respect for difference – towards criteria of cultural belonging and associated practices, it takes on problematic, even dangerous, ethnocentric dimensions.

The critical point emerging from these reflections, which will be taken up in later chapters, is that discourses of the nation cannot be seen as unequivocally supportive of the democratic public spheres. It is possible to assert that the principle of democratic publicity associated with a public sphere is a first-order collective good of modernity, while the idea of nationality can only have that status in some cases. The principle of nationality has always to be considered in relation to whose interests it serves, whether all or only some, both within territorial forms or in the overall interstate context.

CONCLUSION

In this chapter, we have examined, through a number of key theorists, central concepts that are used to place nationalism within long-run traditions of the formation and unfolding of modernity. Of these, three central features can be disinguished. These are, first, the historical construction of a particular structure of centre-periphery relations in Europe that created, in conjuction with the integrative ideology of the nation, a plurality of nation-states. The idea and practice of the nation-state subsequently became a key dynamic in European and world history and powerfully mediated democratic forces of representation, participation, publicity and the generalization of right. The emergence of the nation-state model brought nation building to the heart of the institutional construction of later modernity with highly ambivalent consequences both in its European homeland and in its later export to other parts of the world.

The second key concept is that of the national habitus, which clarifies how national cultures become formed out of the interplay of state activities, historical experiences and cultural interpretation and memory. National habituses have an enduring standing where there are continuities of territory and cultural-political experiences over time and they suggest that in some important instances – Japanese, Russian, American, British, French to name but a few – national cultures and dispositions can be relatively long run. This is not to preclude for a moment that the later construction of national identity out of such materials, but also out of the contemporary play of interests and ideologies, can substantially change such long-run cultures. The concept of national habitus goes a long way to clarifying the inter-textual components of national identity formed out of class cultures, national experience, state activity and contemporary situations.

The third feature to receive consideration is the relationship between nationalism and the public sphere. In this connection it was argued that while nationalism contributed to the formation of a model of horizontal social integration that contributed to the advent of this central category of modern democracy, the relationship between nationalism and the public sphere has proven historically equivocal, sometimes supporting the universalistic idea of the inclusion of all in procedures of democratic publicity but often undercutting the play of public reason in the preferement for authoritarian, inegalitarian and ideologically partisan discourses.

NOTES

1 See, for example, Roger (2000) who argues both structural/functional explanations of nationalism exist alongside cultural explanations in Gellner's work.

2 See the account of the relationship between differentiation and integration in Chapter 2.

3 In research for the authors' previous work on Ireland (O'Mahony and Delanty, 1998), it became apparent that the sociologically explored relationship between differentiation and integration had scarcely been considered at all despite a huge volume of writing on Irish nationalism. The cultural representation of the presumed need for a powerful nationalist movement in Ireland has occluded consideration of the social context of that nationalism as a movement of resistance to differentiation and to certain aspects of the modern form of integration. The social logic of the nationalist movement in Ireland was a call for a different kind of integration that in fact amounted to a certain kind of de-differentiation. In general, more detailed consideration of this relationship is vital to understanding the social implications of nationalist movements.

4 We make extensive use of the excellent selection of key texts of Rokkan that has appeared under the auspices of the European Consortium for Political Research (ECPR) (Flora et al., 1999). See also Rokkan (1975).

5 Neilsen (1985) would also add here that transaction within peripheries. Its obvious correlate, transactions within centres, could also be added. However, Rokkan was interested in transactions across boundaries and to take into account intra-territory transactions would have further complicated his model.

6 Such large-scale territorial systems correspond roughly with what Eisenstadt and others would identify as civilizations. Civilizations correspond to broad container categories that may produce different national or regional variations. (See Chapter 1).

7 See Greenfeld (1992), Scheff (1994a, 1994b), Tambini (1998).

8 See Gellner (1964, 1983, 1987, 1994, 1998). See also Hall (1998).

9 See Chapter 6 where a fuller account of periods of nationalism is presented.

10 For example, Anderson (1983), Calhoun (1997), Gellner (1983), Taylor (1998) Weber (1976).

four
nationalism and culture

In Chapter 3 we remarked on the cultural turn in the social sciences as a major aspect of their development over the last 30 or so years. The various manifestations of these developments have been far reaching as older traditions have been revised and new ones actively created. These developments lie at the heart of much new thinking apparent in the study of nationalism. In this chapter, we will explore a number of theorists that we consider represent this turn such as Smith, Eisenstadt and Giesen, Hobsbawm, Hedetoft, Calhoun, Yuval-Davis and Anderson and also consider the argument of others that add additional insight, supportive or critical, as appropriate. The theorists selected for consideration have been chosen because they stand as key figures in vital debates on the status of culture in nationalism, offer theoretical depth, or extend the thematic range beyond the 'normal paradigm'.

At a general level, the most striking feature of interpretive writing on nationalism is its radical theoretical and methodological difference from structuralist inspired accounts such as Rokkan and, as we shall later see in Chapter 5, even more so the combined structure/mobilization approaches. On other fronts, we distinguish interpretive analysis proper from the theorists covered in the last chapter by the degree of autonomy allowed to cultural processes, mindful that the latter theorists do not exclude culture and in some cases such as Elias have it as the centrepiece of their analysis. The emphasis on cultural autonomy of the interpretive tradition in the sense understood here is characterized by an expressivist orientation that takes its distance from causal, instrumental and, somewhat less clearly and consistently, normative orientations. This expressivist orientation is not as in the classic hermeneutic tradition that of actors or subjects but the expression of nationalist collectivities. It is characterized, therefore, by the belief that nationalism represents a way of viewing the world that offers a certain unity of form, although also high levels of distinctiveness in the expression of that form. It combines the idea of a solid core based on a presumed understanding of nationalist ways of thinking and communicating and the manifold expression of that way of thinking in a variety of situations. What is essential to this mode of theorization is the perspective that structural forces do not overpower cognitive and communicative processes, but instead that such processes very often break free from such structures and craft their own reality, whose resonant cultural power can overcome situative constraints. This is particularly apparent when new nationalist cultural models become widely diffused and lead to new interpretations of their situations by nationalist actors, a phenomenon that is pronounced at times of epochal shifts in nationalist cultural models of the kind described in Chapter 6. A particularly important example is the articulation of the principle of national self-determination that helped provide a distinctly nationalist inflection to the course of nineteenth- and early twentieth-century social mobilization.

Interpretive accounts of nationalism hinge on the key 'supply-demand' relationship between the historically creative implications of cultural innovation in nationalist ideas on the one hand and their reception and interpretation in the socio-cultural life-world on the other. This emphasis has the effect of placing the creation, consolidation and formative impact of national identity within the broader culture of civil society. A subordinate relationship within this tradition is that between the life-world or civic culture and the institutional core. Interpretive writing rarely spends much time on this relationship, vital to the social implications of nationalist ideas and mobilizations, but in some versions it is given some consideration. The exception to this general rule is, of course, the claim that national identity has contributed significantly to democracy and remains vital (Canovan, 1996; Miller, 1993, 1995).

Important, therefore, for the intepretive approach is, on the production side, the generation of nationalist content within the cultural public sphere and, on the demand side, the cultivation of innovative and critical nationalist publics or the maintenance of established national identity-bearing publics. These dynamics are additional to the historical role of the nation form in shaping the category of public sphere itself in the first place, introduced in the previous chapter and itself a further concern of the interpretive tradition. The concentration on processes of cultural innovation and institutionalization in the national lifeworld does not mean that this style of scholarship eschews political questions entirely. No plausible account of nationalism could in fact do so. All traditions of scholarship accept that nationalism is located somewhere in the interstices between the culture of the lifeworld and the cultural foundations of the political sphere, where either or both of these dimensions of culture and politics can be regarded as stable or volatile depending on theoretical and normative orientation. However, the political dimensions of nationalism tend to be regarded in most, although not all, cases of interpretive analysis as downstream of primary processes of identity formation in the lifeworld and not themselves to act as first-order generators of identity, as is emphasized in different ways in some mobilization and institutionalist approaches.

In this chapter, therefore, we explore key aspects of interpretive writing on nationalism organized around two central questions: the question of the modernity of the nation and the question of the nature and normative import of the nation form.

THE QUESTION OF THE MODERNITY OF THE NATION

The general contours of the debate arising from this question have been well described already in a number of general books on nationalism (Hutchinson, 1994; McCrone, 1998; Ozkirimli, 2000). The debate, which by now has many strands and protagonists, addresses the historical origins of contemporary ethnicities and nation-states. In this short treatment, we cannot follow the various strands of the debate between different kinds of primordialists, perennialists, ethno-symbolists and modernists.[1] The core of the debate lies in the question of the degree to which modern nation constructions are dependent on real rather than imagined historical experiences of nationhood. These historical experiences, whether real or imagined, are taken on both sides to relate necessarily to a popular sense of ethnic belonging and territorial attachment and not simply to the beliefs and values of elites. Hence, the argument that pre-modern nationalism really existed depends not simply on demonstrating that elites held positive views on the existence of national bonds, but on actually demonstrating the active popular recognition of these bonds.

83

From one standpoint, the focus of this book on modernity and nationalism could be taken to include treatment of whether nationalism is particular to modernity or when in modernity it arose and achieved distinctive form (Greenfeld, 1992). However, this is not our primary interest. This interest lies in exploring how the structural and cultural dimensions of modernity interrelate with the *modern* nation form. The debate therefore assumes interest for this standpoint insofar as the historical longevity of the nation is essential to understanding its modern construction or otherwise. This question fuses with the one oriented to the intra-modern question of the diachronics of nationalism within modernity itself. The historical perspective is not exhausted by demonstrating the continuity or non-continuity of pre-modern and modern ethnic or national identification, but arises in relation to the setting of a temporal framework for the analysis of nationalism in modernity itself.

Seen in relation to these questions, the issue of the point of the debate as currently framed does raise itself. There is no doubt that the question of whether nations existed in pre-modern times is an important and interesting question, but what is less clear is in what ways the existence of such pre-modern nations should be important to modern nations, even if continuity could be asserted. What is at issue here is the very stake of the debate seen from a modern perspective. Anthony Smith, according to Hutchinson (1994), holds to the view that the parameters created by the national past set boundaries to 'invention' processes in modernity. What this must imply if it is to be relevant to scholarship of the modern nation is that the historical concretization of these parameters is essential knowledge for understanding their range of actual or possible variation in the present. Something like this position emerges in Smith (1986, p. 97). Here, he argues that ethnicity is a cultural bond that survives over generations composed of symbolic, cognitive and normative elements common to a unit of population, of practices and mores that bind them together, and finally of shared sentiments and attitudes that differentiate them from other populations. On these foundations, it is possible to distinguish between the durability of ethnic forms – say Japanese, German or Irish – which is treated as analogous to a common form of life or socio-cultural lifeworld and the transformation of ethnic contents or traits. Earlier in the same text, Smith claims that the lack of enduring ethnic components is likely to constitute a serious impediment to 'nation-building and that such endurance requires that we think through the meaning of modernity as adumbrated by a few of the classical sociologists' (1986, p. 17). This orientation to modernity – Smith refers to Durkheim and modernization theory – recognizes that older types of social structure and culture 'persist within the most contemporary modes of social organization and culture' (Smith, 1986, p. 17). Roughly put, the argument would be that nations cannot be built without historical foundations, that such historical foundations can be assumed to exist, and that scholars cannot understand why nations can or cannot be built, or the cultural forms they may or may not take, unless they understand the historical foundations.

This position on the surface seems fairly consistent with aspects of the argument outlined in Chapter 3 on the existence of certain long-run structural and cultural trends that could influence the form of modern nationalisms. Smith's approach, however, when looked at closely differs from the respective approaches of Rokkan and Elias as outlined in that chapter. Rokkan attempted to place the structural and cultural factors he perceives as important to nation building within a structural account of modernity itself. By contrast, Smith's approach is predominantly cultural and is not *systematically related to* structural developments. Neither does he choose the strategy of Elias of exploring the cultural interpretations of social relations and transformative events that underpin national cultures, not ethnic identities, and that persist over time in the national habitus.

Elias holds to the broader frame of national culture or habitus while Smith seeks to demonstrate continuities of identity. It is a much more difficult challenge to undertake to demonstrate continuities in ethnic or national identity from pre-modern to modern times than it is to demonstrate continuities in culture. As Hedetoft (1999) observes, culture is not equivalent to identity.[2] Enduring common cultural characteristics may be a base for different kinds of collective identity over time. For example, cultural forms present in a supranational empire may later become incorporated into different national identities and may subsequently again emerge as important bases of an emergent transnational identity. Elias provides an example that we have already cited of common ethnic and linguistic fundaments shared between Germany and Denmark, but today producing quite different national identities.[3] The admission of the possibility of common cultures without continuous identity allows identity to be seen also as something that may involve a creative rather than a derivative relation to culture, a perspective that is at the heart of the constructivist position. Insofar as Smith's basic position makes it difficult to see this constructive relation in operation, he may be seen, following the argument in Chapter 2, as a theorist of generalized identity. However, even in this respect incompatibilities arise in that the general functionalist standpoint is one that is built on the rupture between tradition and modernity, even in the Durkheimian version that Smith supports, and is not a good base for demonstrating modern and pre-modern continuities of identity. In addition, in the modern neo-functionalism of, for instance, Münch and Alexander collective identity is produced and sustained through patterns of argumentation and opposition not on the basis of semantic coherence over a long time frame, a coherence that sometimes happens but is improbable.

The most basic problem with Smith as a theorist of continuity of identity between pre-modern and modern times, as distinct from being an insightful theorist of nationalism in general, is that the grounds for deciding the *degree* of possible continuity can only be ascertained from investigation of actual modern identities. This is the case because if it is accepted, as it now generally is, that all identities are subject to continuous construction processes then the question becomes an empirical one of the degree to which such construction involves innovation in or maintenance of existing identity patterns. But Smith's concentration is more on pre-modern identities than on modern ones. The attempt to demonstrate the actual existence of pre-modern nationalism by Smith and others (Gorski, 2000) does not help to decide the extent to which pre-modern identity constrains modern identity formation, although of course it can be used to rebut the claim that nationalism is exclusively a modern phenomenon. To address the question of continuity satisfactorily involves demonstrating that such continuity exists through commensurate consideration of pre-modern and modern identities.

As observed in Chapter 3, Elias has demonstrated how such a task could be conceived by linking the formation of national cultures and identities to social mechanisms of cultural generation. A related research programme is proposed by Eisenstadt and Giesen (1995). The authors address themselves to what they note as the emerging theme of collective identity in sociology. At the core of the programme is the idea that collective identity is a social construct 'produced by social carrier groups which act within a particular situation and within a framework of symbolic codes' (1995, p. 77). The symbolic codes in question are characterized by the authors as primordial, conventional and cultural. The primordial code, the first ideal type of collective identity, relates to identities built on structures of the world that are assumed to be given and not subject to change, such as gender and generation, kinship, ethnicity and race. The second ideal type of collective identity is the civic one and this is based on familiarity with implicit rules of conduct, traditions and social routines that define and demarcate the boundary of the collectivity. A third ideal type of collective identity is the cultural, which links the constitutive boundary of them and us to a particular relation between the collective subject and the sacred or transcendental realm. The authors apply the action-oriented concept of social carrier groups and the semantic one of the coding of collective identity according to these ideal types to two case studies, drawing from their respective previous work on Japan and Germany. The results of these studies emphasize the importance of first cultural codes and later primordial codes in Germany and the importance of primordial and civic codes in Japan. The German case exhibits less developed civic codes and the Japanese one less developed cultural codes.

What is especially interesting from the standpoint of the significance of pre-modern to modern nationalism is the way in which the Japanese case study, based on other work of Eisenstadt (1995b), claims that Japanese collective identity comprising of principled primordiality and some weaker elements of civility crystallized relatively early, 'probably' as early as the eighth century out of Japan's encounters with other societies or civilizations (1995b, p. 93). It is clear from this that while primordiality may be a constructed and reconstructed category in the authors' eyes, it can indeed go back a long way and exhibit a degree of stability over a relatively long time. This work of Eisenstadt and Giesen counts as interpretive in the sense we are employing the term because even though the wider work of the theorists does examine the interplay between culture, structural differentiation and agency (Eisenstadt, 1992, 1995a; Giesen, 1998) the categories of structure and agency are subordinated in this case to the relatively autonomous capacity for semantic persistence of cultural patterns.

The positive prospect opened by this research programme is a semantically enriched specification of boundary-drawing mechanisms that may simultaneously be applied to the rules of membership of collectivities and also to the effect of membership rules on the rules and social consequences of the distribution of resources within collectivities, especially of public goods. There is, however, one particular consideration that would, in our view, need to be addressed if such a programme were generally to contribute to showing how pre- and early modern identities could be regarded as foundational for modern nationalisms. This involves specifying how carrier groups actually operate, bearing in mind that in most modern societies and many pre-modern ones such carrier groups will not have unified visions of the identity code that should prevail and elements within such groups are likely to relate in different ways to enduring elements of tradition. In such differential constructions of tradition, new traditions are themselves created and may become institutionalized as opportunities and constraints for further action. This process has the effect of adding greater reflexivity and contingency to social orders and to require that more attention be paid to the relationship between the logic of culture and the way in which culture is actualized through the logic of practice. The illustrative short-coming in this respect is revealed in the fact that the authors do not systematically address the critical issue for national identity of the unstable relationship between nationalist elites and mass publics engaged in the negotiated, tradition-reconstructing production of a cultural order. This is under-emphasized in favour of a predominantly elite-driven and temporally long-run model of cultural innovation and continuity, which gives too much to the creativity of elites and too little to the dynamics of interpretation in literate, participative societies.

87

The other side of the argument is represented by variations on the modernist position, which is basically united in the idea that modern identities involve qualitatively new mechanisms of identity production predicated on a quadruple revolution in the modality of societal communication. There is an infrastructural revolution in the way the printing press creates new capacities for the production and dissemination of information and opinion, an instrumental revolution in the communication of purposive knowledge and facts, a normative revolution in the rise of democratic publicity in a public sphere, and an expressive revolution in the production and consumption of new literary forms and styles within a literary public sphere. The intensification of networks and relations for communicating diverse dimensions of knowledge leads to the elaboration of institutionally specialized communication systems such as law, bureaucracy, science, education and so forth, developments that both underpin greater societal differentiation and correspondingly greater requirements for a new kind of integrative communication. Such integral communication is not only solved by the discourse of the nation, it is also addressed by discourses of democratic participation, discourses of social regulation in the sense of Foucault, discourses of social and legal justice and discourses of collective, aesthetic sensibility. It therefore cannot be assumed that intensified communication will necessarily lead to nationalist outcomes. This depends on the situation and inter-group dynamics (Breuilly, 1982). However, the nation discourse has a decisive role in specifying membership rules and external boundaries and a big role (and sometimes also a decisive one), in specifying normative and affective rules within such constituted boundaries.

The modernist position is further united by the sense that the complex reciprocal relationship between differentiation and communication and the specific rise of integrative communication of a nationalist kind is qualitatively different from early- or pre-modern nationalism. While this position is certainly subject to rebuttal by early modern scholars (Gorski, 2000), such rebuttal tends to be ignored by modernists, while the state of scholarship in the crucial dimension of demonstrating why early modern structures and cultures should be important for understanding later nationalism remains underdeveloped, in spite of the work of Smith, Eisenstadt, Elias, Rokkan, Greenfeld, Gorski, Armstrong and others. As observed earlier, there is certainly scholarly requirement for sustained treatment of this issue. But modernists on the whole do not feel the need to be excessively troubled about this. The imaginary of modernism stretches back to the infrastructural revolution of the printing press but really gets going in the differentiation/integration dialectic that opens up at the end of the eighteenth century. Hobsbawm dates his book on nationalism from 1780 (Hobsbawm, 1990). Calhoun (1997) claims that by the end of the eighteenth century the discourse formation was fully in play and that it had transformed ethnicity, cultural patterns and state formation. Kedourie (1994) and Breuilly (1982) see nationalism as bound up with German romanticism, in the former case resulting in a sustained ideology critique of the ideas themselves. Gellner (1983) casts an eye backward to the vernacular revolution created by printing, but his decisive period of concentration is the nineteenth century. Perhaps only Greenfeld (1992) and Anderson (1983) of the 'classical' literature really examine the early modern period, in both cases in a somewhat qualified way. Greenfeld locates the birth of the idea of the nation in early sixteenth-century England but then claims that it takes two centuries before it takes root anywhere else, a view challenged by Gorski (2000) who claims that similar ideas of the nation form, linked to biblical cultures, were present in the early modern Netherlands also.[4] Finally, the full flowering of nationalism in Anderson's account of an imagined community can only happen after the full flowering of literacy in late modernity.

These basic positions on the starting point of modernity articulate with at least two wider types of ontological commitment to the underlying emancipatory/repressive dynamics of modernity, that emphasize one or the other dimension. The repressive dimension articulates with a completely or generally ideology critical one with respect to nationalism. The ideology-critical perspective in the work of Hobsbawm, but not that of Kedourie, is associated with those who see modernity as characterized by antagonistic social relations that are politically expressed as a clash of ideologies. In this struggle, which encompasses the three main ideologies originating in the nineteenth century, conservatism, liberalism and socialism, nationalist ideology towards the end of the century takes on the form of elite legitimation through the invention of national traditions. It therefore finds its place in the interstices of other ideological conflicts, for example as ideological support for a liberalism deficient in mass appeal. In Kedourie, the idea of repression remains but quite different from Hobsbawm is tied to a normative critique of what he describes as nationalist doctrine. The main point of the critique is that nationalism results in proposals for national self-determination for unique peoples that offers basically the wrong solution, often worsening rather than improving situations of inter-group and international conflict. Kedourie's position is basically an anti-utopian realism, not unlike that of Canovan (1996). Gellner also carries an ideology-critical perspective, in this case directed at the self-misrecognition of nationalism as a backward-looking folk ideology when in reality it is the indispensable carrier of the high culture of modernity. This, of course, logically carries the implication that the historical folk dimensions of nationalism are bogus. By the same token, the semantic idea of the nation associated with Greenfeld, Anderson, Calhoun and also Giesen (1998) tends to stress the more emancipatory implications of the innovative culture of the nation as it fuses with the communicative transformations of modernity.

89

The latter of the two positions, emphasising semantic form, is more likely to connect to longer run cultural currents, albeit in an unsystematic, assertoric manner, than the former ideology critical one. Only Anderson and Greenfeld take up this issue in any sustained way and only Greenfeld gives precedence to the nation over other modernization variables, although the implications of Calhoun's emphasis on the relative cultural autonomy and creative impact of the nation in the early modern period goes some distance in this direction. The arch-modernists are therefore the ideology critics for whom the real history of nationalism should be dated to the late eighteenth century. At the heart of this position may well be that nationalism has to be seen as modern to sustain a modern ideology critique and especially it needs to be rooted in the advent of mass societies. Gorski (2000), taking issue with this position, claims that nationalism qua ideology also existed in pre-modern societies and cites a series of historical studies, including his own, that support this contention.

Our reflections lean to the view that understanding the use of nationalist ideas in the early modern period is important to understanding certain dimensions and/or certain manifestations of modern nationalism, but that its inclusion is not mandatory for many or even most analyses of the latter. It should also be accepted that just as in the modern period, ideas of the nation in the early modern period constituted only one among several discourses of collective identity, including identities generated by the centralization of the state itself which cannot be reduced to the discourse of the nation (Kedourie, 1994; Zubaida, 1989). These alternative discourses or, also in the sense of Rokkan and others, structural configurations, offer potential for later incorporation in modern nation discourses. Following the distinction drawn earlier between culture and identity, they do not have to be actual discourses of the nation in one period to become incorporated in the nation discourses of a later period.

THE MODERN NATION FORM

Already in this chapter, we have drawn attention to the important distinction for interpretive analysis between the form and appearance of the nation. In line with the basic differences between different interpretive positions outlined earlier, the nation form tends to be either regarded as constitutive of modernity (the constitutive position), although the estimation of its true contribution may vary, or as a reactive growth to a modernity that has been constituted by other means (the ideology critical position). The almost universal distinction drawn between civic and ethnic nationalisms, between the nationalism of the older western nations of England, France and the United States and the more ethnic eastern nationalisms is refracted in this difference in a particular way. Both sides, broadly speaking, accept that a distinction can be drawn between these two kinds of nationalism. The ideology-critical position, however, sees identification with the nation, which in this view always *tends towards* ethnic or national particularism, as being inherently problematic, unless highly qualified by other kinds of identification of which the most important in the literature are democratic and class identification, although ethnic and, from certain standpoints, gendered identification also rank highly (Habermas, 1999a; Hobsbawm, 1990; Kedourie, 1994). It is best, perhaps, to exclude Gellner from such considerations because of the idiosyncratic formulation of his critique, as noted in the previous chapter.

Contrariwise, what might be called the constitutive position views the nation form as neither a new departure within late modernity nor at constant risk of degenerating into pathology. Instead it is placed as both a cultural emanation of civil society, a legitimate expression of affective and normative bonds of identification, and a politically significant discourse of equality and participation. The latter position hereby places the nation in the ranks of the constitutive structured forms of the culture of modernity along with publicity, privacy, law, science and art.

With regard to the relationships outlined in the introduction to this chapter, both positions make a connection between the sphere of cultural innovation and the civic culture as the primary connection, although the emphasis is different. The ideology critical position places its emphasis mainly in the sphere of cultural innovation where nationalism emerges as an unstable culture, high in agency and lacking normative legitimacy, with an important but highly problematic relationship to the institutional core of modern societies. As against this, the constitutive position sees nationalism as temporally co-extensive with modernity, as anchored in the cultural life form itself, as a legitimate basic form of modern identity with tendentially positive 'civic' consequences for the exercise of political authority. It therefore sees its task as comprehending the relatively stable realm of the national habitus, part of the broader civic culture, whose function in modern society its historical reconstructions anticipate. It views the task of explicating nationalism as predominantly that of explicating the forms and implications of a structured and enduring culture. It is not at issue between the two positions that excessive nationalism may have disastrous consequences in certain cases. What is at issue is whether nationalism itself is either intrinsically problematic (Kedourie, Hobsbawm) or tendentially so (Calhoun), a position at variance with Smith, Anderson, Greenfeld and many others.

The constitutive position has two major tendencies in explicating the discourse of the nation that may be designated cognitive-aesthetic and normative. Both tendencies have dominant diachronic versions and subordinate synchronic ones. In the first case of the cognitive-aesthetic version the dominant diachronic position is most influentially represented by Anderson, whose book on the theme of imagined community has gained significant standing within the literature on nationalism. The basic position is by now well known and needs little explication. The nation is a cultural form that fills the void left by the dissolution of traditional communities in modernity. It creates, with the help of the related developments of print capitalism and vernacularization a particular kind of 'horizontal-secular-transverse time' imagined community of the nation. The imagined community that is the nation is limited in that it cannot in principle extend to all of humanity and it is a community because it is based on feelings of horizontal comradeship that persist regardless of inequality and exploitation within particular nations. This is a variation of Elias's idea of inegalitarian feelings of identification with the nation (Elias, 1992), but Anderson does not theorize extensively the possible ideological role of the discourse of the nation in its negative moment, the recurring capacity for degeneration into chauvinistic populism or worse. Instead, against those 'progressive cosmopolitan intellectuals' who insist on the near-pathological character of nationalism, he emphasizes the capacity of nations to inspire love and 'often profoundly self-sacrificing love' (Anderson, 1983, p. 141). It is in the attempt to grasp such real but intangible abstractions that Anderson's book finds its mark. Whether one likes the form of community generated

91

by nationalism or not, it has remained through much of modernity a mode of expressing a sense of belonging that touches on basic needs of the human form of sociation itself. It is not in doubt that these basic needs are addressed by other means also, and it is an argument that they could be better met by non-nationalist means, but for good or ill nationalism as an aesthetic form departs from the mundane towards the sublime, from reason to emotion, which is why the kind of language and perspective that Anderson and some others are willing to use is needed for its theorization, a type of hermeneutic culturalism.

Anderson's work is also of theoretical interest in that while never alluding directly to the theory of the public sphere, especially the literary public sphere, it nevertheless makes a major contribution to how the substantive culture of nationalism can be seen in relation to it.[5] It does this in a predominantly diachronic manner showing the origins of the national imaginary in earlier cultural forms – the dynastic realm, religious tradition – and also showing how the diffusion of print technology and its outputs depended on the historical development of capitalism. In a major contribution from a semiotic perspective within cultural studies that can also be regarded as cognitive-aesthetic in its approach, Ulf Hedetoft attempts to compensate for what he correctly sees as a diachronic bias in the recent literature on nationalism, including Anderson's own account (Hedetoft, 1995). From this perspective, a developed synchronic approach is necessary to correct for the excessive attention to particulars that arises from the use of historical methodology. The kind of synchronic approach that Hedetoft proposes is one based on semiotics in which nationalism is conceived in terms of the production, distribution and interpretation of signs. Hedetoft wishes to move from the *a posteriori* construction of collective identity in the diachronic approach, whether in its interest in the operations of real or fabricated memory or combinations between them, to a synchronic attention to the universals of nationalist thought. The sense in which he uses the term 'universals' is a loose one and could be rendered as 'general contemporary structures of nationalist thinking'. This synchronic approach has two dimensions. The first is a concern with the structural and argumentative influences on the production of nationalist signs, the second with the processes of the interpretation and internalization of such signs. The distinctive national variation on such interpretive patterns, reconstructed out of research interventions by interview and survey, amount to different national habituses. This approach, therefore, is both subjective and structured and shows how a relational methodology giving equal in-depth treatment to its different component (national) parts and (individual) subjects are important in showing how the semantic form of nationalism actually operates. They therefore correct against the recurring problem that nationalism is seen as constituting either too much of modernity in some recent approaches or too little as in previous approaches.

The second tendency in the constitutive approach is to link nationalism to normative learning processes. This tendency is well represented in the work of Calhoun and Greenfeld. In these accounts, early modern nationalism is connected to the establishment of basic structures of modernity. Greenfeld (1992, 1996) sees nationalism not as a response to such structural factors as industrialization and urbanization but as one of their causes. Nationalism emerges earlier and is fundamental to the establishment of egalitarian foundations for social order and the collectivization of authority that made later institutional developments such as capitalism, science and the modern state possible. The relationship between the transformation of the principles of social order and the building of the modern state is a theme addressed by Calhoun (see also Calhoun, 1997). Dealing with the period of the emergence of civil society and the establishing of the principle of legitimacy to bind relations between this civil society and the state, Calhoun sees nationalist rhetoric as an extension of the republican doctrine that expresses this new relationship in participative terms. The subjects of such rhetoric 'nations' came to be understood as historical entities bearing rights, will and the capacity to decide on the fate of governments. The nation represented the emergence of a popular community integrated by new forms of communication and by its normative role as arbiter of good governance. Giesen (1998) refers in similar fashion to the establishment of a democratic nation code in early nineteenth-century Germany by the *Bildungsbürgertum*, the educated middle class, philosophically best represented by the doctrine of left Hegelianism with its combination of liberalism and fairness (*juste milieu*).

93

In the cases of Greenfeld and Calhoun in particular, the establishment of the linkage between nationalism, the transformation of civil society and democracy is fundamental. Although there is much evidence of dysfunction and repression associated with nationalist collective identity, this kind of identity is fundamentally modern and reversion to its ideal-typical origins in linking society and democracy, however modified by new circumstances, remains an important component of the well being of societies. The synchronic dimension is subordinate, not necessarily because it is less recognized, but because it is a derived synchronic position. The normative learning processes of early modernity are not re-examined in the light of their intrinsic merit and new circumstances so much as re-applied in new circumstances.

While remaining diachronic in emphasis the perspective changes radically when one turns to the work of Kedourie, Hobsbawm and others. In Kedourie's influential book (1994), a distinction is drawn between the democratic and the nationalist idea of the nation. To the French revolutionaries, a nation meant a number of individuals who have signified their will as to the manner of their government. In the vastly different theory of 'diversity' propounded by the philosophical movements of organicism and historicism associated with nationalism, a nation becomes 'a natural division of the human race, endowed by God with its own character, which its citizens must, as a duty, preserve pure and inviolable ... [and] ... since God has separated the nations, they should not be amalgamated' (Kedourie, 1994, p. 51). Unlike Calhoun, who sees the positive side of embedding the early modern ideas of individuality within the community of the nation, Kedourie sees the kind of individuality promoted by nationalism as a contributor to the exclusive, organicist and foundation-less tenets of the doctrine. 'Individuality', according to the reading, involves the willingness to subsume individuality to complete absorption of the individual in a state. Kedourie links such ideas to the origins and to the pernicious consequences of the doctrine of self-determination of nations that had empirically led to the multiplication of European states based on the nationality principle in the century to the immediate aftermath of the First World War. In his view, such a principle flew in the face of the kind of realistic supranational multiculturalism that had established more pragmatic and less doctrinal foundations for the constitution of political territories.

It is Kedourie's merit that his work throws up such large and complicated questions about the discourse of the nation that a generation of scholarship might still be required to answer them, although in some ways a generation of scholarship *has already* been applied to Kedourie's questions since the book first appeared in 1960, with no end in sight. The first such question is raised in relation to his insistence on the importance of nationalism as a doctrine – nationalist doctrine as creative of nationality. This has two major implications. The first has to do with his assertion of the centrality of nationalist historiography in bending the facts through creating fictitious historical grounds for nations that did not exist in the sense that we today, since German Idealism, understand nationalism. The second has to do with the importance of nationalist doctrine itself to the kind of nationalism that floats free from the enfetterment of other discourses and evaluative criteria beyond its own ethnocentric standards, which has wreaked such havoc in twentieth-century history. This second question raises two further subquestions. The first has to do with whether the doctrine of national self-determination has proven a beneficial principle and practice in recent world history, the second with what qualifications of nationalist doctrines are required by other doctrines in order to civilize it.[6] It is so to speak our prejudice in this book that Kedourie's questions, if not necessarily his always pessimistic conclusions, remain topical. They remain topical in that hatred of internal or external enemies as much as horizontal comradeship or love has been associated with nationalism within and beyond the European ambit on which his attention was mainly concentrated. They remain topical because Kedourie's problematization of nationalist discourse on a normative level, above all the organicist roots of primordialism, has not been disproven and the equation of nationalism, democracy and egalitarianism too easily made. They remain topical also because just such equations of nationalism, egalitarianism and democracy, extending from moral connections within the nation to moral imperatives for the formation of nations, put too much emphasis on self-determination as a principle rather than a mechanism among other mechanisms for creating and maintaining viable territorial boundaries. These considerations are receiving renewed attention in relation to the questions of transnationalism and cosmopolitan democracy, as we shall examine in the later chapters of this book.

One such question that can be derived from Kedourie, although not *his* question, is what happens when the nascent democratic nation code meets other codes. According to Giesen (1998), the democratic nation code broke down in Germany in the second half of the nineteenth century with the rise of the labour movement, a classic instance of the problems in realizing the distinction asserted by Lefort, and by Marx before him, between the assertion of right and the generalization of right (Lefort, 1988). This goes to the heart of the question of the relation between democracy and the nation itself. Can an enlightenment and early post-enlightenment perspective on this relation really suffice for grounding the democratic significance of the nation code given that nations have existed without democracy and with partial democracy ever since.[7] Can it suffice also given that extensive social interests within the nation-state – women, slaves, ethnic and racial minorities, social classes – remained unintegrated into either the nation or democratic discourse until many more struggles were waged?

95

These kinds of question form the background to the contributions to the collection of essays on the invention of tradition by Hobsbawm, Ranger and their collaborators (Hobsbawm and Ranger, 1983). The thrust of these essays is consistent with a later observation by Hobsbawm (1990) who distinguished between the largely beneficial consequences of nationalism until the last quarter of the nineteenth century and the regressive and dangerous forms it took thereafter. This temporal distinction is supported, in a very general sense, by the well-known historical events and processes that reflected an out of control nationalism after the turn of the century, until the return to sanity after the Second World War with the contained 'civic' nationalism of the established nation-states and the extensive wave of de-colonizing nationalisms in the developing world. Hobsbawm (1983a and 1983b) places in this context the difficulties experienced by political elites in securing legitimation in emergent mass societies after 1870. He describes the need for stable, legitimating rituals in a period of rapid social change associated with increased state activity, the extensification and intensification of communication, the rapid growth of cities, the advent of mass suffrage and, of course, the permanent threat or actuality of war. The idea of inventing tradition is distinguished from the networks of convention and routine that modern societies need to establish for functional reasons, for example, bureaucratic organization and corresponding rituals. The invention of tradition, as against such routine traditions, requires the creation of *public rituals* that induce feelings of permanence and invariance, not least in relation to specific aspects of national traditions such as the monarchy in Britain. Even though these invented traditions may be of recent origins, they have a metaphorical standing in symbolizing the long continuity of identity-securing national traditions. With the passing of time, the very recency of their origins may become forgotten and they gain the aura of timelessness.

The idea of invented tradition in the hands of Hobsbawm and others is a kind of practical semiotics that has certain resonance with the theoretical architecture of the 'analytical semiotics' of Hedetoft. The distinction made in the former between the creation of the nation from above but its interpretation and reconstruction from below is echoed in the latter with the distinction between the objective context of the production of national culture and the subjective context of its interpretation. As with Hedetoft, the role of the discipline of history is brought into relief in that a new task opens up before contemporary reflexive academics, the history of history or for that matter the sociology of history. For some historical materials and writers have knowingly or unwittingly become absorbed into the project of constructing the nation from the Victorian period forward, thereby generating problems for the idea of the continuity of traditions, the long history of the collective consciousness of the nation. In its stead is placed a kind of 'hermeneutics of suspicion' as the building blocks of national tradition are placed under permanent scrutiny to ascertain to what extent they conform to the ideologies of the times of their creation rather than the 'true' contents of the national past they seek to narrate (Trevor-Roper, 1983).

In a revealing insight into differences between the constitutive and ideology-critical perspective on nationalism, Calhoun (1997) has criticized Hobsbawm and Ranger for, in his view, accepting that long-run primordial ethnic traditions would be legitimate but invented traditions are of recent and perhaps manipulative creation (Calhoun, 1997, p. 34). He objects to this on two grounds. First, he says that all traditions are to some extent constructions and, second, that even the most recent and fabricated constructions could be real in their effects if people believed in them. It is hard to find support for these criticisms. It may be that highly indirectly, as the logical opposite of invented traditions that Hobsbawm, Ranger et al. could be regarded as claiming that long-run primordial expressions of ethnicity become in some way 'legitimate', but to our knowledge no claims to this effect are made. Furthermore, they never say that invented traditions are not real in their effects, however manipulative the intent of their production. In fact, the argument actually depends on their being believed and practised, therefore having this function. Otherwise, they would be the reclusive preserve of unknown antiquarians. Third, the point that all traditions are constructions could be transformed into a positive aspect of the position. Since this is so, the context of production and reception should be considered systematically, thereby adopting a reflexive, constructive view of culture as subject to conscious change by social actors. These reflections again draw attention to the synchronic deficit of interpretive analysis that at base can be traced back to the overextension of the historical provenance of the concept of nation. The truth about the 'invented tradition' perspective is that it is a successful but limited partial theory that exemplifies the requirement to consider the productive and receptive context of nationalist messages and rituals more systematically.

A final ideological critical interpretation of the discourse of the nation is ideology critical as much by its exclusion from other theories as much as by its intrinsic critical intention. This is the analysis of the relationship between nationalism and gender conducted by writers such as Yuval-Davis (1997), Mosse (1985) and Jawardene (1986). Yuval-Davis proposes an analytical schema for nationalist projects that has definite similarities to that of Eisenstadt and Giesen, not least because it is *analytically* neutral, although of course it can and does acquire significant evaluative content in application. She wishes to depart from the 'dichotomous' civic-good and ethnic-bad conception of nationalism popular among many writers in building her analytical schema. This involves distinguishing between constructions of nations based on discourses of origins, constructions of nations built on culture and the civic dimension built around citizenship. Especially the first two constructions map well onto Eisenstadt and Giesen's primordial and civic categories and Yuval-Davis's civic dimension bears at least some relation to the former writers' reflexive or cultural codes, especially in the form outlined by Eisenstadt (1998).[8] For each of these nationalist projects she instances crucial aspects of the relationship between gender and the nation. In relation to the discourse of national origins, which in her view tends to be more exclusionary than other nationalist projects, she considers the question of women and the biological reproduction of the nation and efforts to control marriage, procreation and sexuality. In relation to cultural projects, she draws upon Armstrong's idea of symbolic border guards (Armstrong, 1982), expressing the claim to distinctiveness of a form of life, and considers gendered symbols as a major aspects of such boundary maintenance. This formulation is quite close to Mosse's account of the rise of male-bonded fraternities as a major identity marker of nations around the turn of the twentieth century (Mosse, 1985). Finally, she considers the citizenship and nationalist project not simply in relation to right to belong, but also general citizenship rights and the formal and informal rules that apply especially to the entitlements and obligations of women.

Yuval-Davis's and other work on the theme of nationality and gender draws specific attention to an absolutely central but largely neglected theme within the study of nationalism. The implications of the specification of nation codes for social relations extends more widely than the case of women, to ethnic distinctions, social classes, religious distinctions and others. As we shall address in the next chapter, there are inputs to nation codes derived from the interaction and relative powers of social groups in various situations and times; a code-building process that is an institutionalized consequence of such interaction; and an output relation that has to do with the institutional effects of these codes on the social groups involved – or excluded – from their construction. The building of a national identity has therefore an important effect on social relations through its codes of inclusion and exclusion and also by what these codes mean for categories of people.

CONCLUSION

The general importance of the kind of interpretive work described in this chapter has to do with emphasizing the relative autonomy of culture as it operates through the discourse of the nation. A significant aspect of this project has been to free the theme of the nation either from disregard or ascription as an unmitigated pathology of modernity. This has allowed the nation to emerge as a basic cultural component of modernity along with others such as instrumentalization, the autonomous self, reflexivity, gender, publicity and more. The general state of theorization of such cultural structures, although advancing, is still not well developed, especially in their relation to other dimensions of modernity such as networks, institutions, and patterns of agency. What appears lacking in relation to the nation is replicated also in other areas and is, on the one hand, the need to identify global and regional epochs of nationalism through historical-sociological reconstruction. On the other, there is a requirement for a more developed synchronic framework considered within and sometimes across those epochs. At present, the relative undevelopment of the synchronic dimensions has meant too great a dependence on diachronic categories such as the relationship between communication networks and imagined community, the nature of status inconsistency and the expression of ressentiment, the nation and the development of solidary communities and so on. This has created a kind of dependence on linear and predominantly positive evaluative readings of the nation as equivalent to modernity itself, as a discursive form, or as an imagined community and having difficulty in handling regressive social change.

What appears to be needed is the specification of smaller temporal sequences and the development of synchronic frameworks at least on three levels; modernity as a whole, epochs of modernity, and character-istic types of nationalism within each epoch. Such a turn to synchronic analysis would carry new requirements as to the theoretical focus of cultural studies of nationalism that point, as we shall develop in the next chapter and also in Chapter 6, to richer analytical frameworks with greater openness to variation. The hermeneutic approaches to the nation discourse, which have united interpretive work to the present, and that have been on the whole very productive, should be retained. But they might operate in a more tentative manner in which the nation is conceived more as a shifting set of signifiers that 'remains a floating representation ... [whose origins] ... the stages of its foundation and the vectors of its destiny are, therefore, constantly being displaced and are always subject to the decisions of social actors – or those who speak for them – who want to establish themselves within a duration and a time which allows them to name themselves' (Lefort, 1988, p. 232). Such an approach would not preclude establishing the important linkages between the nation and the normative content of modernity but always with the requirement of keeping in mind that the nation is not per se the normative content of modernity and that it always has to be considered and reconsidered in relation to other normative learning processes and its own pathological outcomes in given eras and cases.

99

NOTES

1 For an excellent discussion, see Ozkirimli (2000).

2 See also Delanty (1995a) on this distinction.

3 See also Hedetoft (1995) on German/Danish cultural relations.

4 It should be noted that Greenfeld does allow for the possibility that the Netherlands also germinated the idea of the nation in the modern period but she does not explore this further (Greenfeld, 1992, p. 14).

5 The absence of reference to the public sphere may owe something to the fact that the translation of Habermas's key work did not appear in English until 1989. It also undoubtedly owes something to the fact, as previously argued, that the public sphere no less than the nation have remained underregarded theoretical categories in the social and political sciences.

6 Regretfully, the further normative and empirical consideration of this question exceeds the space limitations of this book. For thoughtful contributions that oppose Kedourie's basic stance, see Miller (1995), Canovan (1996) and for an intermediate posi-tion see Habermas (1996).

7 The German case can be taken as an example in the nineteenth century.

8 Eisenstadt and Giesen in fact gain analytic refinement by adding the dimensions of what they describe as resource distribution and entitlements, broadly citizenship questions, to all collective identity codes but these dimensions are more developed and extensive in the reflexive-transcendental codes.

five
nationalism, agency
and social change

In Chapter 2, we outlined the transformation in the social sciences in recent times, with renewed attention being paid to culture and agency as dynamic and creative entities. The two aspects of transformation are related but far from identical. In the case of nationalism, the turn to culture drew more from older traditions of locating nationalism within structural configurations than did the turn to agency. It also drew from a longer hermeneutic tradition of interpreting the nation that became reinvigorated and re-applied. The turn to agency, while of course in certain limited ways drawing from long-run traditions of empirical inquiry, marked in some of its forms at least a qualitatively new kind of empirical-theoretical endeavour, as it introduces an expanded range of contexts and levels of analytic attention. Agency, in the context of nationalism, can refer, among other phenomena, to large-scale collectivities such as nations or nation-states, to meso-level collective actors including nationalist movements and ethnic groups, to political entrepreneurs, to the opinions of individuals, to political or cultural entrepreneurs, to the enflamed masses, to deliberating publics, to military or other violent action.

It is not, of course, the case that theoretical approaches that we have been designating structural-developmental or interpretive have excluded agency from their concerns. However, in developmental approaches in particular, the long time periods brought into consideration involve a definite reduction in the perceived contingency of action, what might be called the reification of action. This is evident in Rokkan where he only occasionally refers to nation-building elites or monarchs, with the public only appearing on the stage in the indirect form of references to mass society. In Elias the actors are more varied, since he provides an instructive model of how to relate agency to long-term structural and cultural change. However, inevitably only the main actors of particular epochs are really considered in any depth, monarchs, would-be monarchs, and the nobility in the medieval period and from the early modern period onwards, the main social classes. Elias's model may also be difficult, but not impossible, to transfer from the relatively stable context of the big

European nation-states to other parts of Europe and the world where related processes of territory formation, social stratification, state building and cultural interpretation patterns do not inhere in a single territory over time or are otherwise constrained and fragmented. The work of Gellner involves highly abstract accounts of possible nationalist action as a response to logic of industrialization and cultural standardization but does not help to explain either the general or specific character of national mobilization.

In relation to interpretive approaches, the nature and implications of nationalist agency is also undeveloped and where it is considered, as with the reception of Hobsbawm and Ranger's collection on invented tradition, or in the debate between Brass (1977, 1979) and Robinson (1977, 1979) on the capacity to relate strategically or manipulatively to tradition, it tends to become a matter for heated controversy. Agency becomes squeezed in interpretive approaches due to the way in which the cultural object 'nation' is elevated to the central focus of attention to the neglect of sustained period-specific concentration on social mechanisms and inter-textual contexts that go to produce it. The agency that results tends to be the agency of a historical macro subject, the collectivity of the nation, that becomes defined relatively early in modernity and subsequently floats above the cultural contexts of nationalist situations, the formations of mobilizing cultures and the analysis of the public resonance of nationalist messages. This cultural account of the nation form is important in its own as a broad context-setting exercise for the cultural analysis of nationalist agency. As the nation form is pivotal to modernity its application is nonetheless limited to nationalism as a de-differentiating, integrative counter-moment to the differentiating logic of modernity that shapes the cultural unity and meaningfulness of forms of life. As we have observed previously, the form of the nation is considered without sufficient reference to other institutionalized cultural forms, through which its elements are in part refracted. Of specific relevance to this chapter, the approach has difficulty in addressing the social mechanisms implicated in the recurring construction of nationalist cultures. In this way of thinking the nation becomes a generalized identity in the sense of Smith. Its a priori influence on cultural innovation inhibits detailed consideration of the open horizons of any given point of departure, such as episodes of cultural creation or instances of symbolic contention. This is not so problematic for characterizing modernity-long, or for that matter even longer, dimensions of nationalism. It does become so when the creativity of action in specific contexts is under-emphasized or disregarded, when eras of authoritarian nationalism are not addressed in a sustained, intrinsic manner, or when the inputs to the formation of national societies at various times and places are not followed through into an equivalent treatment of long-term outputs or consequences.

The point emerging here is not that the general contribution of developmental and interpretive approaches is wrong; it is that the approaches are not sufficient, especially if we are concerned with phenomena that are most pertinent to the present as, to take just a few examples, the way in which self-determination was defined and institutionalized at the beginning of the twentieth century, the relationship between nationalism and emancipation in postcolonial societies, the rise of right-wing xenophobic nationalism, the de-institutionlization of aspects of the national identities framed out of the nineteenth-century nationalist mobilizations, and the reconsideration of the nation-state as a sufficient form of political organization in the face of globalization trends. Such examples require greater contextual precision and greater attention to forms of agency and the range of outcomes of agency. Furthermore, the empirical-theoretical outcomes of work geared to such considerations need to be re-absorbed into general theories to provide new orientations for further points of departure.

In this chapter, we propose to scratch the surface of such a task by providing an account of and reflecting on approaches to nationalism that contribute to an understanding of nationalist – and ethnic – agency. We will follow three kinds of approach. These are, first, approaches that are well integrated into structural accounts: second, approaches that show weaker integration both with existing structural and cultural accounts; and, third, approaches that explicitly question the degree to which non-political structures are relevant in many cases of nationalist action.

STRUCTURES AND ETHNIC MOBILIZATION

There exists a significant body of literature, largely American, exploring structural factors that underpin ethnic collective action. The allusion to the existence of this literature may indeed seem a strange way to begin, as if this scholarship were some previously undiscovered remote island. However, on the whole, there is little reference to it in the mainstream literature on nationalism that we have been reviewing, at least from the moment we concluded our treatment of Rokkan and Gellner, or indeed there is equally little reference the other way round. There are only a few exceptions to this tendency including the work of Michael Hechter (1975) on the Celtic periphery of Great Britain and that of Paul Brass (1985, 1991). There are some suggestive explanations for this state of affairs. The literature is largely American and reflects American concerns with ethnic relations in a multiethnic society within a long-established political territory. The literature is centrally concerned with mobilization but from a structural perspective using case and variable analysis that pays only indirect attention to the interpretive concern with the narrative of the nation form. The literature is predominantly on ethnicity, whose study for good or ill has tended to be divorced from that of nationalism or, put somewhat differently, ethnicity is treated as categorically different from nationalism although intrinsic to it.

All of this raises the question of why consider it here. Part of the reason lies in a particular reading of the relationship between nationalism and ethnicity. A subtle version of what is generally accepted to distinguish nationalism from ethnicity is provided by Van den Berghe (1983)[1] that a nation is 'a politically conscious ethny, claiming statehood rights on the basis of common ethnicity'. The crucial words here in our reading are 'statehood rights' rather than simply 'state', as in other versions, since the former holds the possibility of such rights being addressed without the objective of forming a completely autonomous, independent state and hence the acceptance of the reality of predominantly multiethnic states in a world context. This means that nations can exist without separate states, but with the aspiration to or reality of statehood rights, and hence by extension so can nationalism, a point forcefully emphasized by Williams who regards the term 'nation-state' as a 'muddled and intellectually dangerous term' (1994, p. 53). This, of course, does not exclude the possibility that many ethnic groups will only see their aspiration to nation status fulfilled by the gaining of an autonomous state of their own. The general point arising here from our standpoint is that to establish too clear a distinction between nationalism and ethnicity is not helpful since it excludes those many cases in which states are established on the basis of compromises between different ethnic groups, who could paradoxically be regarded as nationalist movements before such compromises. The tendency to regard nationalism as the view that a given state structure should represent the culture and interests of just one ethnic group reflects a tendency in vogue in Europe in the nineteeth and first half of the twentieth century but it cannot be sustained in a global context.

The second reason why this literature is important is that ethnicity is an important component of nationalist action, even where nationalism is regarded according to the strict criterion of the possession of or aspiration to an independent state by ethnic groups. Third, we know a great deal about ethnicity from certain empirical-theoretical standpoints and even if it is only indirectly relevant to nationalism in certain cases because it deals with intrastate ethnic relations with no aspirations to the transformation of state structures, the insights gained can certainly be re-applied to cases of nationalist movements that do implicate such transformation. Finally, the literature in question is to a large extent a literature on collective action that is valuable in itself, while also offering important indications for how other accounts of collective action can be used in an additional or substitutive manner.

Neilsen (1985) describes the general orientation of this approach as a macro-sociological theory of collective action that depends on finding systematic relationships between structural characteristics of a society and the success of a particular solidary group in recruiting participation resources from the social environment. Williams (1994) puts it similarly but somewhat more broadly in specifying that it is the structure of intra-societal cleavages and the history of relations between them that provides the global context of constraints and opportunities on ethnic collective action. Williams is, however, aware that though theories of ethnic conflict have characteristically been focused on intra-societal processes such as internal colonialism, split labour markets, economic competition and assimilation, increasing attention is being paid to state power and inter-societal processes by among others Brass (1985) and Gurr (1993).[2] The work under consideration here is therefore centrally concerned with the structural conditions of ethnic mobilizations and conflict. The question that unites much of the work is in what ways and with what consequences are ethnic groups embedded in social structures within or across 'societies'? This can also be formulated as a relative question of the degree of success ethnic groups have in mobilizing solidary resources against other competing social bases for identity and interests (Neilsen, 1985). Formulated in this way, it does echo, at least faintly, our critique of the 'inter-textual' limitations of interpretive work and related work in political theory. Nationalist collective identities must be placed in the context of other identities, especially if wide-ranging claims are made about their contribution to social integration.

105

Ragin (1979) provides a valuable synthesis of three perspectives on ethnic mobilization that could be labelled structural in the sense just described, development, reactive ethnicity and ethnic competition. The developmental approach we have already covered and as we have seen in the case of Rokkan only indirectly contributes to explaining mobilization. This approach explores the establishment of functionally based cleavages on a national scale which requires that the process of structural differentiation erodes the cultures of the different 'value communities' within the borders of the nation-state. What is also basic to this approach is the erosion through modernization processes of the distinctiveness of the cultural expressions of socio-economic cores and peripheries. This approach is clearly insufficient to address the persistence and renewal of ethnic mobilization, even in developed states such as Canada, but it does explain why in some cases ethnic mobilization does not occur – the functional cleavage becomes superordinate – or does occur – the functional cleavage could not be established or could only be established imperfectly. Although its weaknesses tend to be more stressed in the later literature, the developmental approach, as we stressed in Chapter 3, remains important for placing ethnic and nationalist upsurges in the broader context of long-run social change.

The second approach is that of reactive ethnicity, which, to the contrary of the developmental approach, argues that structural differentiation may actually increase ethnic distinctions, because not a universal but a particularistic distribution of roles and resources may accompany it. Such a distribution can lead to an ethnically based cultural division of labour, because the inferior cultural group 'are assigned to inferior positions and receive inferior rewards' (Ragin, 1979, p. 621). According to Ragin, Michael Hechter and, interestingly, Ernest Gellner are the two main proponents of this approach. While both authors share a similar basic position in relation to uneven effects of modernization, Hechter's takes the theory further into the province of explaining the *processes* of inclusion and exclusion and possible responses to them in specific cases (Hechter, 1975). This leads to an emphasis not on sharp cultural markers of difference, as in Gellner, but more subtle ones. Hechter also frees up the temporal association of ethnic mobilization with industrialization and thereby places the conditions of mobilization in a broader political and economic framework. It would probably be fair to say that Gellner provides some basic structural assumptions and Hechter additionally applies them to the more specific contexts in which collective practices are actually situated.

The third approach is the ethnic competition perspective that can be led back to classic theories of nationalism and ethnicity, such as those of Deutsch (1953) and Barth (1969). A common theme among proponents of this approach is that ethnic relations are likely to be stable when different ethnic groups occupy distinct structural positions in a division of labour. This stability may not survive if, due to processes of social change, this structural autonomy changes and ethnic groups now compete for roles and resources. Ragin describes how Hannan (1979) advances two propositions of ethnic competition theory that seem at first glance somewhat paradoxical. The first is that modernization erodes ethnic distinctiveness by connecting distinct populations and eroding small-scale ethnic collectivities. However, modernization also increases ethnic mobilization as the scale of any peripheral mobilization has to be considerable in order to have an impact on centres which, through modernization, have grown in scale, resources and cultural confidence. A similar view of these twin developments is used by Olzak to characterize not just ethnic competition theory but the study of ethnic movements in general (Olzak, 1992). Tilly also advances the viewpoint that modernization increases the scale of collective action in general, of which ethnic collective action could be regarded as one manifestation (Tilly, 1986).

Olzak (1992) presents the latter two theories as *both* being instances of reactive ethnicity divided into Marxist – reactive ethnicity as described following Ragin – and competition perspectives. She characterizes both positions as constructivist in contrast to a previously dominant primordialist perspective that viewed ethnic and racial distinctions as based on ancient cultural and perhaps genetic differences. Contemporary perspectives regard ethnicity as a *reaction* to inequalities in power, income and other rewards. Racial and ethnic boundaries are socially and politically constructed and the content of ethnic categories such as language, skin colour, or cultural attributes is assumed to be 'essentially arbitrary' (Olzak, 1992, p. 7). Olzak also emphasizes the important point just raised through Neilsen that a pivotal question for such reactive theories is the empirical investigation of what conditions lead to ethnic as distinct from other kinds of mobilization. She claims that by placing ethnicity in relation to other possible loyalties 'new questions about the causes of ethnic collective action arise'.

Macro-sociological accounts of mobilization of this kind are both theoretically and empirically sophisticated, but they operate with a relatively small range of core variables, largely socio-economic with a cultural inflection. The relative narrowness of the basic concerns has in certain respects proved an advantage as it has facilitated the development of tested theoretical propositions that allow for clear lines of argument. It also allows the subsumption of a multiplicity of cases within the core theoretical framework. Since the work by and large proceeds with similar empirical-analytical assumptions to studies of other possible linkages between independent variables and mobilization, most notably class, it contributes significantly to clarifying the conditions of separateness or connectedness of ethnic and other mobilizations. The insights gained in this exercise allow also for wider theoretical reflections on how national identities connect with other kinds of identity. The general strength of the approach is such that there are few examples of nationalist mobilization that could not be, at least *partially*, informed by its central insights.

However, its status as a partial theory in most situations may be revealed by two critical reflections we would like to make. The first has to do with the rationalistic perspective that imposes an instrumental framework on motivations to participate and other cultural dimensions of ethnic identification and activity. Olzak (1992, p. 41) asserts that the preferred theoretical orientations of resource mobilization, rational choice theories of group solidarity and research on social movements 'underscore the importance of specifying theoretically how incentives, resources and organizations combine with changing levels of niche overlap – between ethnic enclaves – to produce ethnic collective action'. Incentives involve calculations of costs and benefits; resources include income levels, membership size and information networks; and degree of organization includes levels of hierarchy, leadership and success of former mobilizations.

A recent development in studies of ethnic mobilization from the ethnic competition perspective, as well as American work on social movements, is to stress the resource mobilization paradigm over that of rational choice. This involves a preference for examining the manifest organizational expressions of collective action as opposed to the constitution of the possibilities of *any* collective action out of the preferences of individuals. It also involves a separation of the basic concepts of collective solidarity and collective mobilizations, and subjects them both to distinct empirical consideration in order to discover the linkages between them, rather than assuming as in some versions of rational choice theory that strong group solidarity automatically translates into collective action (Olson, 1965; Olzak, 1992). Solidarity in this reading is an indispensable condition of collective action but this collective action is only realized if other conditions are met, principally the existence of certain structural arrangements, the accumulation of appropriate resources and the available level of organization. An interesting feature of the work on nationalism and ethnicity from this perspective is that its independent variables are what could be called *social opportunity structures* for collective action arising from the nature of intra-societal cleavages. This is different from recent work on social movements that stress political opportunity structures as the basic context of mobilization (McAdam, McCarthy and Zald, 1996), although the resource mobilization paradigm is held in common. What is noteworthy in the latter development is its recent inclusion of a more extended, integral treatment of culture as a process of the 'framing' of collective action. It is not just resources, incentives and organization that count; it is the interpretations of situations made by mobilization actors to improve their inner coherence and to diffuse their messages successfully into the external environment. This certainly has the effect of weakening the instrumentalism of the basic action paradigm as the moral and expressive, as well as instrumental dimensions of culture are taken to mediate between context and action and therefore to create additional possibilities for action or inaction.

However, even in these developments culture is positioned downstream of structure and organization in the overall scheme. The fundamental initiating conditions of mobilization lie in the interplay between structural and organizational questions with culture coming in later. What is neglected in these approaches, going back to ideas proposed in Chapter 2, is the creative role of culture when fused with certain characteristics of collective action. In particular, the process of collective identity formation may itself create a new perception of structural and resource configurations that acts as a propadeutic to collective action by, for example, generating new models of collective learning. The actual, objective existence of discrimination or competitive relations between groups then itself becomes an element of a wider process of the instrumental, moral or affective *construction* of the situation by collectivities. The role of collective identity as a dynamic process is further enhanced when internal cleavages *within* ethnic collectivities or national movements results in claims about the general benefits of certain courses of action that may, for example, only benefit *some* of the collectivity, i.e. elites. The many examples of populism worldwide attest to the extent of this situation. A further dimension of the issue arises when collectivities set the requirements of cultural identification above material resources as a motive for action. In this case, collective identity involves the articulation of a constellation of values that not only influences the expression of instrumental preferences (Eisenstadt and Giesen, 1995) but also what might be called the preference for different kinds of preference, instrumental, moral and expressive.[3] This suggests that although this tradition is in line with Barth's constructivism, it is so within a predominantly instrumentalist framework that neglects the creative relationship between culture and action.

The second critical reflection arises from a problem raised internally to the tradition. Williams (1994) draws attention, following Lichbach (1989), to the 'diverse and contradictory' findings of a research review by the latter that indicates support for every conceivable relationship between economic inequality and political conflict. Williams himself notes that this 'disconcerting' finding has been variously attributed to problems of research design or statistical modelling and to deficiencies in formal models and theories. He also notes in what could be taken as a general critique of the predominance of structure within the theory tradition that: 'We must acknowledge that satisfying explanations of collective conflict cannot be confined to multivariate "accounting" in which a cluster of conditions are shown to precede or accompany the outcome of interest' (1994, p. 71). He goes on to say that timing and sequence must be analysed as well and cites, citing Sewell (1987, p. 17) to the effect that: 'System level outcomes depend not only on the configuration of actors, motives, and resources but also crucially on the sequence in which action occurs.' Consideration of the sequence in which action occurs involves a shift from structure-outcome relations to micro processes of action. Such micro processes in complex, unclear situations tend to involve higher levels of contingency. This confuses attempts to clarify what precise structural factors are at work in 'determining' outcomes and accordingly hinders generalization to other situations. Acceptance of the contingency of action also involves greater recourse by actors to situated cultural framings that make sense of their situation and offers them a way forward. Such contingent relations to interests and interpretations creates a high level of variability and complicate attempts to construct logics of action. The focus on the actual situation of action suggests the need for a more inductive, less teleological approach to identifying the presence and assessing the potency of embedded pre-existing structures. In any case, as Williams himself suggests, the move from structure-outcome relations to the logics of action already implicates far-reaching reconsideration of the view that action

109

is mainly or completely structurally determined in favour of seeing it as more autonomous and constitutive.

THE CONSTRUCTION OF STRUCTURES BY AGENCY

The approach described in the previous section, given the emphasis on the structural determination of action, could be placed in relation to the framework outlined at the end of Chapter 2 in the following way. The structural implications of modernization processes for the institutional core impact selectively on ethnic groups which culturally interpret their structural situations in ways that sometimes gives rise to political mobilization. That approach is characteristically content with demonstrating the causes, kinds and extent of mobilization. By contrast, the approaches considered here, while similarly interested in the explanation of mobilization, are also interested in the reverse process of the implications of any given mobilization for the cultural and institutional orders. There is also a different value attached to symbolic contestation as a mobilization strategy. The approach, therefore, also incorporates cultural innovation as frequently representing the initial step towards political action. The cultural order of modernity is therefore seen as of fundamental importance and the interplay of cultural structures and communication processes together have a powerful bearing on the form that national identity takes. However, the emphasis on cultural structures and processes does not exclude the structural shaping of group political cultures although the emphasis is on the dynamic interplay of these cultures as they become culturally concretized and carried by collective actors.

The most developed theoretical example of this tradition is Klaus Eder's book on history as a learning process, which explores what the author views as the pathological development of political modernity in Germany (Eder, 1985). Eder traces the historical origins and significance of modern national identity in a way that has affinities with the interpretive tradition and political theory alike. He outlines how the decline of princely authority as the representative apex of a society of integrated individuals results in a society integrated beyond political authority in common experiences of a socio-cultural lifeworld. In this process, the cultural order of the life-world takes over as the basis of societal integration from the functional order of state authority. This experience of a common life-world is captured, according to Eder, by the concept of nation. National identity becomes the starting point and reference for what he describes as an evolutionary new form of collective consciousness. This form of collective consciousness has a political function since it offers a basis for mediating between the differentiated ideologies emanating from within civil society. On this basis, Eder goes on to identify a pathology as the partial or complete destruction of the structural potentials of a society in the course of its development. It consists of damaging or destroying the possibility for argument over which a historical development path should have validity. The advent of a pathology signifies that the prevailing collective political identity is no longer adequate for the task of translating the societally available learning potentials into an institutional framework that gives voice to legitimate and socially significant difference.

Eder sees modern political associations as a key to generating the intersubjective contexts of experience in which moral-normative learning can take place. For the first 70 years or so, of the century from 1770 to 1870 in Germany, such moral-normative learning had taken place but in the period after the 1848 Revolution up to German unification this was no longer possible. Political associations, under increasing political pressure, were no longer able to generate the basis for a successful collective identity through processes of rational and representative argumentation. Instead, there was a narrowing of the space of political consciousness arising from, on the one hand, a liberal-conservative social compromise and, on the other, from a conservative-democratic institutional compromise that left in place authoritarian government. As a consequence, politics was dominated by a rightwards orientation that excluded many liberals and the growing working-class movement and vital social interests were substantially excluded from political deliberation. By the end of the nineteenth century, without the possibility of wide-ranging, representative argumentation, politics became reduced to a question of power.

111

What emerges from Eder's account of the formation of German political culture is above all the insight that national identity is *normally* both a constructed and contested phenomenon. German development was pathological not because national identity was contested but because it was not contested *enough*. It is true that national identity can also be regarded as a unifying basis for political argumentation and therefore has a substantial reality above competing parties. But the moral-normative status of such a quasi-transcendental *modern* collective identity is derived from, not antecedent to, argumentation between political traditions that reflect current interests but also have an eye to the future. The fundamental question for Eder is whether competing conceptualizations of the future that reflect collective learning can be mediated and the outcomes institutionalized in society. In modern societies, the key to this translation lies in the quality and representativity of social communication and the degree to which such communication can be separated from non-communicative power.

The importance of these ideas lies in the capacity both to take national identity seriously but also to create the theoretical tools to criticize its substantive form where appropriate. National identity does not float free of political traditions and communication between them. Its true significance must be led back through communicative practices between political traditions to underlying social interests. Eder's approach therefore involves a social constructivist account of the building of national identity. But it also has an eye for the institutional consequences of what actually is built for society as a whole and for social groups within it. This approach does therefore move on from either a defence or a critique of the function of national identity per se to consideration of national identity as a socially construction that can vary with circumstances and agency.

Eder's work is interesting in another respect also. It conceives of the processes of formation of national identity as intra-societal. He resists the temptation to compare Germany with England and France, preferring to see the roots of the German pathology not in some long-run lack of synchrony with these earlier nation-states but in intra-societal communication processes themselves, which as we have seen degenerated in the latter part of the century to 1870. This approach does not need to exclude comparison, though comparative analysis was not Eder's purpose. A comparative approach built on Eder's work, or more generally on constructivist foundations, would add a new dimension to existing comparative work on nationalism. This has focused, first, on comparison of general national situations, often grouped according to typologies; secondly, on specific variables that are taken to shape system outcomes in a number of cases; thirdly, on comparison within a macro-regional framework as with Rokkan and Tilly; and, fourthly, on the comparative semantics of identity-building processes as with Greenfeld and Eisenstadt and Giesen. A constructivist approach on Eder's lines would additionally draw attention to the comparative role of the discourse of national identity as it effects the capacity of different societies to thematize the range of social interests and cultural traditions present within it. Of course, restrictive conditions would have to be placed on this kind of comparison. It would have to compare societies sharing a similar political system, at a similar level of development and in some measure internally stable and not determined from outside by an alien state. Such an approach would open the way to a more nuanced treatment of the role of nationalism and national identities from the standpoint of their contribution to the internal development paths of different societies.

The opportunities and difficulties with such comparative work are modestly advanced by a previous work by the current authors (O'Mahony and Delanty, 1998). Again this work is not comparative, but it does have distinct theoretical affinities with that of Eder and therefore adds another case to the approach. The authors explored the question of how it was that a national movement that has the reputation of an emancipatory struggle against external-English and internal-confessional domination produced such a socially conservative society in the twentieth century.

Unlike Germany, the Irish case involved not a process of unification on the basis of linguistic and cultural common features but of secession from the United Kingdom framework. However, like Germany, the successful Irish national movement did take place in an era of nationalism that has become characterized as predominantly authoritarian reactionary (Hobsbawm, 1990). The authors analyse the different wings of the Irish national movement following Hroch's (1985) pioneering work on small-country national movements and diagnoze the gradual rise to ascendancy of social conservatism and ethnic-romantic nationalism within that movement and within the broader public sphere that it came to dominate. The success of this cultural form of national identity in fact anaesthetized the sharp social conflict that had characterized the phase of the pre-Independence national movement proper. The middle-class elites who gained social dominance were subsequently able to develop a national identity code that emphasized their values of conservative romanticism and they had preponderant influence in building an institutional order that was largely consistent with those values. As with Eder, the societal critique lies in the narrowing of deliberative politics away from an adequate representation of available social bases and towards a form of populist, 'democratic-authoritarian' legitimation of the dominance of a particular social class and of a generally conservative culture. The point of both critical studies is to demonstrate that the form which national identity took involved an excessive emphasis on a romanticized cultural discourse of the nation that became a substitute for normative learning and argumentation among national groups. They involve a detranscendentalization of the concept of national identity in the light of the social mechanisms of its creation and the institutional implications of its substantive forms that involves quite a different emphasis from some interpretive work.

The now classic work of Hroch (1985, 1993) offers a somewhat different approach but one still concerned with the relationship between nationalist movements, situations and outcomes over time applied in this case to the smaller nations of Europe from the eighteenth to the twentieth centuries. He identifies three time periods and four typical wings in the national movements of these countries. The temporal distinctions are, first, the initial scholarly interest in the nation's history and culture towards the end of the eighteenth century; second, an active avant-garde with considerable societal impact by the middle of the nineteenth century; and, third, the mass movement proper which tended to take off towards the end of the nineteenth century. In this phase, nationalist movements can be subdivided into various wings: clerical-conservative, liberal-democratic, socialist and revolutionary. Hroch distinguishes the three phases of the national movement as phases A, B and C. He considers the essence of nationalist agitation to arise with phase B and to involve the 'effort to spread the idea of national identity in an environment which until that time recognized several different identities'

(1985, p. 95). Hroch observes that distinct from ethnic identity, national identity in the cases he studies expressed a relationship to a large social group that should have a fully formed social composition, be composed of citizens enjoying equal rights, acknowledge a body of 'higher culture' in the national language and combine awareness of common origin and destiny to create a historical 'personalized' collectivity (Hroch, 1985, p. 96). The various phases of nationalist agitation involve various thresholds of transition that involve moves from patriotic to national agitation, from agitation to mass appeal and from mass appeal to success for its cultural, social and political goals. Since Hroch's comparative study is specific to a genre of nationalism, movements for self-determination in small-nation contexts, he is able to place the national movement reasonably confidently into a structural context, basically from the expanded scholarship of the romantic enlightenment, to growing social mobilization among elites, including peripheral elites, by the mid-nineteenth century, to the increased level of social communication of mass society, including literacy, schooling and market relations.

Although Hroch's interest is comparative analysis of nationalist mobilizations in a range of comparable cases is different from the normative-critical single-country focus of Eder and O'Mahony and Delanty, his work illustrates the constitutive power of movements to shape situations. Hroch's account does not really analyse the movements' relations with wider society, especially the crucial diffusion of nationalist ideas to wider constituencies in phase C, but it does make plausible that an action category, national movements, carried within them, in Eder's sense, a model of learning that found institutional resonance and had institution-shaping effects. The two wider questions of the normative implications of these movements for the societies in question and the comparative dynamics of how nationalist ideas became societalized would be interesting topics for further research. Some aspects of these themes are taken up in the kinds of analysis outlined in the next section.

NATIONALISM AND POLITICAL AGENCY: A CONTENTIOUS ACCOUNT OF NATIONALISM

Recent work of Brubaker (1996, 1998) and Beissenger (1996, 1998), develop an older tradition of viewing nationalism as a political phenomenon and add to it a wider range of theoretical and empirical approaches drawn from modern developments in social theory and social movements research. This tradition downplays the significance of cultural innovation, above all the role of intellectuals, in favour of viewing nationalism as primarily a form of contentious political action. It is both constantly contentious (Brubaker, 1998) and most transformative of political and social structures during cycles or waves of nationalist contention, an idea drawn from social movement theory. Taking each of these ideas in turn, Brubaker supports Gellner's critique of the nation-centred concept of nationalism linked to the doctrine of self-determination. The idea underpinning the nation-centred concept is that nations are real, enduring entities whose tendency is to seek independent statehood in modern social and political conditions. As we have seen, this is a position that has excited much controversy. Brubaker launches the most radical critique we have so far encountered. He does this on the grounds that nationalism is not always state seeking and, even in cases where it is, nationalist action is not *only* state seeking action. Further, nationalism can flourish *after* the reorganization of political space on nationalist principles. Brubaker (1996) identifies distinctive forms of this kind of nationalism in the 'nationalizing' nationalism of successful nation-states where one 'national' group seeks to impose its priorities and values on others or trans-border nationalism, like the Hungarian, where a national group within a nation-state monitors the welfare of their own 'exiled co-nationals' who are minorities in other states. His most striking formulation is that the Soviet state in its nationality policy, not pre-existing national allegiances, was the primary factor in creating the conditions for contemporary nationalism in the former Soviet Union (see also Chapter 7). Brubaker claims that it is an 'illusion that nationalist conflicts are susceptible of fundamental resolution through national self-determination' (1998, p. 279) because the nation belongs to the class of 'essentially contested' concepts and 'chronic contestedness is therefore intrinsic to nationalist politics, part of the very nature of nationalist politics; and that the search for an overall 'architectural' resolution of national conflicts is misguided in principle, and often disastrous in practice' (1998, p. 280).

115

Beissenger (1996) whose field of study is, like Brubaker, the former Soviet Union and eastern Europe, develops the idea of nationalist cycles of contention. In doing this, he first distinguishes between 'quiet' and 'noisy' politics of nationalism. Quiet nationalism occurs in periods when existing state institutions remain dominant and nationalist contestation either seeks to prevent challenges to official concepts of nationhood or, alternatively, prepares for direct contestation. The noisy politics of nationalism comes to the fore when political opportunities broaden and political institutions come under direct challenge and contest. The noisy politics of nationalism is associated with those periods in history when nationalist contestation takes on the form of a series of linked mobilizations that are described by the term 'cycles of contention'. He identifies the French Revolution as unleashing the first tide of nationalist contention and successively the 1848 revolutionary year, the small-country nationalisms that swept the Russian, Ottoman and Austro-Hungarian empires, also including Ireland and Norway, in the second half of the nineteenth century to the First World War.

Other such periods include the rise of fascism in Europe, the wave of decolonization that followed the Second World War and, of course, the recent nationalist outbreak in Eastern Europe. In historical perspective, he sees these cycles of contention as bound up with the notion of territorial boundedness and the expansion of communication that gave rise to the modern social movement and its particular variant, the national movement. Cycles of contention of these kinds are collectively characterized by an opening of state boundaries that undoes the hardening of boundaries that is a product of the activities of state institutions in more normal times.

Beissenger asserts that when considering the reasons for the spread of nationalism, it is not processes of communication or 'contagion' that are important but political activities through which the 'hitherto impossible, implicit, and inconceivable come to be viewed by large numbers of people as thinkable, desirable, and even conventional' (Beissenger, 1996, p. 104). It is not entirely clear why communication should not count as part of the political activities that Beissenger describes. He speaks, for example, of social movements disrupting institutionalized orders of meaning to bring about 'discursive transformation in society' (1996, p. 105). The answer must lie in the view that communication is part of normal processes of the diffusion of ideas, leading ineluctably to nationalism-induced change. This impression is enhanced by the emphasis Beissenger places on events, especially events marked by violence that takes on symbolic status when used by nationalists to advance their case and inflame the wider population. This view might be supported by the kind of multiple regression analysis that Beissenger conducts which, for example, demonstrates the very strong connection between the degree to which a group mobilized in non-violent demonstrations over republican border issues in the former Soviet Union and the degree to which it engaged in ethno-nationalist violence (Beissenger, 1996, p. 140, footnote 26). Nonetheless, it remains puzzling that Beissenger follows the tradition of social movement analysis in building an analysis around cycles of contention and the opening of political opportunities and diminishes the significance of communication, though making reference to the work on symbolic framing and the construction of master frames by Snow and Benford (1992).

The significance of communication to mobilization is stressed by Brand who adds the concept of cultural opportunity structures to political opportunity structures in order to specify more fully the dimensions of the context for the production and reception of nationalist messages by proto-nationalist publics. Brubaker (1998) appears to adopt a similar position in questioning the assumption that it is politically profitable and relatively easy for elites to stir up nationalist passions, to evoke the anxieties, the fears, the resentments, the perceptions and misperceptions, the self- and other-identifications. Nonetheless, while elites' purposes may not be demonstrably served by attempting to mobilize nationalist sentiments in this manner, such symbolic mobilization is intrinsic to creating and sustaining the kind of nationalist mood that is indispensable to the realization of nationalist goals.

The general contours of the approach adopted by Beissenger and Brubaker is relatively clear. They offer a radical, political version of constructivism that combines substantive-analytical and normative goals. From a substantive and analytical standpoint, it seeks to portray nationalism not as a long-run concept fashioned in the cauldron of ideas but as crucially linked to the subject matter of political science, the state–society nexus. In respect of this emphasis, it operates with a double orientation to normal and extraordinary periods of expression of nationalism; the first characterized by institutional hegemony and latent protest and the second by institutional crisis and manifest opposition. The emphasis on either latent or manifest forms of mobilization in transformative periods indicates the active shaping of nationalist politics in such periods by actors acting with will and consciousness. Also present in this approach is a less pronounced normative critique of the concept of self-determination. Brubaker, in particular, takes up this issue and leaves no doubt, even without mounting a sustained normative critique of the concept itself, as distinct from its scholarly use, that a one-sided emphasis on its implication leads to an essentialist and highly problematic nationalist politics.

117

CONCLUSION

The various theories of nationalism considered in this and previous chapters reveal a field that, due to the explosion of scholarship in recent decades, has become more contemporaneous with developments in the wider social scientific field and actively contributing to the redefinition of a central aspect of the culture of modernity. It is also becoming more common after long neglect to find the nation becoming a theme in social scientific studies not centrally concerned with nationalism per se. The greater scholarly contemporaneity of recent work on nationalism, no less than the salutary reminder provided by events, has had the effect of making nationalism more visible, in the process posing a challenge to the central concepts of modernity that have now to grapple with this elusive, hydra-headed and semantically volatile phenomenon. The inescapable sense of the authors of this book, however, is of a field still in gestation whose central questions and debates have not yet fully formed. True, some theoretical traditions appear complete, but as we observed in the case of interpretive or ethnic mobilization theories above this can be at the cost of innovative paths of development.

We conclude this chapter by drawing attention to some central problems in the current state of theory and research and more by implication than recommendation suggest some new avenues of research. The first of these problems is the overemphasis on the diachronic perspective as outlined by Hedetoft (1995). This manifests itself in a kind of narrative stream about nationalism and modernity that only highly elliptically places it in the context of social integration and social change. It is not the least of Gellner's contribution to nationalism studies that he did try to develop a synchronic theory by introducing industrialization as a central category, but as is now widely accepted this was simply too limited an approach to place nationalism squarely in the evolving context of integration and change. A promising approach might be to place episodes of nationalism within an account of the reciprocal developments of collective actors and institutional orders in modernity, exploring how different models of the nation appear as solutions – at least for some of the parties – in given states of argumentation and conflict between social groups within the possibilities offered by the wider institutional framework. This observation has the implication that a more developed historical sociology of nationalism is needed that would provide better empirical-theoretical foundations for characterizing eras of nationalism. The tendency for a different, general account of nationalism to concentrate on different phases, for example, Calhoun on the late eighteenth century and Hobsbawm et al., on the late nineteenth century not to mention the medieval and early modern contributions, leads to a certain fragmentation of lines of argument. Some stabilization of eras of nationalism in the form of a sociological account of characteristic forms of social integration and conflicts in different periods and places would be very useful. It could also take in the essential dimension of the international state system. Some indications of a move in this direction were laid out in the first chapter of this book and some pioneering proposals are made in the next chapter.

118

The second point is very much related. In general, our perception is that there is underlying normative debate about the contribution of nationalism to modernity as a whole, to particular eras, to the welfare of particular groups and to the path of development of particular societies. Apart from the political theorists and critically oriented sociological works – such as previous work of the authors – this is largely a latent debate. It might be better if it were enjoined more explicitly and the kinds of normative contribution or disbenefits associated with nationalism at various times and places and for various groups made more clear. This is very much connected with the previous point on the need to develop synchronic richness in that the specification of the social, cultural and institutional orders of particular eras is a prerequisite for making and debating normative judgements. Some preliminary steps as to how this could be done are proposed in the next chapter. Developments in this direction might also open the door for a more sustained treatment of the important but completely underdeveloped relation between nationalism and ideology.[4]

A third problem is the absence of significant interchange between different disciplines and different theoretical traditions. The framework outlined in Chapter 2 partially begins that task in drawing attention to the need to integrate different mobilizatory, cultural and institutional aspects of nationalism within simultaneously operating diachronic and synchronic perspectives. Once more, developing prospects for genuine exchange and interchange between theory traditions will as much as anything depend on progress in the first problem/task outlined earlier, the development of a societal model for different eras of nationalism and above all, the elaboration of such a model for the present conjuncture. Pioneering work of this kind might open up the imagination of nationalist theorists and researchers to boundary-spanning innovation that could rework existing developmental, interpretive and constructivist traditions to address current lacunae in the general theory of nationalism. Such a move, drawing off the enormous richness of case material, might in turn enrich the comparative and singular study of nationalist cases by embedding nationalism in the theory of modernity in a more stable, yet flexible manner.

NOTES

1 Cited in Williams (1994).

2 This is similar to the point raised by the praise and critique of Rokkan by Tilly in Chapter 4.

3 Further development of this idea can be taken from Habermas's account of communicative action (Habermas, 1984).

4 Initial steps towards considering this relationship in the Irish case are taken by the current authors in O'Mahony and Delanty (1998).

six

towards a typology of forms of nationalism

Much can be lost by always speaking of nationalism as a single phenomenon, for in fact it has many different forms. Moreover, some of these forms tend to be more prevalent in specific eras. Understanding the variety and the incidence of these forms makes for a richer and more differentiated picture of the phenomenon. It also helps in making judgements about the contribution of nationalism, respectively to the maintenance of order and to the introduction of social change. In this chapter, therefore, we build from our positioning of nationalism within the dynamics of modernity and the interpretation of this relationship by various theories. Here, we attempt the double task of differentiating between the different forms of nationalism and placing the incidence of these forms within a historical sociological framework spread over the last two centuries.

We begin with the following typology that attempts to summarize the main kinds of nationalism that exist in the modern world.[1] Beginning with some remarks on pre-modern nationalism, the following ten kinds of modern nationalism are discussed:

- state patriotism
- liberal nationalism
- reconstructive nationalism
- integral nationalism
- irredentist nationalism
- secessionist nationalism
- cultural nationalism
- religious nationalism
- transnationalism
- the new radical nationalisms.

There is a general historical pattern to these types of nationalism, although this is not to be interpreted too precisely. The variety of nationalisms makes this impossible. However, in the terms of historical emergence, a sequential logic can be roughly indicated.

PRE-MODERN NATIONALISM

We begin with pre-modern nationalisms since a great deal of debate concerns the uniqueness of nationalism as a creation of modernity. This question of the modernity of nationalism depends largely on two criteria, the periodization of modernity and the definition of nationalism. If we follow the understanding of modernity as a process of interacting dynamics behind which lie civilizational processes outlined in Chapter 1, it can be argued that modernity did not simply arise with the European Enlightenment and French Revolution, but was a gradual and multilevel process. The emergence of modernity can be traced back to the sixteenth century in many parts of Europe, and there may be traces of modernity in the late medieval world. In particular, in those parts of Europe where the Reformation made a significant impact, some case for the existence of early forms of nationalism can be made. In the case of creole nationalism we find a blending of native and settler cultures. In Latin America this became an important basis of nationalist movements from the early nineteenth century. In this sense, then, nationalism was a product of long-run historical processes of cultural mixing.

A large body of literature has documented the emergence of nationalism in late medieval and early modern Europe.[2] Major medievalists such as Marc Bloch and Johan Huizinga believed that national consciousness existed as early as the eleventh century in England, France and Germany.[3] What is clear from this literature is that most early forms of nationalism were connected with state formation which fostered the idea of a national political community. In many cases, such as England and the Netherlands to mention the most notable, the cause of radical Protestantism was often linked to nationalism. Greenfeld, for instance, argues that modern nationalism began in Reformation England and not, as Kedourie argues, in early nineteenth-century revolutionary Europe (Greenfeld, 1992). Hebraic mythology played a major role in shaping English national identity around the Puritan cause in the seventeenth century. This was an age that had experienced many kinds of popular revolt, most of which were not connected with the Reformation. However, it is clear that many pre-modern notions of the nation were quite different from the modern usage. Thus the concept of the nation in the Holy Roman Empire of the German Nation did not refer to the masses but to the elites. Many early modern references to the nation meant nothing more than the ruling elites who represented the nation. The republican idea of the *patrie* was predominantly absent from these conceptions of the nation. The early Latin notion of *natio* referred to a community of descent defined by birth and in the early modern period the term was often used to designate foreigners.

It may be suggested that the emergence of modernity's dynamic of democratization in fact played a role in shaping *some* of these early forms of national consciousness. Gorski (2000, p. 1450) documents how the Dutch word for 'nation' becomes a synonym for 'people' in the sense of a group united by ancestry, language and customs during the Dutch Revolt against the Spanish in the 1560s. As an identity and as a movement, national consciousness certainly did exist in some cases in the early modern period. A general conclusion might be that if the French Revolution is not taken as the exclusive reference point for the emergence of modernity, a more differentiated understanding of nationalism is possible as having its roots in pre-modern contexts. The radical impulse in modern nationalism, while being greatly shaped by the Jacobin political heritage, has had clear origins in earlier stages in the emergence of modernity when political struggles were largely articulated in the form of popular revolts against absolutism. However, there can be little doubt that the idea of a sovereign people, the civic nation and notions of self-determination did not become significant until the advent of modernity and the creation of a public culture based on secularism, democracy and individualism.

STATE PATRIOTISM

122 In one of its most pervasive forms, nationalism has been the ideology of the existing state; it refers to the dominant national identities of the established states in their attempt to extend power over their minorities and regions. In this sense, many pre-modern states did exhibit nationalistic tendencies, although it was primarily an ideology that was confined to the elites. As a popular ideology, nationalism has been more a feature of modernity. While figuring in cases of popular revolt as discussed earlier, a major expression of modern nationalism is in the national identity of the established state. We term this kind of nationalism 'state patriotism'. Unlike radical forms of nationalism this type is largely affirmative, a product of *étatisme*, serving to integrate the masses into the official political culture of the central state through, for instance, a national system of education and the codification of a national language.[4] Hobsbawm has argued that until the twentieth century, when it often became a subversive ideology, nationalism has been on the whole the nationalism of the existing states (Hobsbawn, 1990). There is some truth to this, for nationalism has very often been simply loyalty to the existing state, as opposed to nationalism as a movement. In other words, nationalism 'from above' as opposed to 'from below' is not a state-seeking kind of nationalism but a form of national consciousness. The obvious examples of this kind of nationalism might be early modern Spain, Tudor England and in modernity proper, Britain, France, China, and imperial Russia. These examples involve a national project of state legitimation. For instance, British national identity emerged first around parliament and the struggle against monarchy, from the end of the nineteenth century it was recodified

around the monarchy and empire. French national identity was defined by reference to the republican values of the revolution and came to be a strongly state-centric understanding of nationhood.

State patriotism is practised more or less by all nation-states and it is for this reason that it should be seen as distinct from the more extreme doctrine of integral nationalism, (discussed later, see p. 126). This, of course, implies that state patriotism continues wherever there are states seeking to build patriotic allegiances. It is the dominant expression of American Nationalism since the Second World War. A modern form of state patriotism is often described as constitutional patriotism. This form of patriotism is regarded as a manifestation of a civic nationalism, a term that connotes the existence of bonds of common purpose within a constitutional framework of procedures, rights and obligations. This version of state patriotism is associated with relatively stable, democratic nation-states in the twentieth century and in particular after the Second World War.

LIBERAL NATIONALISM

Nationalism entered the modern age primarily as a revolutionary movement, closely allied to the ideas of the French Revolution. In Chapter 1 we discussed this in terms of the Jacobin thrust in modern politics, the revolutionary ideology of the total political transformation of society by a self-appointed elite. The primal Jacobin moment was never entirely subdued and it remained a recalcitrant force in modern politics, making nationalism a very potent and destabilizing force. However, one of the dominant kinds of nationalism that was to prevail in the nineteenth century was liberal nationalism, which while having a revolutionary, romantic dimension to it was strongly republican, universalistic and civic in its self-understanding.

Liberal nationalism – which may also be termed republican nationalism – arose in the early nineteenth century in the aftermath of the French Revolution, whose ideals became the basis of movements as diverse as radical liberalism, nationalism, romanticism and historicism. Unlike the nationalism fostered by the established nation-states, liberal nationalism strictly speaking involved a small number of movements that sought to attain statehood for allegedly historical nations. The most famous example of this kind of nationalism was the case of Italian *risorgimento* nationalism, but also includes nineteenth-century Irish nationalism, Greek nationalism and the German liberal nationalists. But it was the Italian case that epitomized the liberal nationalism of the post-Enlightenment period in Europe. The *risorgimento* itself captures the mood of the new wave of nationalism that swept across Europe after the revolutionary period: the resurrection of the historical nation as a mature nation-state. The *risorgimento* combined the cherished belief of

123

the Enlightenment in human emancipation through self-determination with the romantic belief in the heroic personality fighting for freedom. This combination of liberalism and romanticism that was typical of the European mind of the mid-nineteenth century provided the intellectual justification for nationalism. One of the earliest examples of liberal nationalism was the Greek nationalist movement, which began in 1821 and led to the independence of Greece from the Ottoman Empire in 1832. The Greek cause was immortalized in 1824 with Lord Byron's death at Missolonghi in the name of the Greek nation. His death inspired romantic nationalism, with many causes, as for instance Hungarian romantic nationalism, emulating the symbolism of the heroic poet. The fact that the Greek nationalist struggle was able to claim the European inheritance of classical antiquity undoubtedly enhanced the popularity of nationalism as the cause of freedom.

Liberal nationalism largely took for granted the nation, seeing the task to be the pursuit of statehood. Conservative nationalism, by way of contrast, was able to take the state for granted and saw the task to be the creation of nationhood. Liberal nationalism was mostly republican and gained the support of the educated middle classes in several countries where the pattern of state formation was weak, such as Germany and Italy, and others such as Ireland and Norway. It could be described as a European transnational movement for it expressed a revolutionary consciousness that expressed the right to live only with those presumed to share a similar national character. The Young Italy movement that Mazzini founded in 1831 to promote republican nationalism spread to many countries, such as Ireland, Hungary, Turkey, Poland, and there was also a Young Europe society to further the cause of a Europe of republican states.

Liberal nationalism has mostly ceased to exist in the twentieth century as a republican kind of nationalism. It was primarily based on the civic conception of the nation that arose with the American and French revolutions. The case of Poland, however, represents one of the most enduring expressions of liberal nationalism in the nineteenth century, leading to the re-establishment of the Polish state after the First World War. It may be suggested that this civic tradition continued to offer resistance to communism after 1945. In central Europe the liberal tradition of nationalism was a basis of the civil society movement of the 1980s.

A slightly different version of liberal nationalism was the American republican tradition. This differs from the European tradition in that in it the nation was conceived of in more pronouncedly civic terms. The European liberals tended to stress the historical origins of the nation, and in many traditions liberal nationalism was inspired by cultural and romantic notions of the nation. But the founders of the United States saw the nation as much as the state to be a civic project that had to be created in an act of historical foundation necessitating rebellion from

European tyranny. Thus the American nation was seen to lie in the Constitution of the United States and not in an ethnic or historical people. Indeed, the First Nation Americans were excluded from the civic nation on precisely these grounds. However, since the American Civil War, American nationalism has been predominately shaped by state patriotism rather than by republicanism.

RECONSTRUCTIVE NATIONALISM

In the second half of the nineteenth century a distinctive kind of nationalism emerged in the older imperial states, such as the Ottoman Empire and Japan. It was primarily a project aimed at reconstructing or reforming the existing state by adapting it to the conditions of modernity. The transition of the Ottoman Empire into modern Turkey is the best example of the codification of a new kind of state patriotism that took over certain ideas from the nineteenth-century legacy of liberal nationalism. Mustafa Kemal (later Ataturk) represented, on the one side, republican, secular European nationalism and, on the other, adopted this as the official state patriotism of the modern Republic of Turkey since the deposition of the Sultanate and the abolition of the Caliphate in 1922. Much of the nationalism of the Middle East followed this model, whereby the secular, military and republican national state was established in predominantly Muslim societies and spear-headed modernization.

125

In Japan the Meiji reform, which led to the abolition of the early modern Tokugawa shogunate and the restoration of imperial rule, represents another major example of a nationalist movement that was a response to modern state formation. The Meiji restoration of 1859 established a central state based on the imperial institution, a project that was aimed at the modernization of Japan through the adoption of westernization but in ways that were specific to Japan.[5] Reconstructive nationalism has been more common in Asia than in Europe, where the emergence of capitalism and modernization preceded state formation. In Asia the nation-state was often an agent of modernization. In China modern nationalism emerged after the fall of the Qing dynasty in 1911 and the resulting nationalism was characterized by a strong hostility to the entire Manchu tradition, seeing the authentic Chinese nation to reside in the historical Han people of the Middle Kingdom, and in opposition to the western powers, which had been attempting to make China open to conquest. From the Boxer Uprising in 1900 to the Cultural Revolution Chinese, anti-imperialist nationalism was the means by which China was reformed for a project of radical modernization. Further examples of nationalist movements that derived from the reform of an existing state might be Imperial Russia under Peter the Great or Iran since the Islamic Revolution of 1979. In the former case westernization was a means of creating a new Russian identity and in the latter Islam was the route to a new and anti-western nationhood.

INTEGRAL NATIONALISM

German nationalism since Bismarck was different from the liberal nationalism that preceded national unification in that it was primarily a state project. Integral nationalism was typically a product of the first half of the twentieth century. One of its major figures was Charles Maurras, the founder of *Action Française*, who promoted an anti-Semitic and reactionary nationalism that sought to reverse the heritage of republicanism and liberalism as an exclusionary one. This kind of authoritarian Catholic nationalism excluded the Jews from the French nation (Sutton, 1982). This kind of nationalism that was also embodied in Hitler and Mussolini placed the nation above all else, demanding absolute obedience. Maurras's nationalism differed from fascism only in its belief in monarchy, it shared the basic obsession with the nation as an aesthetic essence that transcended human will. Integral nationalism can be seen as a more extreme version of the state patriotism that was typical of many of the established states in its absolutism and militarism, combining a total identification of nationhood with the state, hence the term integral nationalism. However, the basic principles of integral nationalism were tendentially present in many of the major nation-states in the early twentieth century. Germany, of course, was the country where integral nationalism predominated over other kinds of nationalism. But this was true also of Japan since 1912 and Italy under the fascists. Integral nationalism is also the most potent example we have of how the tendency in all of nationalism to postulate a non-social principle as the basis of the social order. However, this particular kind of nationalism, which is less important today, reduced very significantly the tension between nation and state that is typical of almost all kinds of nationalisms.

IRREDENTIST NATIONALISM

Many kinds of nationalism that emerged in the nineteenth century did not confine the national community to the boundaries of the existing state. Irredentist nationalism sought to extend the nation-state over the allegedly historical territory that had to be 'redeemed'. This kind of nationalism can be named after the policy of *Italia irredenta*, or unredeemed Italy: the struggle of the unified Italian state to recover territory from Austria, principally Trento and Trieste.

Once the principle that a nation should be housed in a territorial state became widely accepted, irredentist nationalism was inevitable, for the simple reason that few states were mono-national. Irredentist nationalism is a territorial nationalism and has been a powerful force in the politics of the twentieth century, with many states struggling to gain territory allegedly part of the historical nation. Despite the foundation of the Irish Free State in 1922 (later the Republic of Ireland) the aim of incorporating the territory of Northern Ireland remained the primary aim of republican nationalism, which since independence became essentially an irredentist nationalism. The question of Alsace-Lorraine was also an example of German and French irredentism, except in this case two nations could claim the same territory on grounds of nationhood. Irredentist nationalism, too, has been central to German integral nationalism and has been an inevitable part of territorial disputes involving national minorities. It has been a potent force in the Balkans, and one of the main expressions of Serbian nationalism in its territorial claims on Croatia and Bosnia-Herzegovina. In these cases irredentist nationalism has often been the other side of the coin of secessionist nationalism.[6] However, in general it is clearly best to see irredentism as a product of the nationalism of the established nation-state, and in particular of the newly established nation-state, as in the cases of Ireland and Italy. Irredentism has remained an enduring component of most nation-states involved in major disputes of territory. This is especially the case in Central and Eastern Europe where national boundaries have rarely remained constant in history.

127

SECESSIONIST NATIONALISM

Secessionist nationalism is one of the most prevalent forms of nationalism since about 1870 and has taken many different forms, from devolutionist movements to liberation movements from colonial rule. Secessionist nationalism is one of the principal expressions of 'nations without states', although it is important to point out that not all stateless nations (for example Catalonia or Wales) are secessionist. Some early examples of secessionist movements that embodied nationalist consciousness were the Dutch Revolt of the 1520s, the Greek independence movement and, from the late nineteenth century, nationalist movements in Norway, Finland, Ireland and Iceland. The early secession of Belgium from the Netherlands in 1839 may also be cited but it is questionable if this was due to a nationalist consciousness. In many cases national consciousness arose only following independence. In the Balkans several states were created in 1878 following the San Steffano Treaty and the Congress of Berlin in that year: Serbia, Bulgaria, Rumania, Montenegro. The principles of liberal nationalism and political expediency largely lay behind many of these new states, which did not arise out of secessionist nationalism but political expediency on the part of the Great Powers.

Prior to the end of the First World War, secessionist nationalism was relatively marginal as a mass movement. Thus in 1898 Crete refused simple independence from the Ottoman Empire, preferring instead to become part of the Greek state.

In the twentieth century secessionism was much more prevalent and the principles of liberal nationalism were often submerged in ethnic nationalism. In 1960 the United Nations passed a controversial resolution recognizing the right to independence of all colonial peoples. Although the interpretation of that principle has been debated, the basic right to self-determination has been widely accepted in principle. With the rising tide of secessionism two principles collided: the sovereignty of the state and the right to self-determination. Secessionism was often violently resisted by the established states as well as by other political ideologies, such as Marxism.[7] Given the diversity of peoples, the principle of self-determination did not clarify who was the collective self, for few countries could claim to be based on a single ethic nation. The result was frequently civil war, forcible integration, partition, population exchanges, even genocide. Nevertheless, the principle of self-determination has generally continued to be applied as a solution to the problem of secessionist nationalism or the problem posed by expansionism. In the case of the break-up of Yugoslavia in the 1990s it was widely accepted as the only solution and received the backing of the European Union and the United Nations. Within Western Europe secessionist nationalism has been confined to a number of isolated cases, such as the Basque separatist movement, Corsican separatism and in Northern Ireland. In India, the separatist nationalism in Kashmir and in Punjab have continued to undermine the state-led project. Colonial liberation movements frequently took the form of separatist nationalism, as in the example of Arab nationalism since 1919, colonial liberation movements in the Pacific or in Africa since 1960s, or the older colonial liberation movements in South America from the 1820s. One of the main problems with these kinds of nationalism is the problem in sustaining, in particular under the conditions of independence, the spirit of emancipatory nationalism. Another problem is that many of these movements, as is strikeningly apparent in the case of Arab nationalism, are expressions of highly different contexts and groups. Arab nationalism was never entirely a response to western imperialism, since not all Arab peoples experienced colonialism (Kramer, 1993, p. 173). It is for this reason that we can say not all secessionist nationalism is a creation of stateless nations – in many of these cases the nation followed in the wake of the state. Instrumental in this regard are state policies of 'ethnicization'. Some major contemporary examples of secessionist nationalism are Kurdish, Tibetan, Palestinian liberation struggles. One of the main differences between these kinds of nationalism and earlier colonial liberation struggles in Africa is the prior existence of a national consciousness.

ETHNIC NATIONALISM

In the majority of cases secessionist nationalism has been based on radical ethnicity, or at least politically mobilized forms of ethnicity. Ethnic nationalism can be discussed separately since it is not always secessionist in its aspiration. It can take several forms, of which the two must prevalent are ethno-linguistic nationalism and ethno-regionalism. In recent times language has become a powerful marker of ethnicity and of national identity. Many forms of nationalism are based on identities shaped largely by language. The Quebec nationalism is entirely based on the fact that the Quebecois are French speakers, Welsh nationalism is primarily based on language as are the two dominant groups in Belgium, the French-speaking Walloons in the southern parts and the Flemish speakers in the northern regions. Ethnic nationalism can take a radical form in outright secessionism, but in many cases it is expressed in demands for regional autonomy or federal status. In the case of Quebec, Wales and Belgium there is also a notable constitutional aspect to the nationalist struggle and an almost total absence of violence.

Ethno-regional nationalism refers to a wider range of movements that mostly have been nurtured within the federal structures of larger territorial states. Such movements can be based on a mixture of ethnic traditions such as language, religion, territory, distinct social customs and descent. Such movements may seek independence as a short- or long-term aim or may seek autonomy within the existing state. Regional nationalism in the north of Italy is an example of a regional nationalism that is based on a variety of factors, which are largely regionally specific and non-ethnic. Scottish nationalism is an example of an ethno-regional nationalism and, like many of its kind, it is divided between secessionism and moderate devolutionism.

CULTURAL NATIONALISM

As used here cultural nationalism is a form of nationalism that does not take an explicitly political form. However, we include it in the present discussion because of the fact that almost every kind of nationalism has in some way defined itself by reference to culture and cultural nationalism. Cultural nationalism is a distinct form of nationalism not radically different from ethnic nationalism insofar as it is based on largely cultural markers of national identity. As a non-state-centric form of nationalism it refers more to manifestations of national identity expressed variously in national literatures and music, cultural policies on the preservation of heritage, and some of the taken for granted assumptions of national identity in the everyday. It makes sense to classify this kind of nationalism as distinct from ethnic nationalism since it is not a nationalism of political mobilization. While it can of course be a basis of nationalist mobilization, it primarily concerns national identity in the sense of national awareness. In some of its most famous historical forms it was deeply unpolitical and even hostile to political nationalism, as was evidenced by the antipathy of Irish cultural nationalists to the Republican movement in the late nineteenth century. Cultural nationalism in this sense was founded by Johann Gottfried Herder in the second half of the eighteenth century with the doctrine that all nations are culturally and historically unique (see Herder, 1969). A stronger version was expressed by Fichte in 1807–08 in his *Addresses to the German Nation* (Fichte, 1922). In its time it was compatible with the *patrie* of liberal nationalism, giving to it a romantic dimension and a justification for secession in the name of cultural pluralism. Enlightenment cultural nationalism was democratic in spirit and had little in common with the 'blood and soil' nationalism of the twentieth century.

We can speak of cultural nationalism to mean simply the nationalism that is the basis of the nation-state, as expressed in cultural policies such as museums and national heritage, in education, in tourism. Michael Billig terms this 'banal nationalism' in the sense of the nationalism of everyday life (Billig, 1995). Cultural nationalism legitimates the more explicit political forms of nationalism by anchoring them in everyday life. Cultural nationalism is evident in societies where there is a tension between nation and state, for instance, Australia. The most notable feature of the Australian conception of the nation is its uncertain relation with the state, which has been historically a foreign body alien to the people who lived under it. Thus, Australian expressions of nationhood are not defined primarily in the codes of statehood but in more cultural codes.

RELIGIOUS NATIONALISM

Religion and nationalism has always been a complicated relationship. On the one side nationalism has served as a kind of modern political religion for many people, in many cases commanding the complete dedication to the national cause. On the other side nationalism has been a predominately secular force in modernity. This ambivalence is present in Zionism. Zionism emerged in the latter half of the nineteenth century. One of its early founders, Moses Hess, saw how the *risorgimento* nationalism of Mazzini could be an example for the Jewish people in their quest for nationhood. Inspired, too, by Enlightenment philosophy and socialism he evolved the notion of a national destiny that was extremely influential in shaping modern Zionism. Later kinds of Zionism developed these philosophical ideas into a political theory of Jewish ethnicity based on Israel and the quest for a national state. While Jewish messianic and religious thought played a role in shaping Zionism, it was more than a simple appeal to Biblical themes, it was a political movement aimed at the creation of a state. In this sense it encapsulated all the elements of modern nationalism. Zionism was a secular, modernizing and anti-religious ideology that sought to crush the hold of religion and traditional values over the Jews. That is why the ultra orthodox Jews still regard the state of Israel as blasphemous.

Religion has played a role in many modern nationalisms, notable examples being the role of Catholicism in Ireland and Poland. However, in these cases religion became pivotal only at particular points in history. In Poland and Ireland, Catholicism certainly played a role in anchoring the political identity of nationalism in a cultural identity. However in these cases, nationalism was always more than religion. In Ireland, Catholicism – although always significant – became a major part of the national identity only following the Civil War that occurred in the immediate aftermath of the foundation of the state and was an expression of the ideological exhaustion of the predominantly Republican movement (O'Mahony and Delanty, 1998). Much the same happened in Poland since the fall of communism (see also Chapter 7). It might be suggested that it is only in recent, 'postmodern' times, that religion and nationalism have become closely linked. In this sense then, modern Shi'ism is perhaps the really major example of religious nationalism. With the demise of the Enlightenment project of modernity, religion has re-entered the political arena, and nationalism is more likely to accommodate religion than in the past when secular and republican ideas dominated.

TRANSNATIONALISM

Most of the nationalisms discussed until now have been specific to distinct nation-states. A huge area of nationalist consciousness is transnationalism or long distance nationalism. Some of the major antecedents of contemporary transnationalism were pan-nationalist movements, such as pan-Arab nationalism, pan-Slavism or pan-African nationalism. German expansionism in late nineteenth century and early twentieth century had a transnational dimension to it, as in the Pan-German League. However these particular ones have not endured and crystallized into distinct national patterns. An important exception is the case of Zionism and diasporic nationalism. With globalization and international migration, transnationalism has become a growing feature of the contemporary face of nationalism. It is primarily sustained by global migration, internet and global communication, transational networks and multiple identities. Transnationalism is not necessarily a movement that aims to create new states, although in many cases that is the aim as in, for example, Kurdish nationalism. In a great many instances, transnationalism is an expression of ties, which can be quite flexible, between migrants, the country of origin and, in the case of Chinese transnationalism for example, of kin states (Ong, 1997; Ong and Nonini, 1997). Not all kinds of transnationalism are de-territorial. The case of Kurdish nationalism is an important reminder of an significant nationalist movement that while being largely directed against the Turkish state is based on the existence of Kurdish people spread over parts of Turkey, Iraq and Iran.

THE NEW RADICAL NATIONALISMS

A growing feature of western societies in recent years in a new version of the old integral nationalism. It is, however, quite different from the older integral nationalism in that it is predominantly focused on immigrants rather than on enemy states. The context for its emergence is not war and jingoism but immigration and the diminishing ability of the welfare state to maintain social integration. The xenophobia that it fosters is less sustained by biological notions of racial superiority than by social and economic arguments to restrict citizenship laws and, in the case of the EU member states, by opposition to the EU. Moreover, such nationalist movements are, with some few exceptions, generally marginal and do not have the support of the mainstream political parties. We discuss these kinds of nationalism in more detail in the following chapter.

132

THE TYPOLOGY AND ERAS OF NATIONALISM

In this section, we attempt to make some temporal ordering to the accounts of the types of nationalism covered in this chapter. We will do this by situating these cases with reference to the framework laid out in the first two chapters, but especially Chapter 2. We will also try to show how the theoretical traditions laid out in Chapters 3, 4 and 5 relate to these different eras of nationalism.

When modern nationalism is considered on a general level, it becomes immediately apparent that it can only be understood in relation to the international context, on the one hand, and the mechanisms of social integration on the other. In relation to the first dimension, as we have seen, in relation to Rokkan, Tilly and Elias in Chapter 3, the interstate and inter-nation context has a vital bearing on both the cultural-political models and practical feasibility of nationalism. Nationalism cannot be properly understood from within the confines of single territorial entities. It has to be placed in the context created by the interplay of different territories. In relation to the second dimension, nationalism must also be set against the prevailing models of social integration and their political feasibility. This means, as we have stressed throughout the previous chapters, that it must be placed in the context of other ideological systems and society as a set of institutions and social relations. As a general rule, nationalism gains in potency in historical conjunctures when both dimensions, international relations and social integration, are subject to dislocation and fragmentation at the same time, and to lose at least some of its shaping power in periods of stability.

This leads to the question of what these historical conjunctures are and how nationalism features in them.[8] Allowing for all the caveats that must attend this kind of exercise, four main historical conjuctures, or as we shall term it 'eras of nationalism', may be discerned. These are, first, the period from about 1770 to 1870; second, the period from 1870 to the end of the Second World War; third, the period from 1945 to about 1989; and, fourth, the period from 1989 to the present.

The first period covers the formative period of modern nationalism, which most agree arose out of the stir of ideas and events associated with both the French Revolution and the Enlightenment and subsequent reaction to them. From the standpoint of social integration, this period involved the play of three major cultural-political forces: the question of civic and political rights clarified in the Enlightenment and later in the cauldron of revolutionary politics and the nineteenth-century questions of class and the nation. For most of the period to 1870, the proletarian lower orders were only peripheral players in the political cultural clashes of the time. These clashes tended to be sharpest and most salient between disaffected elements of the middle class, whether liberal or radical in persuasion, and some sections of the nobility who were opposed to arbitrary and bureaucratic forms of rule. The era of class politics was only beginning to gain momentum at the end of the period of the bourgeois liberation movements. The international context was marked by the French attempt to export the Revolution, admittedly mostly in the highly adapted, ideologically reduced form of the Napoleonic military-bureaucratic colonization of European territories and by subsequent attempts, crystallized in the interstate settlement of 1814–15, to contain both French imperium and the flowering of a multiplicity of destabilizing nationalisms that arose in response to it.

The Congress of Vienna was actually quite explicitly directed against nationalism – which Metternich regarded as one of the greatest dangers of modernity – and emphasized the legitimate rights of monarchs, not the rights of nations to self-determination. It may well be conjectured that much of the long peace that subsequently ensued owed much to the success of this interstate order in containing the forces of nationalism. Nationalism, however, was merely contained in the period not eliminated, remaining a recalcitrant force always ready to errupt. As we saw in Chapter 2, the nation was increasingly becoming an important foundation of political community and the ideological work of national movements continued apace in the period.[9] This process was greatly assisted by growth in literacy, the fact that the Enlightenment was nationally

133

mediated and that the production of nationalist culture fused with the late Enlightenment expression of romanticism. The depth of national feeling in the period became briefly prominent in the 1848 Revolution, sometimes described as the 'springtime of the peoples' when one fault line of the struggle of middle class and nobility against arbitrary rule was joined by another, the struggle of emergent nations such as Poles, Danes, Germans and Italians. Of these types listed, the most emblematic nationalism of this period was liberal nationalism with its emphasis on the translation of emergent national cultures into political-constitutional orders. It would be easy to assert that this nationalism could afford to take on liberal and constitutional clothes only because the international order was so repressive of wider expressions of nationalism. The aim was to the great powers's status quo, which placed Britain and Russia as pre-eminent and Prussia, France, Italy and Austria–Hungary secondary but important. There is indeed much truth in this view. However, in the European context, much hinges on the German case, which certainly appeared in its cultural-national form to have been more open to internal and external compromise prior to 1848 than after it. If the German case really was a context for learning through exploration of the nation idea in its interplay with internal and external forces, then this era might indeed be regarded, as it generally tends to be seen, as a highly qualified but 'progressive' exploration of the principle of nationality.

The era from 1870 to 1945 is by contrast generally seen as problematic and regressive, an era when ideas and practices of nationality got out of hand. In the international context, this era is characterized by the rise of a Prussian-dominated united Germany to a prominent role in the European order and by the creation of overseas empires, mainly in Asia and Africa, by European powers. Both these developments had a destabilizing effect on the European order as the internal alignment of German politics fuelled dissatisfaction over its international standing. The dissolution of the 1815 interstate settlement was further hastened by the internal problems of Russia and Austria–Hungary. The outcome of the First World War and the Bolshevik Revolution to the East merely exacerbated instability as the post-war settlement excluded Germany and Russia from a prominent position in the interstate order and coupled this with the advocacy of the divisive principle of national self-determination. In relation to social integration, this era was marked both by the rise of mass democratic forms of government and the gradual emergence of the class cleavage as the dominant principle of political alignment, a development, however, that was only fully institutionalized in some parts of the world after 1945. In the interim, as a response to the rise of democracy and class, movements such as conservative authoritarianism and fascism gained in potency, carrying alternative, corporatist principles of social organization.

The dominant nationalisms in this second period were integral nationalism, especially of the major fascist states, Germany, Japan,

Italy, Spain and also towards the end of the period, the communist authoritarianism of the Soviet Union but also other states such as Croatia, Hungary and Poland, and a whole host of secessionist nationalisms, driven on by the post-First World War implementation of the principle of self-determination. In this period, therefore, nationalism became closely associated with right-wing, often non-democratic, authoritarianism. More generally, the extension of the suffrage had created the conditions for the new forms of mass publicity for which the inclusive collective identity represented by nationalism was highly functional. In this respect, nationalism was also becoming a cross-class phenomenon. The creation of empires in the period by the European states also put in place the conditions for a new wave of anti-colonial nationalism, that only matured fully in the next era of nationalism.

The period from 1870 to 1945 was therefore a period in which the interstate order outlined in the Congress of Vienna had gradually imploded, leading to an era of nationalism, which especially from the turn of the twentieth century was relatively unconstrained by the balance of power diplomacy or by successful and enduring transnational states, as it had been in the previous period after the post-revolutionary turbulence. A relative stabilization of the international order was to be the case once more after the Second World War, in the third era of nationalism from 1945 to 1989. Europe, which had been at the heart of two world wars, introduced two new, relatively stable international orders centred respectively on the hegemony of the Soviet Union to the East and voluntary cooperation between the western nation-states in military cooperation with the United States and economic and later political cooperation with one another through the European Economic Community. The model of de-colonization at first appeared to offer some optimism for developing countries in this period, but it was later to run into trouble with the consolidation of authoritarian regimes and simmering ethnic strife. The model of social integration, especially in the developed countries, enjoyed considerable success with its tenets of political democracy, the institutionalization of class conflict in the welfare state and economic growth. The more coercive model of communism in Eastern Europe, and also in China and elsewhere in the world, in a certain sense also worked, in some cases raising living standards appreciably and avoiding social fragmentation and chaos.

Of the types of nationalism addressed in this chapter, the most emblematic of this period was a modified contemporary state patriotism, also including reconstructive-type nationalisms in the developing world. A second important emblematic nationalism of the period was the more diffuse kind of cultural nationalism in everyday life. The first, state patriotism, expressed the desire for rebuilding in the post-war period and the need for citizenry to identify with political institutions. In key parts of the world, especially Western Europe and Japan, this was

135

initiated under American hegemony, although America was not remotely as careful in attempting to engineer the conditions of democratic identification in the more proximate area of South America. State patriotism with a strong reconstructive element was also a major force in the communist world, the wider developing world and in North Africa and the Middle East. In these forms, clearly with many exceptions for short- or long-run democratic systems, the emphasis was on deliberately inculcated loyalty within an authoritarian setting and with a severely delimited public sphere. This indicates one of the principal modalities of the expression of nationalism in this period, the maturing of the state as a culture-producing and culture-controlling organization in its own right, a development already presaged in the previous period with the rise of propaganda and censorship.

The period from 1989 to the present has seen many of the controls on the expression of nationalism gradually released. The demise of Soviet communism, the re-ordering of eastern Europe and new global dynamics have created an entirely new situation, more suited to nationalist mobilizations. Many of the postcolonial regimes set up in the first de-colonizing wave have proven unstable and complex ethnic conflicts have become the order of the day in many parts of the world, including Indonesia, many parts of Africa, and the Indian subcontinent to name but a few typical flashpoints. There has been a resurgence of ethnic conflict in the developed, capitalist world in a long wave of anti-systemic movements from the late 1960s. There has also been a rise in ethnic, race and stranger hatreds all over the world, in part at least due to the relaxation of the strong normative controls on expression of such sentiments with distance from the Second World War. The relatively successful model of social integration of the previous period has also somewhat unravelled, further contributing to a renaissance of violent and exclusivist kinds of nationalism. Some areas of the world have regressed absolutely in terms of prosperity and fairness such as some of South America, much of the developing world, the former Soviet Union, and much of Eastern Europe. The rise of Islamic movements in Afghanistan, North Africa and the Middle East has not only signalled the end of assumptions about the attainability of convergent modernization in these parts of the world, but has contributed to to the rise of intrastate and international violence, the former witnessed in Afghanistan and Algeria, the latter most typically in the Iran–Iraq conflict. The developed, industrial world has seemed prepared to live with a permanent disadvantaged underclass and though there has been an enormous absolute increase in wealth, relative poverty has increased among some sections of the population, heightening the climate of intolerance towards racial minorities, immigrants and asylum seekers.

The emblematic nationalisms of the contemporary period are various, including ethnic nationalism, religious nationalism, radical nationalism

and a continuing cultural nationalism. With respect to ethnic nationalism, it has often been observed that contemporary conflict is much more
within or across the borders of pre-existing states than previously. In
any case, ethnic mobilizations have become more prominent all over the
world and is probably the most typical expression of contemporary
nationalism. Running it close on a world plane is religious nationalism,
most notably the resurgence of Islam, but also Hindu nationalism in
India, Zionism in Israel, the religious identifications of the Balkan
protagonists among many other examples. Radical, xenophopic nationalism in the West and elsewhere is also on the increase, as we shall
consider more extensively in the next chapter. Finally, banal, cultural
nationalism has become more important as a source of collective identity as normative commitment to democracy has declined, especially in
the West. The development of these other forms of nationalism have
also signified an erosion of the power of state patriotism in the contemporary era. However, there have been interesting countervailing
moments, as we shall discuss in more detail in Chapter 8, to do with
the worldwide increase in the number of democratic countries and the
emergence of enhanced kinds of transnational institutions such as the
European Union that can reduce the potential for national conflict
within particular regions of the world.

The question arises as to what 'logic' underpins this evolution of the
overall impact of nationalism and the mutation of its dominant forms.
Given the unpredictable nature of nationalism and the coexistence of
radically different forms in different eras, it is only possible to offer
some tentative interpretations as to such a logic. The first pattern that
might be observed is that nationalism thrives in periods of rapid and dis-
locating social change, especially the social challenge of accommodating
new classes or class fractions thrown up by such change and requiring
a new model of social integration. The advent of a middle-class dominated civil society in the eighteenth and early nineteenth centuries,
whether or not one can confidently speak of a 'bourgeois ideology',
posed the first social challenge to monarchical absolutism and resulted
in the first sustained attempt in the modern period to establish intellectual roots for nationalism as a critical component of the political and
cultural identity of civil society. This is what theorists such as Calhoun
and Kedourie in their different ways understand as the period in which
nationalist ideology was first created and applied. The Industrial
Revolution also had an immense socio-demographic effect. The wave
of new proletarians and the construction of their political parties
commenced in the latter part of the nineteenth century and in many
countries they commenced a slow movement from the periphery to the
core of society and politics. Other classes and class fractions ranged
against them, either opposing their advent into the political mainstream
or seeking to curtail it, the residual nobility, the lower middle classes,

rural populations, professionals. These classes often appealed to the nation and tradition against the Godless proletarian internationalists and the revolutionary spectre they carried. The kinds of analysis carried by Hobsbawm and Elias among others is particularly useful for capturing this period of contradiction and nationalist authoritarianism. Over the course of the twentieth century the working class was absorbed by the nation project and ultimately recompensed by gaining a share of rising prosperity in the developed countries. More recently, in the last period, a new social cleavage between the prosperous and disadvantaged has opened up in many parts of the world, providing a new social basis for various kinds of state and substate nationalisms.

A second pattern can perhaps be built around the role of the state. The first wave of post-revolutionary nationalisms in nineteenth-century Europe were emanations of civil society against the state, seeking to establish a new cultural basis for connecting the two spheres. However, it is only in the second period after 1870 that the state – and the establishment generally – becomes an instititutionalized, that is to say continuously and intrinsically, a cultural producer of nationalism. Nationalist movements in civil society increasingly became movements for state power, rather than producers of new cultural imaginaries. Once a nation-state was established, or a new political regime constructed, it promulgated a code of national identity that represented the outcome of the play of ideology production and social power within national movements and other actors in civil society. With the rise of the propagandistic state from the beginning of the twentieth century, the state increasingly became a creative force as a cultural producer in its own right, needing to have only some cultural base in civil society but over time capable of reconstructing the cultural foundations of civil society itself. Fascist and communist states provide the prototypical example of this trend, both of which relied on the diffusion of ideologies of national integration. The role of the state continued to be central in the period after the Second World War but generally in the more peaceful and less extreme forms of inculcating state patriotism. In a long trend from the Second World War, however, the role of the state at the heart of nationalist ideology production has been in decline. Developed states cannot now afford to go to war with one another, given the likely scale of mutual destruction, and therefore no longer seek to incite the degree of cultural mobilization that would in turn lead to the mobilization of armies. Nationalist conflict has therefore once more retreated to the margins of the developed world, where it exists largely in the form of ethno-regional movements and xenophobia. In the less developed world, ethnic conflict within states or within regions in which state boundaries are highly contested – for example, the Congo/Rwanda, Kashmir, Lebanon, the Balkans – are also more the norm than conflicts between nation-states. Of course, the sum total of all of these conflicts in the contemporary amounts to a worldwide presence of war conditions on an enormous scale.

The third general pattern is provided by cultural interpretation systems. In this instance, what appears to be critical is that representative argumentation between groups in civil society can proceed on a rational plane within the procedures of a public sphere or is otherwise constrained from mobilizing antagonistic sentiments between groups. Monarchical repression in the nineteenth century or communism or state authoritarianism in the twentieth offer good examples of the mobilization of such sentiments. The construction of pejorative national and racial steretypes in the second half of the nineteenth century and also of national habituses based on ressentiment towards outsiders, ethnic others or other nations, as well as the appeals to the blood sacrifice, are instances of how nationalist cultural mobilization appeals to negative emotions (Mosse, 1985). What cannot be stated at this level of generality is that such emotions are always groundless, only that their unchecked expression can colour an era and lead to terrible consequences. The two eras in particular that are so coloured are the eras stretching from 1870 and the contemporary era. Also of critical importance on the cultural level is the nationalism of pivotal nation-states such as Germany, Japan, and Russia. The German example of resentment at the Versailles settlement, coming on top of a long-run feeling of German inferiority, created a climate conducive to Nazism as a redemptive force (Elias, 1992). What is also the case is that such nationalist constructions are intertwined with periods of pessimism or ennui over the conditions of the world, perhaps coinciding with the radical social destabilization that threatens the moral underpinnings of groups habituses. The advent of mass, urban, industrial society, and the winners and losers that follow it, appears to have given rise to one such period of cultural angst, an angst that provided the cultural resonance for movements of reaction by threatened classes. The contemporary period may also be so regarded as one of structural dislocation that is related to a variety of problems generated by globalization, the destruction of much of the communist order, increasing poverty, environmental degradation. What is absent in both these periods of rising xenophobic interpretations of the world are convincing models of social integration that give threatened, and in turn threatening populations a sense of security and freedom from uncertainty. The result is a dangerous escalation in outsider-directed discourses of uncertainty, whose persistence creates the conditions for both symbolic and real violence.

139

CONCLUSION

The discussion in this chapter delineates the two key variables, the international/national dialectic and the availability of workable models of social integration, that facilitate or constrain the expression of nationalism and allow the specification of different eras. The three further dimensions of class relations, the role of the state, and cultural interpretation systems also appear to support the idea that there is some logic to the general extent and characteristic types of nationalism in these different eras. It is possible on the basis of this approach to suggest that there are general macro- and inter-societal conditions that are conducive to nationalism and, depending further on the constellations of social forces and the state of nationalist ideologies and their interpretation, characteristic forms of nationalism may be produced in different eras. To speak of nationalism as an integrative counter-moment to differentiation and disenchantment, as we did in Chapter 2, needs to be further specified in the light of these historical sociological reflections. In particular, the question must be posed of why, if it is integrative, does it tend to be most prominent in periods of social upheaval? The answer to this question is not easy. The integration of some cultures and peoples often arrives at the cost of others' disembedding and alienation, a process particularly pronounced in periods conducive to nationalist mobilizations of all kinds. The answer must therefore be tentative in suggesting that nationalism is integrative more as an aspiration for some kinds of common cultural foundations of political communities than as a secure mechanism for such integration. Sometimes this aspiration is realized, paradoxically most successfully in eras of nationalist quiescence, and sometimes the aspiration is merely a propaedeutic to further conflict, as those excluded by the proposed national identity mobilize against it.

140

To this first, difficult question, a second question also unavoidably follows as to the normative status of nationalism. How can we judge which kinds of nationalism are generally to the good and which to the bad. A succession of thinkers have followed Kohn's (1955) distinction between western and eastern nationalism as respectively good and bad nationalism. There is, of course, some obvious truth in this if comparative nationalist outcomes are considered over a long period. However, we would suggest that attention must be deflected to the general conditions that give rise to and shape various forms of nationalism in different eras. The normative content of particular nationalist ideologies and programmes must be considered in relation to a whole plethora of conditions such as the international order, ethnic configurations, social inclusion and exclusion, postcolonialism and others. The only certainty here is that normative judgement is indeed difficult. However, at a more general level, it can be asserted that socio-political conditions and cultural interpretation patterns in certain eras do take nationalism into dangerous terrain. It is indeed salutary to reflect that the present is one of these eras.

NOTES

1 For another useful typology, see Alter (1989). See also Hall (1993).

2 On pre-modern nationalism, see Armstrong (1982), Coulton (1933), Dann (1986), Forde et al. (1995), Gorski (2000), Marcu (1976), Ranum (1975).

3 See Bloch (1964), Huizinga (1959). For a discussion see Connor (1993).

4 See Watkins (1990) and Weber (1976) for examples relating to the consolidation of the nation-state in France. In relation to British national identity, see Colley (1992) and Corrigan and Sayer (1985).

5 For an analysis see Delanty (2002c).

6 On the difference, see Horowitz (1992).

7 The Austro–Marxists opposed the division of the Austrian–Hungarian Empire into nation-states in 1919 on the grounds that the resulting national consciousness would be a disaster for a progressive socialist movement.

8 An extensive exploration of this question would, of course, lead to a full-length book by itself. What follows is a brief, illustrative account that offers insight on how the topic could be taken forward.

9 In Chapter 5, Hroch's periodization of nationalist movements was outlined. This period saw the combination of the early antiquarian scholarship clarifying the lineage of the nation and subsequent formation towards the middle of the nineteenth century of an ideological avant-garde.

seven

the new radical nationalisms: globalization, xenophobia and cultural violence

In the concluding two chapters of this book, carrying on from the temporally specified typology outlined in the last chapter, we will review the current manifestations of nationalism and reflect on its future prospects. Before doing so, in the following pages, an attempt is made to resume the book through its central theoretical framework and arguments. This will have the additional value of setting the scene for the treatment of contemporary nationalism in the final two chapters.

Two related theoretical perspectives were developed in Chapters 1 and 2 that set up our treatment of theories and forms of nationalism in Chapters 3 through to 6. In Chapter 1, four dynamics of the institutionalization of nationalism within the social and cultural order of modernity were specified, respectively its relation to democratization, state-building capitalism and the intellectualization of culture. In Chapter 2, a schema of four spheres of nationalist activity was developed that distinguished between characteristic innovation processes in culture and in socio-political mobilization, on the one hand, and characteristic embedding processes in the cultural order and the institutionally structured world of social systems, on the other. In Chapter 2, additionally, nationalism was specified as being at bottom a type of collective identity that had different moments, the moment of construction in cultural and political innovation processes and the moment of institutionalization in cultural and institutional orders. In this present part of the book, where we turn to key issues concerning the present and future of nationalism, we wish to tighten the relationship between these different specifications with the aim of showing what kinds of identity construction and institutionalization processes characterize the present phase of nationalism. In order to advance this, let us turn, first, to the fourfold framework of the institutionalization of nationalism in the key aspects of modernity as outlined in Chapter 1, taking each of the dynamics in turn and further specifying them in terms of their relation to nationalism.

The facet of democratization, firstly, leads to the development of a universal framework designed to guarantee the formal equality of all citizens in the national community and to provide a system of institutions that impartially delivers the citizenship rights inherent in the assumption of equality. Although there is a universal core to the ideas of formal equality specified across democratic systems, these can manifest themselves quite differently in different national democratic systems. The dynamic of state building, secondly, can be represented combining ideas of Giddens, Weber and Foucault as leading to a monopolization of power, including monopolization of the means of violence, and certain kinds of categorizing, ordering and disciplining knowledge by the state. It is therefore possible to speak of the national refraction of this general process of state centralization as the building of national power–knowledge containers. The dynamic of capitalism, when combined with the institutional order of nation-states leads to an emphasis on the economy as a basis of national welfare. The division of economic goods is highly influenced by the institutional embedding of the economy in particular nation-states or by ethnic networks that are prominent in particular sectors or spatial areas. Economic critieria alone such as those associated with processes of innovation, network building and efficiency do not define economies. Economies are also embedded in **143** social orders that regulate productive, consumptive and distributive codes and the social forms of nationalism and ethnicity are in different places and times institutionally highly significant or equally highly disruptive. The final dynamic of modernity, outlined in Chapter 1, is that of the intellectualization of culture which has the effect of producing a generalized competence to participate in literate high cultures. The diffusion of high cultures are often conducive to nationalism as the processes often proceed through vernacular appropriation. A crucial aspect of this diffusion of high cultures, highly associated with the extension of the social boundaries of the politically significant *demos*, is the creation of ethnic and national cultures.

These four dynamics of modernity, i.e. democratic rights, order, welfare and a sense of cultural belonging, become refracted in a national direction because the creation of nation-states tends to offer an institutional path for their realization, albeit in a particular national variation. However, 'national solutions' of this kind are often endemically contested by those who perceive themselves constrained by this institutional path in given cases, but excluded from full or any benefits by being defined outside the dominant national community. The presence or absence of sustained contestation, especially the degree of contestation that destabilizes the minimal consensus on which socio-political reproduction depends, distinguishes those more or less successful cases from the many chronically unstable or ill-fated ones. National or ethnic allegiance therefore becomes a primary means whereby the collective goods of modernity become defined and distributed. This automatically implies that the universal and general moment of modernity is not sustained for all people at all times, rather this universality and generality is particular in its application. This tension therefore, embracing variously contestation and consensus over rights of citizenship, the technology of state and the means of violence, the distribution of goods and the basis of cultural identification is at the heart of the politics of nationalism and by extension at the heart also of the politics of modernity.

In Chapter 2, and in subsequent chapters, we distinguished between the institutionalized collective identities that are formed when there is a sufficient degree of absence of contestation over the territorial borders of an actual or would-be state and when there is a sufficient degree of internal absence of contestation over identity. This negative formulation 'absence of contestation' may seem strange but it has wider application than to speak of 'consensus' over boundaries of territory and boundaries of identity for 'absence of contestation', or more precisely absence of destabilizing contestation also includes those many cases in which actual or symbolic violence enforces territorial or cultural compliance by states and ethnic groups to states of affairs from which they dissent. Of course, it remains true that when the impossible case of protracted, destabilizing contestation is left out of the picture, minimal consensus about the nation's territorial boundaries, cultural identities and social projects is fundamental to its prospects of creating a viable institutional path and also to the precise form that path actually takes.

Different from this role of national identity as a fundamental base of social integration, as was emphasized in Chapter 2, nationalism involves another kind of collective identity that arises with its status as a form of protest directed at the domination practised by groups perceived to be antagonistic to the mobilizing groups. This un-institutionalized collective identity is animated by perceptions of inequality and injustice in relation to rights, power, welfare and cultural status of either particular ethnic groups or the nation as a whole. Often, perceptions of inferior status among some social groups will lead to their viewing nationalism as a vehicle for their advancement. The mobilizations associated with this kind of would-be dominant identity sometimes involves taking over the existing institutional framework and employing it to serve new ends and sometimes involves the promulgation of entirely new mechanisms of social integration, as instanced by earlier revolutionary nationalism, fascism and contemporary Islamic fundamentalism.

We sought to outline in Chapter 6 how nationalism tends to be expressed differently in different eras. Eras of destabilization in international regimes, in models of social integration and in cultural world interpretations, in particular, give impetus to new forms of nationalism, and in general to the potency of nationalist identity claims as a basis for mobilization. Nationalist mobilization thrives on insecurity and uncertainty as categories of group belonging become sharpened in the heat of contestation. In contexts of destabilization and uncertainty, nationalism becomes intertwined with new imaginaries of the social, sometimes involving the 'reasonable' promotion of group claims and sometimes involving the moral or physical annihilation of otherness. What makes nationalism so potent and sometimes so dangerous is its capacity to move across the 'cultural' register from fulfilling the role of a mobilizing or institutionalized political ideology to a basis of identity formation and exclusion in everyday life. It is not unique in this but the consequences of how it builds identities and draws boundaries has been more potent than any other comparable modern ideology, most centrally because as it includes some groups it also equally constitutively excludes others, and this exclusion tends to the absolute. This is particularly the case in language based kinds of nationalism. What this means is that nationalism is not about mediated exclusion through engagement with others so much as their complete exclusion from the national collectivity altogether. This is not always a problem as some do not want to be included in the first place and available resources and opportunities may make alternatives possible. But it often is a problem and in that case non-nationalist solutions have to be found or nationalist force employed, often deferring the solution of the problem to another day of reckoning.   **145**

The dissatisfaction and deferment built into many nationalist solutions to boundary setting and identity marking disputes goes some way also to explain what we mean by the term 'recalcitrance of nationalism'. Solutions based on a dominant nationalism are often unstable, sometimes chronically so. This can occur for a variety of reasons. A dominant group may be threatened by the arrival of immigrants. The antagonistic articulation of the cultural and social interests of an ethnic group or nation-state may be re-ignited by internal reassessment or external shocks. Political elites can appeal to nationalism to solve a crisis in state legitimation or to advance their own social interests. As a recalcitrant form, nationalism often functions as a latent cultural resource that becomes manifest, albeit in new circumstances and with shifting cultural content and ownership by new social groups, when there is a real or imagined perception of threat to the collective goods of a particular collectivity, or when an opportunity to avail of more of them is presented by nationalist mobilization.

When we turn to the contemporary period, it is without doubt a period of uncertainty and instability, as outlined in Chapter 6. Much of this has to do with shifts in the international context, the dissolution of much of the communist world and the growing momentum of globalization-led processes. It also has much to do with the weakening of welfarist models of social integration. In this chapter, we turn to the way in which writing on nationalism has tried to make sense of the interaction between these global changes and shifts in the manifestations of nationalism itself in the contemporary period. In the next chapter, we explore postnational or cosmopolitan expressions of political community.

One of the paradoxes of globalization is the emergence of new nationalisms of exclusion, on the one side, and cosmopolitan expressions of community on the other. The two dimensions are not separate, but are products of the same dynamics, namely that tendency within modernity towards an inclusive universalism and an exclusive particularism. Nationalism has often been enhanced by cosmopolitanism, as was the case with the liberal nationalism of the nineteenth century when nationalism was a key aspect of the project of modernity and in many cases was a vehicle of social integration. Today, globalization has set into motion different dynamics that have been widely believed to undermine some of the central dimensions of the project of modernity. The current situation is characterized by the release of political community from the fetters of the nation-state, which while being far from in demise is no longer the sole custodian of community. In one of its most striking forms, nationalism has become a recalcitrant and malign force in the contemporary world. Self-determination has lost its earlier associations with liberal nationalism and has become a legitimation of violence and a radical critique of modernity. No account of nationalism can ignore the extreme nationalism and violent movements that have been so much a feature of social and political change since the great upheavals of 1989. These include the fall of the USSR, the Gulf War, the wars in the former Yugoslavia and Rwanda, the unification of Germany, the end of apartheid, European integration, the spread of the internet, global markets, 11 September 2001 and the growing perception of global problems.

Three main kinds of extreme nationalism can be identified:

- radical right nationalism, in particular in the member countries of the European Union
- radical ethnic nationalism especially in the former communist countries
- radical religious nationalism, in particular in Asia.

This is certainly not a complete list of all kinds of extreme nationalism. It does not include forms of violent nationalism such as certain extreme separatist movements and terrorist organizations that have nationalist ambitions (for instance the IRA, ETA, FLNC, PKK).[1] Although these violent movements are also based on relative minority support, they differ considerably from the kinds of nationalism under discussion in the present context in that (with the exception of PKK) they are not induced by globalization, and indeed may be in decline precisely as a result of globalization which seems to unleashing a wide range of different kinds of anti-systemic movements.

We begin by defining three kinds of extreme nationalism before proceeding to look at the principal theories that explain the new nationalism. We then move on to offer a more nuanced interpretation of the new nationalism. It is argued that while these movements appear to indicate a major rupture with modernity, there are some common strands with the project of modernity, such as a subterranean culture of violence. Under the circumstances of globalization, which can be seen as opening up multiple modernities, violence has been released in a total critique of modernity. However, we stress that this total critique of modernity is itself a product of modernity and has always been a part of modernity but has taken a more pervasive form today as a result of globalization. In what follows, first, the three main kinds of radical nationalism are discussed. Second, we critically discuss five principal theories of the new nationalism. Third, we attempt to advance the debate by looking at these new nationalisms in the context of the globalization and a new wave of anti-systemic movements. In the final section we discuss the cultural logic of the new nationalism. In this context we offer a theory of xenophobia, which extends the notion of symbolic violence discussed in Chapter 1.

THREE KINDS OF VIOLENT NATIONALISM

In the previous chapter we outlined a typology of nationalism and identified radical nationalism as one major expression of contemporary nationalism. We now need to be more differentiated in our discussion and therefore propose to distinguish three main kinds of extreme or violent nationalism. These are:

- the nationalism of the new radical right
- radical ethnic nationalism
- radical religious nationalism.

They all share the following characteristics: a strong presence of fundamentalist assumptions about group membership and hence a high degree of exclusion; the identity of the self – 'the people' – is predicated on the negation of the other; and there is an absolute subordination of the individual to the collectivity. In general these kinds of nationalism are based on authoritarian cultural codes of belonging that contain a high degree of symbolic violence and xenophobia. They are constructed in a way that exclusion is not a consequence but a defining rationale. The 'people' is not itself a sovereign body that is defined by essentially civic and legal norms but a culturally defined project. Racism and xenophobia thus underlie all kinds of radical nationalism (see the final section of this chapter on p. 162). However, these nationalisms are highly diverse and cannot be easily reducible to a core ideological component, such as racism. We also stress the radicality of their projects, which is a contrast to most earlier kinds of nationalism which have been linked with liberal ideas. In earlier modernities the total critique of modernity was performed not by nationalism but by other political ideologies, such as fascism and communism, which sought to create alternative modernities. Today, nationalism is part of a communitarian movement that is playing this role, which is also to be seen as a reassertion of the Jacobin tradition in modernity. The following is a short descriptive account of the three main kinds of new radical nationalism. Our aim here is to be descriptive rather than analytical. A critical analysis of the main literature follows this section.

the new radical right

Radical right nationalism has been more prevalent in the relatively prosperous western countries than in other parts of the world.[2] In general it is driven by party organizations rather than mass movements but differs from small-scale neo-fascist organizations in having a populist basis that has an appeal to certain kinds of 'floating voters'.[3] While most kinds of nationalism are driven by organizations, the nationalism of the new radical right ultimately owes its existence to movement activists and the opportunity structures of electoral politics. Following Herbert Kitschelt's analysis, we can say the nationalism of the new radical right involves more than racism and neo-fascist ideology; it is primarily a combination of a political ideology of neo-liberalism and cultural authoritarianism (Kitschelt, 1995, pp. 28–42). The major representatives of the new radical right advocate radical liberalism in economics but radical conservatism in social and cultural issues. However, there is growing evidence of leftist elements in their discourses. On cultural issues an integral view of the world predominates (Holmes, 2000). Although there is much to suggest that the these parties are moving closer to the left, a neo-liberal stance on social and economic policy dominates their agendas. The combination of economic liberalism and cultural authoritarianism in fact reduces the explicit fascist ideological component in their discourses, for fascism has been historically characterized by corporatism, anti-capitalism and anti-liberalism in economics. The radical new right in recent years are forced to address economic issues and not rely exclusively on a racist, fascist agenda. Indeed many of these movements deny the racist component in their manifestos, claiming that their opposition to immigrants is social not cultural or biological, that it is about protecting jobs not racial superiority (Evans, 1996; Silverman, 1991). This is particularly the case in the European new right movement, which is influential in France where the chief representative is de Benoist. What this movement shares with the older fascist ideologies is authoritarian values with a pronounced xenophobic dimension. While many are in favour of a strong state (e.g. Le Pen), some of the most influential figures are anti-statist and

148

pro-radical multiculturalism in the sense of a strong belief in cultural incommensurability (Taguieff, 1994). This commitment to cultural difference and relativism, which legitimates itself by anti-racism, is also a major departure from the earlier forms of European fascism. The European new right shares certain affinities with the American militia in their strong opposition to the state. For this reason we see the entire new right movement – as well as all kinds of radical nationalism today – as the expression of new anti-systemic movements that go beyond the older right and left.

The connection with earlier forms of European nationalism must be commented on. These relatively new kinds of fascism are not ideologically coherent (with the major exception of the European new right, which has supplied an ideological programme).[4] Although they do offer ideologies which to a degree make sense to some people, and reflect an integral view of the world, on the whole they do not appeal to intellectuals. The intellectual appeal of fascism was a key feature of the earlier forms (Pels, 2000). The ideological component of the new nationalism is considerably narrower and is not addressed to mass publics. Explicitly fascist currents within the new radical right are relatively narrow. Moreover, unlike the older fascism, which was a product of the project of the modernity and gave expression to some of the central values of modernity – the belief in progress, technology, the primacy of the state, politics as art, and charismatic leadership – neo-fascism is defined by the past, not the future. Futurism is absent from it and much of it is deeply anti-statist, as is illustrated by the example of the American militia nationalism.[5] What is to be stressed then is the mixed ideological nature of the nationalism of the new radical right which cannot be reduced to fascism and racism but expresses a strong degree of xenophobia and intolerance. Such forms of nationalism are generally connected with a wider political agenda. It is for this reason that we prefer to use the term the new radical right rather than neo-fascist to characterize them.

radical ethnic nationalism

A related kind of extreme nationalism is ethnic militarism and which has been so much a part of the postcommunist transition. In its milder forms this amounts to no more than what is often called ethno-democracy, the project of fashioning a state around a dominant ethnic core. However, it can also take the more radical form of the expulsion or marginalization of national minorities who are severely discriminated against and in many instances denied citizenship. Ethno-democracy can result in 'ethnic cleansing', which Akbar Ahmed (1995) has described as the metaphor of our time. The case of Serbia under Milosovic is an example of this kind of ethnic militarism. In the extreme case, this will become genocide.

In Croatia, Roman Catholicism has played a role in igniting the flames of violent nationalism against Muslims and Orthodox groups. In its weaker forms it is found in several countries that have emerged from Soviet rule, such as the Baltic republics. However, ethno-democracy goes hand in hand with ethnic militarism and it is frequently the case that neo-fascist ideologies are present. This kind of nationalism is far more populistic than the nationalism of the radical right in Western Europe in that it commands greater support from the population, and can directly appeal to majoritarianism and democratic ideas of self-determination. It may be compared to the integral nationalism of a former period in the western world, in that it is primarily a project that derives from the dominant elites within the state apparatus rather than from marginal groups in society. In this sense then radical ethnic nationalism is more of a state project, as has been the case with most kinds of 'ethnic cleansing', in contrast to the nationalism of the new radical right in Western Europe which is more of an anti-establishment movement, rarely gaining more than 10% of the vote.

Postcommunist nationalism often lacks a coherent ideological component and cannot be compared to western forms of nationalism. Shari Cohen argues that postcommunist societies suffered a severe rupture with history and that consequently current nationalist movements are characterized by historical amnesia (Cohen, 1999). The communist regimes left a legacy of emptiness at the heart of these societies which nationalism filled but in a way that had little to do with earlier traditions of nationalism. The potentiality for a militaristic kind of nationalism was present in cases where statehood had been achieved only within the communist period and where, as in Slovakia, a pre-communist national identity had been weak.

radical religious nationalism

Militaristic religious nationalism is also a feature of the current situation. With few exceptions – such as early modern nationalism and Zionism since its organization as a global movement in 1897 – nationalism has historically been a predominantly secular phenomenon. Even the founder of modern Zionism, Theodor Hertzl, hoped that a Jewish state would be an integral part of European civilization. But religion and nationalism have been revived as potent forces today and in many parts of the world they have found a common alliance. Islam in Iran since 1979 (although currently showing signs of abating) has been a major component of Iranian nationalism. In Algeria, since, 1991 the Islamic Salvation Army has been able to sustain major opposition as has the Islamic Renaissance Party in Tunisia and extreme Muslim *hamas* groups in Egypt and Palestine.

The Orthodox church has become a major symbol of national identity in many parts of the Russian federations and the former Soviet

Asian republics where a new and radical reformist Islam has come into existence. In Georgia, since 1992 following the collapse of communism the Georgian Orthodox Church and Georgian nationalism became linked, and endorsed by Shevardnadze. In Russia, the Orthodox church has witnessed a remarkable revival. Although this confluence of religion and nationalism has not always been a legitimation of violent nationalism, it has proved a potent force in codifying militaristic ethnic projects (Goody, 2001). The secular Israeli national identity is increasingly being challenged by religious nationalism and in many parts of the Arab world, Islam has rekindled extreme kinds of nationalism. In India, religious nationalism has set limits to Nehru's project to build a unified secular state based on the integration of the Hindu majority and the large Muslim minority. Religion is one of the major alternatives to territory or culture in the definition of Indian nationhood (Varshney, 1993). In Western Europe there are few signs of extreme forms of religious nationalism.

Religious nationalism has benefited from the resurgence of religious movements in the 1980s and in the countries where it has taken root there have been strong traditions of the essential unity of religion and politics. This is particularly true in the case of militant Muslim nationalism and militant Hindu nationalism. According to Juergensmeyer (1997) resurgent religious nationalism, while being anti-modernist, is a product of modernity and today it has become a global force (see also Eisenstadt, 1999b; Hutchinson, 1994; Kepel, 1994). It cannot be dismissed as a marginal, irrational movement but is an integral part of the global world. In time of crisis and upheaval, religious nationalism can be a means of empowering marginal groups. In his view, western secular modernity will have to learn to live with many of its beliefs, such as respect for tradition and public institutions of morality. The violent or extreme forms are only one side of a wider cultural force, which can be accommodating, he argues (as is suggested by Iran in recent years).

151

FIVE THEORIES: A CRITICAL ANALYSIS

In recent years there has been a great deal of debate about the new nationalism. Unfortunately, much of it has not been particularly theoretical. We are not short of specialized case studies and a great deal about this nationalism is known and widely documented. But how are we to understand it in terms of a wider theory of modernity? In this section we attempt to assess the current explanations that have either been explicitly given or have been implicit in the literature. For convenience we look at five main approaches that have been adopted. This will provide a useful basis to formulate some general theoretical arguments in the subsequent section.

the return of history

The most common explanation given for the emergence of the new nationalism in the postcommunist constellation is the enduring power of long-run historical forces.[6] This is the argument that is much favoured by journalists and politicians who claim that ancient ethnic and religious hatreds, dormant for centuries, erupted once the iron hand of the communist state was lifted.[7] Tribalism and ancient ethnic hatred is thus given as the reason for the emergence of violent nationalism. According to this explanation, history holds the answer for the current situation which is plagued by essentially cultural forces that are beyond rational comprehension. The assumption underlying these arguments is that western nationalism is primarily civic while in Eastern Europe nationalism is ethnic, with their roots respectively in the 'state nation' or 'cultural nation'.[8] While many commentators are content with vague notions of tribalism, Samuel Huntington offers a more coherent civilizational theory for postcommunist nationalism, but one that ultimately suffers from the same assumptions of historical inevitability. He explains the rise of extreme nationalism as being due to civilizational clashes of the Christian west and the Muslim east where it is cultural and not political conflicts that is the cause (Huntington, 1996).[9] The wider clashes of the great civilizational blocs are likely to be more pronounced in the borderlands between these civilizations and will be expressed, he argues, in violent ethnic nationalism.

There is no doubt that long-run civilizational forces coupled with ethnic factors do play a role in shaping the conflicts of the present day, although this argument must be treated with caution as it is largely an extreme simplification when applied to a particular case. The problem with these explanations is that they become too general and fail to account for obvious exceptions and tend to project back onto history products of relatively recent origin. Thus much of the ethnic militarism in Eastern and Southeastern Europe has little in common with earlier kinds of collective identity (Kaldor, 1993). According to Cohen, postcommunist nationalism is the product of the absence of history, not its return. The conflict in the Balkans did not begin as an ethnic one but became one much later (Cohen, 1999). The cosmopolitanism of the Balkans in the pre-communist period has been widely recognized and this was not due to the strong arm of the state but the viability of ethnic pluralism (Malcolm, 1994). For over 500 years Sarajevo was one of the most culturally plural of Balkan cities. In this context Craig Calhoun has also pointed out that when the Christian rulers who established modern Spain, Ferdinand and Isabella, expelled all Jews in 1492 it was to the Ottoman Empire that they fled, where they lived in relative peace with Christians and Muslims for some 500 years (Calhoun, 1997, p. 59).

It is not to be disputed that nationalism, orchestrated by elites, gave ethnicity form and substance and therefore the claim of the motivating power of 'ancient hatreds' is over-extended and often misleading. Huntington's argument commits this basic fallacy of attributing too much historical continuity. In any event, modern nationalism must be substantially distinguished from its pre-modern antecedents, although such antecedents can play a role in providing certain preconditions. It is wrong to see nationalist beliefs as already comprehensively formed in history and simply released into the present. Such a view neglects the constantly changing alliances and shifting codes in nationalist ideology and mobilization. The following approaches take further these reflections.

internationalism and modernization

An argument that has frequently been applied to Central and Eastern Europe is that the current rise of nationalism is the product of nation-state formation in the post-1919 period when the great powers imposed the western model of the nation-state on southeastern Europe. With the collapse of the Soviet Union, which preserved the nation-state model, the old fault lines have resurfaced in the form of ethnic nationalism, it is argued. In this version of the historical explanation the causes are less purely cultural or ethnic than political and are to be explained by international factors, such as the imposition of a western model of modernization. Denying the existence of ancient traditions or the salience of earlier forms of nationalism, authors such as Eric Hobsbawm argue patterns of state formation were more important than ethnic or cultural forces (Hobsbawm, 1991, 1996). Other authors have argued against culturalist approaches, claiming that processes of nation formation in southeastern Europe were determined by the active intervention of the great powers who imposed their model of the nation-state. Consequently the Balkans are entirely products of modernity, not of backward cultures (Roudometof, 1999). In this view, postcommunist nationalism is a product of the combination of modernization as shaped by internationalism.

153

These arguments concerning the modernity of the Balkans are convincing in that they go beyond purely cultural explanations. However, these explanations also make the mistake of giving too much weight to earlier historical structures of state formation and fail to give due regard to the role of agency. It cannot be denied that structural factors, be they cultural or political, have played a crucial role, but these accounts make little sense in the absence of agency. As argued earlier, for much of the twentieth century there was relative peace in the Balkans, indicating that the earlier reorganization along western lines was not crucial in shaping the current crisis. When international intervention did come it was almost entirely in response to endemic conflicts, and was not itself the primary cause. A more plausible view is one that recognizes the interaction of the structural, the cultural and agency. Accepting that patterns of state formation and earlier ethnic fault lines played a role in shaping ethnic militaristic nationalism, the outcome was never predetermined by inexorable historical necessity or by international intervention. A fuller account would recognize the impact of diverse forms of agency, such as citizen revolts against injustice, corruption and demands for democratic reform. The capacity for these popular revolts to be mobilized by nationalists and transformed into an ethnic project cannot be underestimated.

institutionalism

Recent literature on nationalism emphasizes very strongly the importance of an institutional analysis to nationalism. For instance, Rogers Brubaker (1996) has shown how the seeds of postcommunist nationalism were sown by the policies of institutionalizing nationhood and nationality in the Soviet Union. The Soviet Union was based on institutionalized multinationality which not only tolerated national identification but institutionalized it, establishing nationhood and nationality as central institutional categories, and in doing so, Brubaker argues, it prepared the way for its own demise. His approach, which is influenced by the sociology of Bourdieu but adapted for a institutionalist analysis, sees the dynamics of nationalism being governed by the properties of political fields, not by the properties of collectivities, such as cultural entities like ethnicities. Thus he argues nationalism is not engendered by nations but is produced by political fields of particular kinds.[10] Herbert Kitschelt (1995) takes a similar view in his assessment of the radical new right in Western European politics.[11] He emphasizes the role of electoral dynamics and opportunity structures that these movements depend on, and not purely ideological doctrines. This is a thesis that overlaps with the argument (see next section) concerning the decline in the traditional political parties. Kitschelt argues that one of the main factors that accounts for the rise of the new radical right in Western Europe is the growing convergence of the right and left. The success of the extreme right depends on its ability to find a formula by which it attracts support from both the right and the left.

The advantage of such approaches is that they avoid the excessive preoccupation with culture and ethnicity that is characteristic of the first argument and avoids putting emphasis on extraneous factors such as the international context that is characteristic of the second. By stressing the role of institutional dynamics within the communist period history is demystified by such quasi-metaphysical notions of inexplicable and ancient hatreds. The disadvantage is that while offering a theory of the origins of the new nationalism it does not show how it is institutionalized in the postcommunist period. In the case of Western

Europe, the role of protest and dissatifaction with the main parties, while playing a role in mobilizing support for the radical right, does not explain the long-term institutionalization of these movements. There is little doubt that the new nationalism is more than a protest movement.

transition to democracy

An additional approach to postcommunist nationalism would explain it in terms of the transition to democracy. Such views are influenced by theories of the transition from authoritarianism in southern Europe and Latin America (O'Donnell and Schmitter, 1986). Applying such approaches to postcommunist transition is, of course, complicated by the additional transition from the centralized economy to the free market. Thus the transition is more than a purely political one, but requires the overall restructuring of the society. There is also the fact that major territorial changes to the state have accompanied the transition to democracy.

This general stance that stresses the transition to democracy is also reflected in a widespread view that the new nationalism is a response to the conditions created by the collapse of the political structures sustained by the Cold War and the growing diffuseness of the old political ideologies of right and left. This view was implicit in Huntington's theory, discussed earlier, and is also reflected in Mestrovic's account of, what he calls, 'Balkanization' (Mestrovic, 1994). According to these positions, nationalism fills the vacuum that has emerged with the declining appeal of the established political ideologies and allegiances (Chirot, 1991). In place of the old right and left is a radical and populist conservatism, such as that of the new right in Western Europe (Dahl, 1999) and in the postcommunist societies, radical ethnic nationalism. According to Denitch, nationalism has emerged in contexts where democracy has been weak and become a substitute for democratic mobilization (Denitch, 1996).

Many accounts that emphasize the role of the transition to democracy take a rational choice perspective. Thus Claus Offe, who adopts a rational choice perspective on ethnic politics in Eastern Europe, stresses the rationality of ethnic politics.[12] In his analysis, 'ethnification' is not the expression of some kind of a communitarian longing for cultural identity but a rational strategy to deal with, for instance, the economic need for boundaries, the weakness of state power, the fact that many ethnic minorities are associated with the minorities of a neighbour state and are therefore a source of instability for the new regime. In the absence of stable civic and political cultures based on democracy and citizenship, ethnic politics are frequently rational resources. This situation is summed up in the joke: 'The left has no ideology and the right has no money. What remains is nationalism' (cited in Offe, 1996, p. 71).

155

The argument that the new radical nationalisms are related to the transition to democracy caries some conviction in the case of postcommunist societies, but is of limited relevance to explain other kinds of nationalism, such as the new radical right in Western Europe. The rise of these movements in general preceded the post-Cold War constellation and is not sustained primarily by democratization, other than the recalcitrance of the Jacobin project in modernity. A weakness of the rational choice approach is that it neglects the fact that the transition to democracy in the former communist countries, with the exception of parts of the former Yugoslavia and some other notable cases (e.g. Georgia), has been primarily peaceful.[13] The strategic rationality in extreme nationalist and ethnic politics should not be underestimated, but it should also not deflect from the power of cultural identities. Even if cultural-ethnic identities become resources for strategic choices, they still require explanation in the first instance. However, there can be no doubt that perestroika and glasnost provided the conditions conducive for the emergence of nationalism.

reaction to globalization

156   The rise of globalization theory has been influential in theories of the new nationalism. In one major version of this the rise of extreme nationalism is explained as a reaction to the economic upheaval brought about by globalization. Such explanations do not look to history but to more recent social transformations. Nationalism can thus be explained as a response to diminishing resources and anxieties brought about by new socio-economic insecurities. The assumption then is that radical nationalism can be explained by structural factors such as economic problems, especially unemployment. The argument is that inflation, unemployment, diminishing social rewards in the context of recession predisposes large segments of the population towards xenophobic sentiments. In Western Europe, xenophobic responses to immigration are often explained in these terms. Habermas thus speaks of a 'welfare nationalism', a nationalism that has been fueled by fears of diminishing economic resources for the socially insecure (Habermas, 1991). It was always Habermas's argument that nationalism was a defensive and reactionary force that came with the second generation of bourgeois ideologies in the nineteenth century (Habermas, 1984, pp. 353–4). While playing down nationalism as an expression of agency, such explanations are convincing when applied to postcommunist transition, where the securities afforded by the old communist order disappeared with the transition to market societies.

In a slightly stronger form, it has often been argued that major structural problems in the late communist period led to the collapse of its social and political order leading to the emergence of nationalism. Thus, for instance, major economic disparities between the regions in many former communist countries found expression in nationalist opposition to the centre. Economic nationalism has often been a key aspect of nationalism going back to the late nineteenth century and it can be cited as a plausible factor in the emergence of nationalism today. However, in the past, economic nationalism was a state-led project, whereas today, with some few exceptions, nationalism has been primarily reactive and lacking in economic rationale.

Castells adopts a globalization perspective in his account of nationalism. For him the new nationalism is largely an expression of resistance identities, as opposed to legitimizing identities or project identities. Where legitimizing identities generate civil society and project identities aim at the making of a new kind of society, resistance identities are generated by groups who feel marginalized and threatened by society, which, rather than legitimate or reshape, they reject in the name of a 'communal heaven'. Nationalism is thus an expression of essentially defensive identities, rather than the identity project of many of the new social movements. The age of globalization, he argues, is the age of nationalist resurgence, expressed in the form of reactions to the established nation-states. Nationalism today is more often than not, a reaction against the global elites (Castells, 1997, p. 30). Zygmunt Bauman also argued from a largely globalization perspective (Bauman, 1992). For him, the new ethnic nationalisms are more akin to 'tribes' than to modern nations.

There is then much to suggest that the new nationalism is related to globalization. However, this is better seen as being less caused than induced by globalization. Major socio-economic processes only have an indirect relationship to nationalism, in many cases providing the structural preconditions and opportunity structures for nationalist mobilization. Globalization does not explain every nationalist conflict in the sense of causing it; rather the point is that globalization has opened up new possibilities for the emergence of nationalism as a new anti-systemic movement which is able to redefine the state project as an ethnic one.

The problem with such explanations is that they fail to explain why social discontent is channeled into radical nationalist movements and not to other political parties and movements. Globalization can just as easily provoke leftist movements, as is witnessed by the anti-globalization protests that have accompanied world summits in recent years. Moreover, while economic recession may be significant in many cases, the fact is that much of the new nationalism in Western Europe has occurred in countries that are relatively prosperous and there is no evidence of material deprivation in the support for such movements.

The existing literature on new radical nationalisms has been mostly focused on postcommunist nationalism and the war in the former

157

Yugoslavia. Given the diversity of postcommunist nationalism it is clearly impossible to generalize about radical nationalism in other parts of the world, such as in the rest of the western world and in Asia. We do not therefore propose to offer a general theory of nationalism. Of the five main approaches adopted in the existing literature, we favour, with some qualifications, the fifth one. This is not to deny the validity of the other theories, although we largely reject the return of history theory. The emphasis on the institutional context and the emphasis on the transition to democracy are particularly relevant to explaining the rise of extreme nationalism. There can be little doubt that these kinds of nationalism have assumed the power they have because of globalization which has opened up many spaces for ethnicization, indigenization and localization. The growing trend towards 'third way' style politics in which left and right are being diluted in a new politics of the centre has clearly created a space for the new nationalisms to gain public support. In the following section we attempt to develop the globalization approach to a wider theory of modernity. The main argument is that radical nationalisms are more than a reaction to globalization but are an integral part of the contemporary world and are also deeply rooted in the Jacobin tradition in modernity which today is being reconstituted in a whole range of new anti-systemic movements.

THEORIZING THE NEW RADICAL NATIONALISMS: THE NEW ANTI-SYSTEMIC MOVEMENTS OF THE LATE GLOBAL AGE

As has already been argued, given the diversity of the new nationalisms, ranging from the radical right to radical ethnic and religious nationalisms, a single explanation is not possible. The five arguments discussed in the previous section offer, to varying degrees, valid explanations of the rise of violent nationalism, in particular the fifth theory that nationalism is a defensive reaction to globalization. While the other theories place too much stress on historical preconditions or on structural causes, the globalization argument offers the basis of a more robust view of nationalism. However, in stressing the defensive nature of nationalism these accounts tend to neglect the fact that nationalism is also a form of agency and can be empowered by globalization. It is, of course, a question of perspective but even movements that are primarily defensive can also be proactive. In this view nationalism can be driven by globalization, which must be seen as an empowering as well as a fragmenting process.

This ambivalence is present in Castells's analysis. For him, nationalism, while being primarily defensive, can be empowered by the information society where ethnicity can be reshaped into transnational movements. He claims ethnicity does not provide the basis for cultural integration in the global age because the kinds of bonds that it is based on lose their significance when they are cut off from their historical context: 'Ethnic materials are integrated into cultural communes that are more powerful, and more broadly defined than ethnicity, such as religion or nationalism, as statements of cultural autonomy in a world of symbols' (Castells, 1997, p. 59). This suggests that the new nationalisms can be strengthened by globalization. We only have to consider the case of Sri Lankan nationalism to appreciate the impact of globalization on the nationalist struggles there, for without the support of the transnational diaspora the armed struggle would not be sustainable.

This double dynamic of localization/indigenization and globalization/homogenization – or globalization 'from below' and 'from above' – has also been commented on by Ong (1997), Soysal (1994) and Hedetoft (1999). Many nationalist movements have been empowered and reshaped by participating in the global society that is emerging today in the internet, in diasporas, in new career patterns, in international crime. Global communications offer entirely new ways of mobilization. New ideologies such as those of the radical right have given a legitimacy to extreme kinds of nationalism. Other statements of this general conception of nationalism as a recalcitrant movement in the global age can be found in the work of Benjamin Barber (1996) and Alaine Touraine (1995). Alaine Touraine's interpretation of late modernity in terms of an authoritarian communitarianism, on the one side, and on the other the remnants of the institutions of modernity would support this view, as would Benjamin Barber's account of the contemporary global conflict between 'jihad' and 'McWorld'. A similar notion can be found in the work of globalization theorists such as Jonathan Friedman (1994) and Roland Robertson (1992), who claim that globalization provides the local with the resources to be reinvented. In this sense, therefore, globalization does not merely have a negative impact on national contexts, forcing a defensive posture.

In sum, then, we do not see the new radical nationalism as exclusively defensive, despite its obvious anti-systemic nature. Although it lacks an intellectual project comparable to that of earlier nationalisms, which was able to appeal directly to the Enlightenment and the project of modernity, the extreme nationalisms of today are far from being marginal and cannot be dismissed as a mere backlash against modernity. This brings us to the critical juncture of the transformation of modernity by globalization. Can the new nationalism be understood within the categories of modernity or does it point to a movement beyond modernity? The argument advanced here is that while being hugely different from the earlier kinds of nationalism, the extreme nationalist movements of recent times can be understood as a radicalization of some of the central motifs and dynamics of modernity but ultimately go beyond the horizons of modernity. They are radical in the true sense

159

of the term, as opposed to being merely protest movements. It is this radicality that makes them more than defensive or reactive. In order to understand these movements we must see them as part of the emergence of the anti-systemic movements of the modern age, and not as exclusively as nationalist movements or as defensive reactions to globalization.[14] However, these movements are more anti-systemic than were previous kinds of social movements, such as earlier forms of nationalism which were more easily adaptable to the project of modernity. As argued in Chapter 2, nationalism in modernity had a major integrative role. Today this is no longer the case and many of the new nationalisms are powerful enough to resist what remains of the project of modernity and shape a new modernity in their image. In this we must not neglect the ability of the new nationalisms to articulate an integrative ideology. Lacking the ideological programme of earlier nationalisms, the new radical nationalisms have by default an ideological appeal that has come as a result of the growing convergence of the main right and left parties. The radical nationalisms are a combination of right and left wing political ideology, the discarded remnants of the major movements of modernity. Their popularity is due to their ability to occupy the space left vacant by the new centricist parties of the third way. This in fact means that in Western Europe the radical right are increasingly taking on board leftist elements, such as the notions of equality, anti-capitalism, anti-establishment and social justice which is combined with cultural authoritarianism. The current scenario is that these ingredients may become a functional substitute for the older political ideologies, including those of the traditional forms of nationalism. In this sense the new nationalism is a less than enlightened variant of what Ulrich Beck has called a 'second modernity', in which the second modernity is an attempt to cope with the problems created by the first but lack a programmatic vision of its own (Beck, 1994). In the case of nationalism this means that some of the central dimensions of nationalism persist but have become recalcitrant and destructive forces.

It has already been noted that the central idea underlying modern nationalism is that of radical freedom. It is this powerful notion that has driven and sustained it over the last two centuries. It was noted too that this idea has been central to the Jacobin tradition in modernity and has been the basis of much of the total critique of modernity since the Enlightenment. While the idea of radical freedom has mostly been domesticated by modern politics, a powerful strand in modernity – going back to the romantic movement, the Jacobin heritage, the philosophy of the German idealists and was present in modern nationalism – has sought to overcome the modern itself by appealing to radical freedom. Fascism was one major modern expression of the overcoming of the modern, but it was not to last. Despite reshaping the face of Europe and the world in the first half of the twentieth century, fascism was defeated.

Contemporary neo-fascism is only a small and relatively minor aspect of the new radical nationalisms that have become so prominent in recent years. With communism also defeated, it would appear that nationalism has no major ideological rival today. It is still – even in its most authoritarian forms – the most powerful voice of radical freedom and one that is subversive of the institutions of modernity.

Few ideologies have been able to articulate the notion of radical freedom more than nationalism, making it a recalcitrant force in modernity and never completely tamed by the institutional forces of the state and of civil society. For this reason nationalism and violence have been closely linked, since freedom in its radical form requires violence to manifest itself. Extreme nationalism is therefore essentially no different from other kinds of nationalism insofar as it is driven by the idea of radical freedom. While other kinds of nationalism domesticated violence, many of the contemporary forms of nationalism have a more direct relation to violence. However, it would be a mistake to reduce nationalism in any of its forms to an underlying idea, for it is ultimately shaped by institutional dynamics. Earlier we discussed how modernity is based on four institutional dynamics – state formation, capitalism, democracy and in intellectualization of culture – and argued that the interaction of these dynamics has shaped the particular forms that nationalism has taken in the modern world. We noted that nationalism arose along with the transition from the older civilizational constellations to modernity. By extending this analysis to the present context of postcommunist transition, globalization and the enhanced momentum towards European integration, we claim that the transformation of modernity by globalization sets into motion once again the central dynamics of modernity: but with a difference. Rather than single revolutions, such as the French Revolution or the Bolshevik Revolution, that inaugurated the modern epoch, today there are a plurality of mini-revolutions and a wider range of anti-systemic movements. The Islamic Revolution of 1979 was possibly the last of the great revolutions of modernity. While great epochal revolutions cannot be ruled out, it would appear to be a more characteristic feature of the present age and in line with the dynamics of globalization that there will be multiple sites of conflict. Unlike the earlier movement from civilization to modernity, we cannot speak of a fundamentally new society coming into existence, as certain theories of modernity have announced. Instead, we are witnessing multiple logics, including delayed modernization, demodernization and several overlapping modernities. Nationalism is central to many of these developments. Unlike, for instance, democratization, which stands on its own explicit normative claims, much of the enormous appeal of nationalism has been due to its ability to sublimate other values, such as the aspiration for freedom, autonomy and justice. It is not then globalization that is the primary cause of nationalism, for nationalism is more than a reaction to something but is itself a powerful force in the modern world insofar as it expressed the values of radical freedom. The point is that globalization has created the conditions for the resurgence of radical freedom in a whole range of new anti-systemic movements, fundamentalist movements, anti-capitalist movements, environmental movements, spiritualist movements, ethnic and nationalist movements, and INGOS of all kinds. What is also important to note about these movements is that they are not just liberation movements embodying western values of liberty, cosmopolitanism and individualism. Many of the new anti-systemic movements of the late global age are deeply authoritarian and anti-western. Democracy in many cases is not the desired aim, although paradoxically in most cases they are products of democratization. Crucially, many of these movements have emerged not just out of the life-world and to resist the system, as in Habermas's theory, but in the growing number of transnational spaces that now exist between life-world and system. They are anti-systemic but represent a different kind of colonization, which can be described as one which has a capacity to redefine the life-world and system. This capacity is reflected in, among other things, the construction of new cultural codes, to which we now turn.

162

THE CULTURAL LOGIC OF THE NEW NATIONALISM: XENOPHOBIA AND SYMBOLIC VIOLENCE

The cultural logic of the radical nationalisms has never been fully examined. The central argument proposed here is that the cultural logic of the extreme nationalism cannot be seen as ideologically coherent but is instead based on a recombination of the symbolic and cognitive codes of everyday life. Nationalism entails a political recodification of the symbolic violence embedded in everyday life. The success of such nationalist discourse is due to its ability to resonate with cultural values and ways of thinking that are present in the life-world. To understand this aspect of nationalist discourse is the aim of the present section.

The first and most general point to be made is that the new radical nationalism is a product of the tendencies towards pluralization in contemporary culture. It may be suggested that nationalism has taken to an extreme the concern of postmodern culture with difference, security and belonging. In a sense these core features of postmodern times have been inverted or recodified by nationalism into symbolic violence that is based on authoritarian and xenophobic values. The preoccupation with the self in earlier modernity has been overshadowed by a concern with the other today. In modernity the other was exterior to the self; today, as is exemplified in multiculturalism and postmodern thought, the other is seen as part of the self. But the kind of difference that is expressed in radical nationalism is one of xenophobic fear and reaction to otherness.[15] The denial of the other within the self defines the cultural presuppositions of xenophobic nationalism: 'Difference breeds hatred,' Nietzsche (1996) argued.[16]

We should not see xenophobia as an irrational and therefore an inexplicable psycho-social disposition.[17] Hatred of the other does not explain very much. The term is often used to mean hatred as opposed to fear of otherness (the stranger, foreigners). But there are major differences between hatred and fear as psycho-social dispositions. Fear may lead to hatred but hatred may not lead to fear. Hostility is a term that is also used to suggest something between outright hatred and fear. Moreover, xenophobia is not the same as racism or fascism. Racism is much more explicitly an extreme hatred of particular races and is based ultimately on a cultural and ideological theory of the biological superiority of the self over the other. Fascism is not primarily an ideology about otherness, and in its classic form in Italian fascism the preoccupation with minorities or other national groups was relatively minor. Indeed, anti-Semitism was marginal in the case of Italian fascism. Fascism is primarily an authoritarian political ideology of absolute loyalty to the national state. These distinctions are important to make, particularly in the context of radical nationalism since its presuppositions are not primarily about race or about hatred. The strict meaning of xenophobia, literally fear of the other, should be retained and distinguished from other, related dispositions. This is because, as will be shortly demonstrated, the xenophobic component of nationalist discourse is more about fear of the other within the self than hatred and in much of its expressions explicit racism is not evident. The precise Greek double meaning of the term is of sociological significance: fear of the other/fear of the guest, suggesting in a sense the otherness that is in the self. We are thus making the strong argument that radical nationalism is primarily driven by xenophobia and not by racism or fascism or even as something as vague and ill-defined as ethnocentrism, which is merely the acknowledgment of cultural differences (we are different from them). The implication of this view is that xenophobia, while often being a basis of racism, is quite distinct from racism and from ethnocentricism. Indeed, many of the historical forms of racism did not emanate from xenophobia but from science. What then is xenophobia?

Xenophobia is rooted in the symbolic violence of everyday life from where it derives its primary motivations, but it is also linked to the symbolic violence in cultural worldviews from where it derives legitimation. Distinguishing, then, between the level of everyday motivations within the lifeworld and cultural legitimations, we can discuss the cultural logic

163

of radical nationalism in the following way. The primary motivational sources of xenophobia that derive from everyday life can be resentment, disappointment, anxiety and uncertainty, demoralization and cultural trauma.

Resentment is one of the main expressions of hostility against others and which can be expressed in the more overt form of xenophobia but is more fundamentally a feature of modern life. Nietzsche in the *Genealogy of Morals*, published in 1887, regarded *ressentiment* as deeply embedded in modern culture, an expression of a powerful reactive current in modernity (Nietzsche, 1996, pp. 54–6). It is an opposition to the other within the self and to the other outside the self. In either case it is an attitude that constructs self-identity through negative identity. In order to exist the 'slave morality' requires an other to provide the reference point for the identity of the self.[18] Greenfeld and Chirot have also noted the role of *ressentiment* in non-western nationalism. This nationalism, while taking over western Enlightenment ideas and practices developed at the same time a deeply rooted *ressentiment* of those values and which often became the basis of later xenophobia and aggression (Greenfeld and Chirot, 1994, pp. 102–24).

Disappointment as a result of the disjuncture between expectations and experience is another source of xenophobia. Disappointment with the promises of modernity has led many voters into supporting political causes that have projected blame onto a scapegoat, such as a national minority or ethnic group that is associated with external threat. This might explain how revolutions of rising expectations have often been transformed into reactionary nationalist movements. Several studies of extreme right-wing voting in the Western Europe of the 1990s, emphasize the role of protest rather than right-wing ideology. It would appear that dissatisfaction with democracy more than right-wing ideology is what is significant (Falter and Klein, 1996, p. 53). However, there is general agreement that some ideological predispositions are required for dissatisfaction to play a major role in extreme right-wing voting.

Anxiety and uncertainty also play a role in shaping the conditions that are conducive to xenophobia. Cultural trauma is a more pronounced kind of anxiety that arises as a result of a total breakdown in the social order that leads to a 'cultural shock' (Neal, 1998; Sztompka, 2000). One of the consequences of cultural trauma is a culture of distrust which can easily be conducive to xenophobia and inter-group violence. Such sentiments can be exacerbated more generally by demoralization, which Febrve (2000) argues has become a major part of contemporary culture.

However, xenophobia can be linked to more explicit forms of symbolic violence which have a more pronounced legitimating function in maintaining otherness and in maintaining adversarial frames. Examples of these might include categories as various as:

- racism
- anti-Semitism
- homophobia
- misogyny
- citizenship and nationality
- moral purity
- ethnocentrism
- exoticism.

On these levels, otherness is expressed in more objectivist terms than in the symbolic violence of the habitus, where the otherness of the 'they' is subordinated to the identity of the 'we'. This is the case of racism and anti-Semitism, which are more than forms of prejudice that may arise from ignorance or fear, but are ideologically and often theoretically elaborated. Homophobia and misogyny are forms of hatred that are nourished by some of the cultural practices of everyday life, such as sexism and patriarchy. Citizenship itself makes a fundamental distinction between citizens and aliens, and as such offers a weak cultural basis of exclusion (Mann, 1999). Ethnocentricism is more present in some cultural forms than in others, depending on the relationship between cultural and political identities. If the political identity of the state rests on a prior cultural identity which is primarily defined by ethnic, primordial codes, the cultural identity is likely to exhibit a relatively high degree of ethnocentrism. Moral purity can be a consequence of ethnocentrism, as Barrington Moore has argued (Moore, 2000). Exoticism may also be mentioned as a relatively weak cultural basis of otherness, and this can also be related to the role of fantas (Salecl, 1993; Todorov, 1993). However, it must be stated that ethnocentricism as such does not necessarily result in either xenophobia or racism. Ethnocentricism is simply the view that 'we are different from them', or as in certain kinds of multiculturalism the view that 'we are all different'. Nevertheless the perception or attribution of a cultural difference can lead to prejudice, fear and even hatred.

165

To separate symbolic violence that is expressed in the new radical nationalism into two levels, a strong and a weak level, allows us to trace the relations between the social and cultural sides in a more intricate manner and in a way that avoids conflations of its different dimensions. This involves distinguishing two levels of symbolic violence: one the level of everyday life (i.e. social practices) and on the cognitive level of cultural narratives, rules, adversarial and symbolic codes. In contrast to Johan Galtung's well-known concept of cultural violence as a form of violence that is embedded in culture as opposed to the structural violence in institutions, we see cultural violence as more differentiated (Galtung, 1990). For Galtung, cultural violence relates to those aspects of culture that are exemplified by religion, ideology, language, art and even science, which may indirectly legitimate violence. This neglects the more subtle and less coherent dimension of symbolic violence in the practices that constitute the everyday habitus, where it may also provide an indirect basis for violence, but one that is less articulated than on the cultural level.

Symbolic violence is contained in everyday life in several cognitive frames and symbolic dispositions that express xenophobia or are conducive to it. Fear of the other has arguably increased with modernity, which has brought strangeness into the heart of the lifeworld through immigration, multiculturalism, consumption, tourism, education, and value pluralization (see Kahn, 2001). Fear of the other accompanies modernity's logic of inclusion in the form of a construction of different orders of exclusion, ranging from exotic fantasies to xenophobic neo-Nazism (Theweliet, 1987). Xenophobia is shaped by the logic of exclusion – the separation of the 'we' from the 'they' – and the construction of adversarial frames, requiring a negative identification by which the 'they' becomes an enemy. Carl Schmitt (1970) generalized such relations of enmity to all of politics, which he believed was always about the fundamental division of 'friends and enemies'. But his reductionist philosophy failed to see that the us/them polarity is distinct from the quite different logic of xenophobic politics by which the 'they' becomes first an 'other' and then an enemy. However, the shift from exclusion to adversity is a very subtle one. Most groups are based on a sense of the 'we' as distinct from a 'them'. The potentiality for other-creating mechanisms to become adversarial is always present.[19] For instance, a sense of grievance or an injustice can transform the self-identity of the we into an exclusive preoccupation with the other who is made responsible for the fate of the we. The normal means of coping with this necessity for boundary maintenance against an enemy is punishment sanctioned by law and other civic norms of justice, but other mechanisms can be employed, such as denial (Cohen, 2001). Xenophobia results when the self loses its self-identity and seeks in the other the reference point for its identity. In such circumstances the other ceases to be an enemy as such, but a pathological expression of self-identity.

Cultural codes of otherness can thus arise from the fundamental facts of group identity and can be sustained by adversarial codes which may involve xenophobic dimensions. However, not all adversarial frames become xenophobic, just as not all tightly defined we-groups become adversarial. Xenophobic relations result when the adversarial frames that maintain otherness are unable to maintain exclusion or when the logic of inclusion and exclusion breaks down or becomes diffuse. The claim that is being made, then, is that xenophobic relations do not arise directly from the logic of exclusion and neither do they arise directly from adversarial frames. Such forms of symbolic violence are, to varying degrees, normal. Xenophobia becomes a pronounced pathological force when adversarial frames arise and, crucially, are unable to maintain the fundamental boundaries of self and other. Xenophobia is thus the pathological condition that arises when the self is unable to cope with otherness and is destructive of both self and other. Thus, many forms of xenophobia result from situations where, because of social and political change, the internal other becomes associated with an external other, as in the case of national minorities who become perceived as a threat due to their association with a larger group in a neighbouring state. Especially in situations where the other is so close to the self, the other is generally defined in reified codes and by the construction of a scapegoat, for instance, Jews, homosexuals.[20] Theoretically, then, xenophobia can be understood as akin to the logic of reification, by which the other is a fetish for the self.

CONCLUSION

Because of the latent symbolic violence that is inherent in group dynamics, many forms of nationalism are potentially xenophobic. In Karl Deutsch's famous definition, xenophobia is written into the heart of nationalism: 'A nation is a group of persons united by a common error about their ancestry and a common dislike of the neighbors' (Deutsch, 1969, p. 3). In the extreme case it can lead to ethnic cleansing and ultimately to genocide. In this chapter we have argued for the need to appreciate the cultural logic by which symbolic violence in everyday life and in the habitus of the group can be made to serve adversarial frames on the cultural level and to distinguish both of these from the pathological condition of xenophobia. The implications of this is that extreme forms of nationalism feed off the xenophobia that is present in everyday life and in cultural codes.

Nationalism is part of the global world and will not wither away along with the state, as an older social theory once believed. Ways of living with it will have to be found. In the next chapter we discuss prospects of accommodating nationalism and diffusing it of some of its violent dimensions.

167

NOTES

1 IRA (Irish Republican Army), ETA (*Euskadi To Askatasuna*, 'Euskadi and Freedom', the Basque nationalist movement), FLNC (*Front de liberation nationale de la Corse*), PKK (Kurdish Communist Party).

2 The term radical new right is used by Herbert Kitschelt (1995). See also (Betz, 1994), Ignazi (1997), and Dahl (1999).

3 Examples are FPÖ in Austria *(Freiheitliche Partei Österreichs* – Austrian Liberal Party), in Belgium the *Vlaams Blok* (Flemish Bloc), the Front National in France, the *Centrumdemocraten* (Centre Democrats) in the Netherlands, *Die Republikaner* in Germany.

4 This ideological programme is to be found in the writings of Alain Benoist and the movement known as GRECE. See Holmes (2000).

5 See Castells's discussion of the American militia and patriot movement (Castells, 1997, pp. 84–97).

6 See also Jovic (2001).

7 See also for example Kaplan (1992). The US Secretary of State, Warren Christopher, held this view (see Calhoun, 1997, pp. 61–2).

8 This is a distinction that goes back to Meinecke's classic work published in 1907 (see Meinecke, 1970) Vol is also found in Kohn (1944).

9 Originally based on an article in 1993 (Huntington, 1993).

10 For a similar approach, see Vujacic and Zaslavsky (1991).

11 See also Koopmans (1996, 1997).

12 See Chapter 4, 'Ethnic politics in east European transition' (in Offe, 1996).

13 See Laitin (1995) on Georgia and the conflict in autonomous region of Abkhazia. In the case of Georgia, the civil war itself was not directly connected with nationalism, which was an issue only with regard to the autonomous republics and regions within it.

14 On anti-system movements, see Arrighi et al. (1989).

15 See de Vries and Weber (1997) for various perspectives on violence and difference.

16 For an interpretation on *ressentiment* in Nietzsche, see Stauth and Turner (1988).

17 Hatred is often used as a vague term that is rarely theorized sociologically, as in Hockenos (1993).

18 For Max Scheler in a philosophical work, *Ressentiment*, published in 1915, 'ressentiment' is the condition of modernity itself (Scheler, 1972).

19 For an inspiring analysis of some of the mechanisms, see Gamson (1995). See also
Rothchild and Groth (1995) and Wendt (1994).

20 This can be compared to what Freud called the 'narcissism of minor differences'. See Blok (1998).

eight

debating the limits of nationalism: possibilities for postnationalism

In this concluding chapter, drawing from the materials developed in the book so far, we offer an interpretation of the current status of nationalism. We have argued that nationalism emerged under the conditions of modernization and connected the political project of modernity – the radical project of elites, state formation, etc. – with the cultural project of shaping new identities and new forms of thinking and meaning. In this, as structuralist accounts have always argued, the social project of modernity played a crucial role. Nationalism was thus one kind of reaction to the particular constellation of social, political and cultural forces that shaped modernity. The current situation differs from the past in one major respect: the political project of modernity is less connected with the cultural project. Consequently, under the conditions of globalization, the dynamics of modernity have produced a different field of conflicts which are characterized by greater fragmentation.

A POSTNATIONAL WORLD?

The current situation of nationalism can thus be seen in terms of processes of decoupling, two of which can be specified:

- the decoupling of nation and state
- the decoupling of citizenship and nationality.

Rather than speak of the end of the nation-state and with it the end of citizenship, we need to see how the forces previously contained within the parameters of the nation-state are being released into a global, but very uncertain world in which different logics of openness and closure come into play.

the decoupling of nation and state

With regard to the first process of decoupling, it must be firmly stated that neither nation nor state is coming to an end. Globalization is undermining the project of modernity in the specific sense of the dis-embedding of the political project of the state from the cultural project of nationhood. The previous combination within the nation-state has been the major casualty in the global age. What this means, however, is the separation, or decoupling, of nation and state from one another. In this sense, then, nationalism has been given a new lease of life by globalization. Released from the fetters of the nation-state, nationalism has reasserted itself in the world today in a great variety of anti-systemic forms, ranging from violent new nationalisms to different kinds of transnational movements. In the last two decades, there has been a major swing in international principles of legitimation from states to nations (Barkin and Cronin, 1994). This is not unconnected with the fact that today the nation is easier to accommodate than in the past. Globalization has opened up many opportunities for new nations, the emergence of small economies and transnational actors.

The state itself, for its part, is no longer entirely tied to established cultural traditions for its legitimation. Globalization has the effect of disburdening the state from legitimation by cultural traditions, such as the established conception of the national community or democracy. The state is no longer exclusively a provider state, but is becoming more and more a regulatory state. Thus, it is not so much a decline in the state that is occurring but a major transformation in its functions. Various processes of globalization have the effect of redistributing the functions once concentrated in the nation-state. European integration, for instance, has the effect of relocating functions performed by the nation-state onto the transnational level. However, not all functions are being redistributed. The tendency is for the European Union to take over those functions from national governments that are less effectively performed on that level. The resulting political constellation is a highly complex interlocking network of relations that is spread over national, subnational and the transnational levels. In a sense, this process is no different from earlier forms of state formation, since the state has always been a product of particular relations rather than an entity in itself. This relationalist dimension is more pronounced today with the growing salience of regulatory regimes, on both the national and transnational level. In view of this, it makes little sense claiming the state is coming to an end or is in a major crisis (Hall, 2000). The simple fact of the unification of East and West Germany in 1990 testifies to the power of the state to provide a framework of unity for society. The widespread support for Berlusconi's party *Forza Italia* in Italy in 2001 is also evidence of the viability of the state as a focus of national loyalty. Moreover, monarchies are seemingly more popular than ever. This traditional form of government has survived intact in some of the most advanced democracies, such as in the entire Scandinavian world, and is increasingly becoming popular in Greece, eastern Europe and Russia, where the Romanovs have been redeemed as national heroes. In 2001 the former Bulgarian child-king, Paul II, was elected president of Bulgaria. The Australians voted against republicanism and those countries that do not have monarchies often envy those that do. The world-wide mourning of the death of Princess Diana in 1997 seems to suggest that despite its republican origins, there appears to be a close affinity between nationalism and monarchy.

The argument put forward here is that the state is undergoing significant transformation as a result of the transference upwards to the transnational level and downwards to the subnational or regional levels of many of its functions. This argument does not deny the obvious survival of the state and the continued significance of national economies. Many new elites are emerging and redefining the social and political world according to new categories. As a result the state is becoming more fluid, and thus more open to nationalism and ethnization. The extreme version of this is in parts of Latin American, Africa and the former communist world where the state does not exist outside particular kinds of ethnic mobilization and organized crime.

We can say that with the restructuring of the state, the traditional forms of cultural legitimation based on democracy and national cultures are losing their relevance. Legitimation by public culture is less significant today simply because of the growing number of global spaces, stateless spaces and normative vacuums. Thus, the increased visibility of nationalism in the world today is merely the manifestation of this anarchic situation of extreme social fragmentation, which can of course also be described as one of offering new opportunities for cosmopolitan community. Lacking a political form – akin to the nation-state – 'nations' as articulated by anti-systemic forces all over the world are rebelling against states. The new radical nationalisms discussed in the previous chapter are only one expression of this resurgence of the nation as a recalcitrant force. Other expressions of the decoupling of the nation from the state are the emergence of new regionalist movements, the recovery of the city as a civic project, the growing salience of community beyond the state, as in certain expressions of cosmopolitanism.

In these developments the nation code has been opened up to new codifications of belonging. The most striking feature of these new discourses is the contested nature of national belonging. The nation has been deconstructed in contemporary public discourse. This is because national culture has lost its integrative function. The result is that the nation code is opened up to new interpretations arising from cultural opportunities for new demands for self-determination. The global age has opened up many interpretative cultural models for social actors.[1]

Nowhere is this more apparent than in the case of architecture. Globally, architecture is becoming increasingly important as a cultural space for the expression of identities and consequently architects are becoming ever more a politically influential group. This is particularly

171

the case in the UK, where debates about national identity have been closely linked to major controversies about architecture. But in Eastern Europe architecture has also become a major site of political contestation (Leach, 1999). It is of course true that national identity has always been closely related to the creation of great national buildings, which were intended to reflect the historical achievements of the nation-state. What is different today, however, is that architecture has become more open to different forms of codification, and in the changed circumstances of the current situation it is less controlled by the state. In short, architecture has ceased to be a national project. While British architecture is still one of the most heavily funded by national governments, the discourse of architecture now extends beyond the remit of national governments and has become an open space in which many conflicting projects struggle. Architecture is, on the one hand, shaping new national icons – such as the Millennium Dome – and, on the other, is providing a discourse for the multiplication of urban meanings, as is evidenced by the rise of postmodern architecture and regional development. That is why architecture and urban design have become powerful forms of the expression of new social identities. The contemporary challenge for architecture is to articulate new cultural voices and to embody their conceptions of the social. Such a perspective will see architecture as central to cultural citizenship. Architecture is also increasingly the site of tension between the local, the national and the global; the most striking being between the city, the state and global capitalism. As a result of processes associated with globalization, the state has become separated from the idea of the nation as a cultural project; it has become concerned with the regulation of transnational processes to such an extent that it is no longer the clearest expression of the nation. Consequently, the nation is finding a new embodiment in the city – and more specifically in its architectural design. In the age of global capitalism, the city is also the site of the new means of production, as Saskia Sassen asserts (Sassen, 1992). But this means that the discourse of the nation is more contested.

This conflict about the identity of the city in the global context age is strikingly apparent in the diverse cases of cities such as London, Berlin and Paris. Owing to globalized, information-based capitalism these kinds of cities are national and cultural capitals detached from their regions and globally connected in different ways. In the past the coexistence of the nation, capitalism and culture was what defined capital cities – they were centres of cultural capital and centres of economic capital – but today these structures have become disjoined, making the city the site of new kinds of conflicts and new cultural discourses about politics and society.

While global cities such as London have become the location of major sites of tension between the nation and the city, others reflect a

172

different development. In a spectrum of middle-range European cities, the urban and the architectural form of the city is becoming more and more an expression of regional, city-based identity (Delanty, 2000d). Architecture is becoming a means of allowing the formation of postnational identities. Here, the tendency discernible elsewhere is more pronounced: architecture is becoming a reference point for the expression of social identities that are not defined by the state and history. But, as critics as diverse as Manual Castells and Jürgen Habermas argue, there is the danger that architecture will be drawn into the posthistorical world of global capitalism (Castells, 1996; Habermas, 1989b). In sum, architecture has become the cultural site of major battles between national identity, global capitalism and the city.

The point of this discussion is to demonstrate that the discourse of the nation has become a discourse open to many meanings and codifications. While it may appear on one level that the contemporary world is characterized by more and more nationalism, this is only partly true. While nationalism is certainly enjoying a productive era, what is also occurring is that there is more contestation about the nation. The idea of the nation is contested, pluralized and globalized/de-territorialized; in short, it has become a discursive category characterized by radically shifting patterns of signification and the end of the master discourse of statehood.

the decoupling of nationality and citizenship

The second major example of decoupling processes is the separation of nationality from citizenship. Until now the connection between nationality and citizenship has been taken for granted in theory and practice. To be a citizen was to be a member of a nation-state and thus to have particular rights in return for which certain duties have to be performed. It has been a fact of modern history that the nation-state has been the political and administrative framework in which the rights have developed. The established civic, political and social rights, as described by T. H. Marshall (1992) in his classic work on citizenship, were, on the whole, rights secured by the state. This conception of rights did not question the nation-state as the exclusive model for citizenship. The advent of the mature welfare state in the post-Second World War period reinforced the idea of the nation-state as the sole guarantor of citizenship. The earlier rise of civic and political citizenship, too, occurred within the contours of the nation-state. Thus, whether in the form of the constitutional-democratic state or in the welfare state, the nation-state seemed to be the pedestal of modernity. Existing outside this framework was the relative vacuum of the international order, comprised largely of a politics arbitrated by national governments, constrained only by international law and the necessity for compromise.

Today in the global era this has all changed and is illustrated in the decoupling of citizenship from nationality. Citizenship is no longer exclusively defined by nationality for the following reasons. Post-national membership has become a reality in many parts of the world as a result of the growing presence of transnational processes in people's lives as well as a result of the tremendous impact of globalization on the nation-state. The older conceptions of citizenship took for granted the nation-state as the only viable framework for citizenship and for politics more generally. While the nation-state is still without doubt the single most important geopolitical unit, it has not been able to reverse the worldwide swing towards transnational politics. Major examples of this are the growing importance of such kinds of citizenship as cultural citizenship, ecological citizenship, technological citizenship. It will suffice to comment briefly on these new forms of citizenship.[2]

For several decades cultural rights have being growing in importance, bringing about a shift away from the previous exclusive concentration of social rights and, more generally, the ideal of formal equality. The turn to cultural rights marks a radical departure from all traditional conceptions of citizenship because of its embracing of difference rather than equality as central to citizenship. Cultural rights also, by their very nature, entail a commitment to group rights, in contrast to the previous assumption of the individualistic nature of rights. Cultural rights have, of course, been central to communitarianism, which was not a movement that questioned the nation-state, and have also been central to debates about human rights from the 1960s. However, the significance of cultural rights in undermining nationality has become more pronounced today as a result of the growing mobility and, crucially, organizational capacity, of many groups, in particular migrants and ethnic groups. Some major studies have documented the ability of migrants and ethnic groups to advance demands for rights on the basis of residence rather than birth (Ong, 1997; Oommen, 1997; Soysal, 1994). In the context of the European Union, residence has become more important as a criterion of citizenship than birth. As citizenship becomes more and more differentiated into different kinds of rights and with more and more routes to citizenship, the tie with nationality is breaking down. Although political rights (the right to vote in national elections) have not always been granted on the basis of residence, in many countries there is growing recognition of other kinds of rights, social as well as civic, cultural and even ecological rights.

More generally, citizenship has moved beyond nationality in the emergence of such transnational discourses as ecological and technological citizenship. If citizenship is in the most basic sense participation in the political community, it is evident that participation extends beyond nationality in these critical areas. Technology has emerged as a new focus for citizenship, as is witnessed by debates about the control

174

over and access to information technologies, human reproductive technologies, genetically modified foods, various kinds of genetic and bio technologies. The classic duties of citizenship are no longer simply framed in terms of the duties of the citizen to the state, but concern responsibility for humanity, responsibility for nature and responsibility to future generations. Because of the growing transnational space – as is witnessed by European integration, global civil society, the increased role of non-state actors, such as non-governmental organizations, the tremendous impact of the internet – participation in political community no longer occurs exclusively on the national level. There is much to suggest then that citizenship has become flexible and differentiated (Delanty, 2000b; Isin and Wood, 1999).

This all brings us to the critical question of loyalty to the nation-state and the future of national identity. We have argued that the current situation is marked by separation of citizenship from nationality and also by the decoupling of nation and state. Posing the question of the status of nationalism in this way avoids exaggerated claims of the demise of the nationalism in a new global, on the one side, and, on the other side, claims of a universal descent into violent nationalism. Globalization has brought about a situation in which political community is being reconstituted on many different levels (Linklater, 1998). The state no longer dominates the field which has consequently become more open to many different kinds of social actors, including nationalist movements. In this way, then, globalization has brought about new opportunities for movements as diverse as cosmopolitan political community and nationalism. In the following section we look at some of the major debates on possibilities for postnationalism in a world that appears to be torn between cosmopolitanism and nationalism.

BEYOND NATIONALISM: THE MAJOR CRITICAL DEBATES

In the debate about the limits and alternatives to nationalism four positions can be discerned. First, proponents of internationalism, who see in nationalism a sign of degeneration; second, those who attempt to rescue nationalism from nationalists, arguing instead for a kind of liberal patriotism; third, those who reject nationalism and patriotism altogether for a genuinely postnational cosmopolitanism that goes beyond internationalism and all kinds of nationalism; and, fourth, those who argue for a postmodern transnationalism that combines elements of nationalism and cosmopolitanism.

internationalism

Many of the well-known critics of nationalism presuppose in their rejection of nationalism a radical liberal international order. Figures such as

Gellner and Hobsbawm adhere strongly to internationalism, seeing nationalism as a form of xenophobic degeneration. In the case of Gellner this was an uncompromising commitment to a liberalism rooted in individualism and in the case of Hobsbawm socialism was the only viable alternative to nationalism. However, what is striking is that neither strongly opposed the nation-state as such; what they reject is radical separatist nationalism, especially in its ethnic form. The assumption therefore is that the nation-state in itself is a viable entity. Although this was never made explicit, their attack on nationalism did not question the sovereign nation-state.[3] Their commitment to internationalism reflected an older view of internationalism as a political space in which states were the main actors. This notion of internationalism has its origins in Kant, who, in *Perpetual Peace* in 1795, was one of the first to write about the rise of an international legal order (Kant, 1970). Internationalism has been the focus of a great deal of debate since the 1970s, as reflected in such major works as Hedley Bull's *The Anarchical Society*, but has been overshadowed by the more recent notion of cosmopolitanism (see p. 180–1). Although critics such as Bull were conscious of the movement towards an international society as opposed to an international system and which might be composed of a common, albeit tendentially anarchic, framework of legal and moral norms. Internationalism on the whole stood for a view of politics as shaped by the relatively stable projects of national states (Bull, 1977). This was the neo-functionalist worldview acceptable to the mainstream critique of nationalism, which was predominantly liberal in inspiration.[4] The objection against nationalism was primarily cognitive: nationalism was based on an incorrect view of the world, one based on myth, invented traditions, a distorted view of the national past. The liberal, internationalist perspective seemed the more attractive alternative. For Gellner, in his final book, this struggle – between the closed and communal world of atavistic nationalism and the open world of individualistic, Enlightenment rationalism and internationalism – was an integral struggle to the human condition (Gellner, 1998). In the present context the internationalist critique of nationalism is important because some of the major defenders of nationalism have defined their position against it, rather than to the more recent work on cosmopolitanism.

liberal patriotism

This position has many supporters and has its roots in liberal nationalism. It is broadly the view that nationalism is a benign force in the world. Many of the supporters of nationalism distinguish between nationalism and patriotism, arguing that what they defend is better called patriotism.[5] The distinction between nationalism and patriotism has appeal for third way politicians. In a speech on 'Modern Patriotism' in 1999 Tony Blair said 'Ours is a modern patriotism not a narrow nationalism' (cited in Kahn, 2001, p. 5). In this case patriotism is tied to a communitarian state-led project. By patriotism is meant love of one's community and devotion to ideals beyond mere individualism. Patriotism has its roots in the Enlightenment republican tradition and the concept of nation it is based on is one of civil society as opposed to national society. A wide range of writers on nationalism – Kymlicka, Miller, Tamir, Berns, Viroli – defend this particular kind of nationalism against its violent and atavistic forms. They thus differ from the conservative defenders of nationalism and the more traditional forms of radical secessionism.[6] Patriotism as love of country, then, does not mean 'my country right or wrong' but a civic virtue. This is broadly the position taken by Maurizio Viroli, who admits patriotism is easier to defend theoretically than in practice, where it is often indistinguishable from nationalism (Viroli, 1995, p. 17). Nevertheless, patriotism is a coherent position to take and must be distinguished from the cruder forms of nationalism. In the case of Vitrioli, patriotism has a long history going back to classical thought, especially Stoical tradition. In this sense, patriotism is likened to ancient republicanism, as opposed to its later Enlightenment form. This was the sense of patriotism that surfaced in England during the English Revolution and which saw itself as a continuation of Roman republicanism. The major representative of this kind of, what in fact was, Puritan patriotism in England was John Milton.

177

The communitarian tradition in political thought strongly defends patriotism for its civic contribution to citizenship and as a necessary basis for political community. Charles Taylor is one of the best known defenders of nationality (Taylor, 1990, 1994, 1998). His communitarian philosophy holds that political community must rest ultimately on a cultural community. For him and for other communitarian thinkers, cosmopolitanism is too thin and devoid of cultural content. It is unable to do what nationalism can achieve, namely inchoate group identity and solidarity. This is an essentially liberal view of nationalism, and is also reflected in the work of Will Kymlicka, who has written extensively on national self-determination and the problem of multiculturalism.[7] In his view, certain kinds of national self-determination are defensible and broadly compatible with a liberal philosophy. Whereas Taylor takes a stronger communitarian position on cultural rights, Kymlicka argues from a liberal perspective, albeit one that is less encompassing in its support for all kinds of nationalism. However, as far as nationalism is concerned, liberalism and communitarianism tend to offer a broadly positive view of nationalism. Many liberal positions, such as that of Michael Ignatieff (1994), are, of course, highly critical of nationalism, seeing it as a destructive force in the world, though the liberal position – going back to J. S. Mill – has been generally positive about nationalism (Mill, 1971). It may be suggested that the compatiblity of liberalism with nationalism is that the latter offers a degree of loyalty to the state, thus compensating for the social deficit in liberalism. However, this has not always been the case and many liberal thinkers have been opposed to nationalism. A famous example of liberal hostility is Lord Acton's essay on 'Nationality' (Acton, 1907).

There are several liberal thinkers of a more left-wing disposition who are also favourable to nationalism. Richard Rorty, for instance, sees an important connection between nationalism and social solidarity. In a controversial book, *Achieving Our Country*, Richard Rorty (1998) argued that national pride is an important virtue and one that has been too much neglected by the left, to its detriment.[8] Although a thinker associated with liberal postmodernism, Rorty wrote a strongly communitarian defence of the relevance of nationhood in order to overcome demoralization:

> In America, at the end of the twentieth century, few inspiring images and stories are being proffered. The only version of national pride encouraged by American popular culture is a simpleminded militaristic chauvinism. But such chauvinism is overshadowed by a widespread sense that national pride is no appropriate. In both popular and elite culture, most descriptions of what America will be like in the twenty-first century are written in tones either of self-mockery or of self-disgust. (Rorty, 1998, p. 4)

178   The problem with the academic left, as he sees it, is that it has no project or vision to offer a demoralized country that can at best appeal to a narrow nationalism. For Rorty, there is a higher kind of patriotism than nationalism, on the one side, and, on the other, the preoccupation with cultural politics. In his view the American academic left has become a politically impotent 'cultural left'. Patriotism in the sense of a national project based on national pride can offer an alternative. Rorty associates this with an older leftist tradition that has been forgotten today.

For the British political philosopher David Miller, the crucial question is not whether nationalism is right or wrong in its construction of history but whether it is able to perform valuable functions for a society. In his view:

> Nationality answers one of the most pressing needs of the modern world, namely how to maintain solidarity among the populations of states that are large and anonymous, such that their citizens cannot possibly enjoy the kind of community that relies on kinship or face-to-face interaction. (Miller, 2000, pp. 32–33).[9]

For Miller, the strength of nationalism is that it is precisely an imaginary identity and the main source of solidarity in modern society. His communitarian liberalism sees politics as responsive to human nature and social needs. National identity is flexible and can accommodate a great variety of challenges and situations and is compatible with deliberative democracy and with multicultural citizenship. There is no reason why nationalism cannot be part of a pluralist political culture that is inclusive rather than exclusive, he argues. In this, then, he differs quite strongly from those authors who are critical of nationalism, for instance Kedourie, Minogue and Gellner.[10]

Canovan's account is akin to Miller in her assertion of the importance of strong collective identity that could create affective moorings for democracy. She is more circumspect than Miller, however, in respect of the conditions whereby nationhood can 'in some cases generate collective power of a kind that makes aspirations to democracy, social justice and human rights seem within the bounds of possibility' (Canovan, 1996, p. 115). She criticizes Miller for being too optimistic about the putative benefits of an 'overarching national identity' and for not sufficiently considering the contingent conditions, especially arising from interstate relations, that could generate the kind of collective power referred to earlier. Canovan's realism notwithstanding, she does believe that the nation is necessary because it has the cultural and normative power to bind populations together. On the cultural plane, she cites approvingly Simone Weil's assertion that moderns love the nation because they have nothing else to love (Canovan, 1996, p. 61). According to Canovan, the dissolution of village, kinship, and occupational status has left individuals with nothing to turn to except the imagined community of the nation. On a normative plane, the attachment to nation is fundamental to the loyalties that bind individuals to political entities, acting as a kind of reserve that can be called upon in times of crisis. She considers the nation to acquire in this process a kind of quasi-natural status that is almost dangerous by virtue of a self-evident status that disguises the real dependence of the liberal democratic political community on it.

In the sociological debate on nationalism the main point of contention is whether nationalism is an invented tradition or an authentic tradition. While these critics and others such as Hobsbawn reject nationalism as a fabricated and destructive force in the world, a wide range of writers on nationalism see it in much more positive terms. Such authors who are broadly sympathetic to nationalism include Greenfeld (1992), McCrone (1998), Tamir (1993), Anderson (1983) and Smith (1995). For these authors it is only with states that democracy has any chance of success and nationalism is a necessary basis for political identity in terms of supplying the necessary resources of solidarity and social integration. Even though this position is not explicity stated by Benedict Anderson, it is apparent that his position is broadly favourable to nationalism, which he does not see as primarily based on xenophobia but on a cultural kind of patriotism. Anthony Smith is more vocal in his defence of nationalism as a liberal view of the world and the only realistic alternative to cosmopolitanism, which he sees as unable to defend autonomy, collective identity and freedom.

In sum, liberals, ranging from communitarian liberals to left-leaning liberalism, believe that nationalism can be modified to essentially liberal virtues, such as respect for the individual, tolerance of diversity, human autonomy and freedom. Nationalism, as a culturally based patriotism, provides the liberal polity with the basic ingredients for belonging, solidarity and identity.

cosmopolitanism

In recent times the cosmopolitan position has become a highly articulated stance on nationalism.[11] The cosmopolitan argument differs from earlier kinds of internationalism in its advocation of a strong antipathy not only to ethnic, separatist nationalism but to the very idea of the nation-state, which is no longer seen as a viable entity. This is a contrast to the older discussion about world society or international society, which tended to presuppose a world divided into nation-states seeking only a stronger commitment to an international normative framework. Internationalism thus tended to be primarily based on the overriding belief in international law. The cosmopolitan perspective has accompanied the enhanced momentum of globalization and in one of its most extreme forms is the view that politics today is no longer constrained by the nation-state. This new cosmopolitanism has been partly based on a rereading of Kant, despite the fact that Kantian cosmopolitanism was closer to internationalism.[12] With regard to nationalism, cosmopolitans look to a moral universalism that transcends all forms of particularism, and thus agree with the famous words of Samuel Johnson that 'patriotism is the last refuge of scoundrels' (Johnson, 1934, p. 348). Nationalism is regarded by most proponents of cosmopolitanism as irredeemable and must be rejected (see Kateb, 2000).

180

In a much discussed essay, Martha Nussbaum states the cosmopolitan argument as one that is directly opposed to Rorty's attempt to rescue patriotism from nationalism (Nussbaum, 1996).[13] In her view patriotic pride is both morally dangerous and ultimately subversive of some of the more worthy goals of patriotism, such as equality and justice. These goals, she argues, would be better served by the cosmopolitan ideal of allegiance to the worldwide community of human beings. This argument opposes, too, the weak concession that liberal nationalists make to cosmopolitanism in the form of a commitment to human rights. For Nussbaum it is not sufficient to base national education on the values of nationality with a token commitment to human rights. The alternative she proposes is a framework of values based on a commitment to world citizenship. Four arguments recommending it are as follows:

- cosmopolitan education is a basis for self-knowledge, for the more we know about others the more we know about ourselves
- whether we like it or not the nation-state cannot solve all the problems facing it, especially those relating to ecology, population growth and food supply

- moral obligations to peoples outside the nation-state are equally real and compelling, for territorial boundaries do not constrain democracy and morality
- patriotic values can be dangerously close to jingoism.

In a debate over Nussbaum's cosmopolitan plea, critics representing a wide variety of positions have rejoined. Benjamin Barber and Charles Taylor, for instance, have argued against her version of cosmopolitanism that it sets up too strong an opposition to patriotism, which is more reconcilable to cosmopolitanism than she allows.[14] Taylor – who as we have seen stands for a liberal patriotism – argues that patriotism is an essential part of the modern world and cosmopolitanism alone is insufficient. The question of patriotism thus presents a problem. Is there any kind of patriotism that can be defended from a cosmopolitan perspective? Taylor's position does not give much room for cosmopolitanism and Nussbaum is uncompromising in her rejection of nationalism. Of relevance in this context is Habermas's notion of constitutional patriotism.[15] For Habermas the only viable form of national identity is one that is based on an identification with the principles of the constitution. Originally put forward in the context of debates about the future of German national identity, but relevant to all modern societies, Habermas argues that German national identity has been irreversibly tainted since the Holocaust. Moreover, in the context of multicultural societies, political identity cannot be based on any single ethnic, cultural identity. National identity cannot resist the reflexivity and self-confrontation that is now irreversibly integral to all aspects of life. In this sense, then, a kind of patriotism that is founded on the principles of the constitution is all that is left of collective, national identities. In Habermas's formulation, constitutional patriotism is a minimal kind of national identity.

Most of the major arguments for cosmopolitan alternatives to nationalism are ultimately based on moral universalism. In other words, cosmopolitanism is a moral necessity and is, moreover, as much a part of the modern world as nationalism. This is a position that has been very forcibly stated by philosophers such as Karl-Otto Apel and Jürgen Habermas. These arguments, from the point of view of moral universalism, (see Apel, 2000) are supported by sociological conceptions of cosmopolitanism, with notable contributions by Ulrich Beck (2000), Manuel Castells (1996), Bryan Turner (2000) and John Urry (2000). These positions entail a view of cosmopolitanism as deeply rooted in processes of globalization, which is always more than homogeneous standardization but involves a wide range of responses from the lifeworld. The growing salience of human rights, humanitarianism, ecological politics, global civil society, are all evidence of a real dimension to cosmopolitanism. This brings us to the fourth alternative to nationalism: the postmodern argument.

postmodern transnationalism

One of the most persuasive conceptions of postnationalism is based on the assumption that nationalism and cosmopolitanism are deeply implicated in each other's projects. Liberal nationalism stresses the flexibility of nationalism while being largely defensive of nationalism as a positive force in the world and an essential foundation for cosmopolitanism, which can only be a secondary value. Internationalism, too, makes certain assumptions about the centrality of the nation-state, while being largely critical of radical, secessionist nationalism. Cosmopolitans are more explicit in their critique of both nationalism and the nation-state. A broad range of quite different approaches can be grouped under the heading 'postmodern transnationalism'. This is the view that neither nationalism nor cosmopolitanism contains coherent fully formed identities, but are highly fragmented and hybrid identities. Many forms of national consciousness have emerged out of polyethnic contexts. This was a position that was stated by William McNeil of an earlier period in the history of European societies (McNeil, 1986). He argued that polyethnicity was the norm in history and only with the arrival of the nation-state was this reversed. Reacting against the view that in fact the identities that did evolve in the last 200 years were predominantly primordial and exclusivist, several theorists have emphasized the hybrid nature of nationalism. Thus rather than looking beyond nationalism for a cosmopolitan future, these figures see *within* nationalism the signs of a more reflexive and hybrid consciousness but one which cannot be understood as liberal patriotism.

Homi Bhabha in *Nation and Narration* has outlined an influential conception of postmodern nationalism as a hybrid or 'Janus-faced' construction (Bhabha, 1990). The nation is a narrative that has an imaginary component to it; it is a discursive construction that does not exist outside language. Nations, like all of culture, are not unified or unitary in relation to themselves. He argues the problem of self/other, inside/outside must always be seen as a process of hybridity, incorporating new peoples and different kinds of meanings. This postcolonial view of the nation as contested applies some of the central ideas in post-structuralist thought to nationalism, namely the view that the experience of difference underlies all kinds of identity, including national identity. This means that the nation is always transgressing boundaries, for the self must always define itself in relation to an other. But this other is becoming less subject to narratives of closure today. Immigrants, women, colonial peoples, who have been traditionally marginalized in the discourse of the nation, are playing a bigger role in defining the nation today and as a result the nation is becoming more and more contested. The feminization of the nation – recodifications of the nation by migrant women – runs counter to earlier male constructions of women as the docile voice of the nation (see Anthias and Yuval-Davis, 1989; Yuval-Davis, 1997). Paul Gilroy in *The Black Atlantic* argues that the black diaspora is based on a negotiated identity that is formed out of the experience of exclusion and resistance (Gilroy, 1993). Diasporic identities are not purely negative conditions, or shaped entirely by the dominant culture, its elites as well as publics, but instead are dynamic. Black consciousness, he argues, is transnational, drawing from the Caribbean, the United States, Africa and Britain. In other words, many forms of consciousness are formed in the context of social relations that are located in transnationalized and marginalized contexts. This attempt to rewrite the history of national and ethnic consciousness in terms of marginal voices is a familiar theme in postcolonial theory (see Spivak, 1987). To reveal how the nation can be reread in terms of hidden histories involves a deconstructive approach, which also has a constructive moment in bringing to consciousness subaltern voices. In another sense it is an attempt 'to rescue history from the nation' (Duara, 1995).

Postcolonial, Derridean perspectives on nationalism are particularly popular in Ireland in interpretations of neo-nationalism. As is illustrated in the work of Richard Kearney (1988, 1997) and Declan Kiberd (1995) a new Irish postnationalism has come into existence with the demise of the older forms of nationalism.[16] It is characterized by a shift in the nation code from the state to culture and the rediscovery of marginality as legitimate difference and the self as hybrid.

183

In this view, then, nationalism is never entirely a fabrication of elites, but the site of many different kinds of resistances, in particular those that emanate from the margin. Cosmopolitanism, too, must be reinterpreted in light of this alternative conception of diasporic nationalisms. New conceptions of cosmopolitanism as rooted in concrete contexts, reject the Enlightenment, Kantian tradition of a decontextualized cosmopolitanism (Appadurai, 1993; Cheah and Robbins, 1998; Joseph, 1999; Ong, 1997). In these new works, the emphasis is on transnational, postcolonial cosmopolitanism in which, under the conditions of globalization, national identities are reconstituted as sites of resistance. Like nations, cosmopolitanism becomes pluralized and instead of being founded on an ideal of unattachment, the new cosmopolitanism is a rooted one.

CONCLUSION

The four conceptions of postnationalism discussed in this chapter offer different responses to the limits of nationalism and the challenges of cosmopolitanism. It is evident that the different approaches have much in common. Yet, the differences are striking, not least due to the different intellectual traditions but also quite different political concerns. Nevertheless, in terms of an overall assessment of the current status of nationalism, our contention is that for cosmopolitanism to be a viable option it will have to address the possibility of 'nations without nationalism', to use the title of a book by Julia Kristeva (1993). This means that cosmopolitanism will have to reconcile itself with an understanding of political community based on belonging, solidarity and plurality. In this sense, a self-limiting conception of the nation is not incompatible with the horizons of cosmopolitanism, and there are many examples of national debates on nationhood that point towards a certain cosmopolitanism.

In Germany, for instance, there is considerable interest in postnationalism, ranging from a federal European state to the cosmopolitan notion of constitutional patriotism as advocated by Habermas (Habermas, 1989c, 1994, 2001). In March 2001 the German parliament devoted a special session to debating the possibility of patriotism beyond nationalism.[17] For many, patriotism – as love of one's country – is admissable but 'national pride' is not, for it is too suggestive of chauvinism and xenophobic sentiments. In the UK, British identity has been considerably weakened in recent years. Since the creation of a Scottish parliament, a Welsh Assembly and the reestablishment of a devolved parliament in Northern Ireland, some of the presuppositions of British national identity derived from parliamentary sovereignty have been eroded. The growing debate about the monarchy, the reform of the House of Lords, the race debate, and the unavoidable question of European integration have made national consciousness increasingly more uncertain. Other countries have gone further in pluralism. The Swedish Constitution, for example, now recognizes the Swedish ethnicity to be only one and of equal status with Finnish, Muslim, Sami and other ethnicities.

In view, then, of the obvious reality of cosmopolitanism, nationalism cannot claim a privileged role in defining national identity. The assumption that a society can have only a single, fundamental identity must be rejected. Yet, this assumption is central to much of the specialist literature on nationalism, as in the work of Greenfeld (1992), Smith (1995), Miller (1995) and Canovan (1996). Greenfeld (1992, 1996) provides the most extreme and ultimately untenable formulation of the viewpoint exhibited also by Smith, Miller and Canovan, whatever their internal differences, when she asserts that while national identity is one among many possible identities in the modern world such as class, religious, gendered, linguistic and territorial, she counts it as the 'fundamental identity', the one 'that is believed to define the very essence of the individual, which the other identities may modify but slightly, and to which they are consequently considered secondary' (1996, p. 10). The problem with this argument is not that national identity does not have extensive capacity to do what Greenfeld says it does, mould personal identity, but it does not have the kind of hegemony over other identities that she, Canovan and Miller think it has. This argument fundamentally confuses the capacity of a territorial identity to separate individuals by membership of a political community and its internal capacity within such a community to dominate other identities and learning processes to the extent that Greenfeld can use a term like 'slightly' to designate their contribution to personal identities. Are we then to think of class habitus, gendered experience or religious profession as only 'slightly' influencing personal identity in modern societies? These authors do not consider in any sustained way the rival claims of other collective identities to offer normative foundations for social integration. Without doing so, it is hard to see how normative claims about the centrality of the nation to modern democracy, and still less to a wider conception of the collective good, can be sustained. It is also difficult to reconcile these assumptions with the obvious pluralism in much of the world.

Consideration of the relationship between the collective identities generated by nationalism and other forms of collective identity opens the way to placing the theoretical argument advanced in this book in a substantive, contemporary context. The emphasis throughout this book is that nationalism must be conceived in its relation to other key aspects of modernity and other modern forms of collective identity. The essence of the contemporary cosmopolitan and postnational critique of nationalism is that these wider identities have gained in potency. In particular, non-nationalist identities associated with multicultural societies, transnational institutions, and the rise of an international civil society have undoubtedly become more prominent. While each of these developments must be examined on its own merits, they do appear to form part of a general movement leading to a qualification of the hegemony of the nation-state. This is animated by a combination of resigned realism over what it has historically been unable to achieve, above all, the permanent civilization of the principle of nationality, and by active normative critique of why it has been unable to do so. However, at least some variations on the defence of the nation-state remain on strong ground when they argue that many of the forms that cosmopolitan takes in the real world, so to speak, including globalization and much of the telos of the European transnational project, involves the endangerment of important gains already institutionalized within national civil societies, such as social welfarism. A critical point raised in this connection is that globalization diminishes the cultural, economic and social automony of not only nations but also whole regions of the world, leading to a kind of hegemony of systems over varied, local practices, especially manifested in the systematic production and diffusion of commodities of all kinds. The kind of disembedded, diffuse systemic power represented in the flow of commodities and in the interests of their producers is not respectful of the kinds of normative commitment that historically underpin the more successful nation-states. Neither, so the argument goes, is it likely to offer much succour to new normative claims such as those articulated through the projects of the new social movements.

Where does this leave cosmopolitanism as a viable alternative to nationalism and patriotism? Against the proponents of liberal patriotism, we contend that nationalism should have no more priority than cosmopolitanism, which is gaining in credibility as a normative antidote to destructive nationalism. With Habermas, we argue that all identities – including ethnic, gender, nationalist, religious – must be subject to critical and reflexive self-confrontation; indeed, far from being remnants of pre-modern consciousness, even the most anti-modern movements are products of modern intellectualization and rationalization. However, the same contextualization must be applied to cosmopolitanism, which has shed its origins in the habitus of pre-industrial elites and has entered modern forms of life. Neither the traditional internationalist perspective nor the pure cosmopolitan stance offers adequate rejoinders to nationalism. In this we accept some of the critical arguments against cosmopolitanism, which needs to be more sharply distinguished from globalization (Brennan, 1997, 2001; Zolo, 1997).

The fourth position, postmodern transnationalism, while offering alternatives that appear to be excluded from the other stances, suffers from too much focus on marginality, transnational mobility and on identity as flexible and hybrid. Accepting that identity is far from fixed and primordially rooted in historical heritage and memory or in the designs of elites, but is always contextually constructed and open to contestation, it remains the case that some forms of identity are a good deal more stable than the postmodern accounts suggest. This is the essence of the twofold theoretical account of collective identity presented in this book, as being both innovative and susceptible to institutionalization and stabilization. Postmodern sensibilities, and the various symbolic and rational choice strategies that take up from the basic fact of such fluidization, make a contribution to clarifying both the stakes and dynamics of change in a period in which the claims to hegemony of certain kinds of identity are more and more contested. However, by way of contrast, identity patterns that at one period appear impossibly conflictual and opposing have also shown great capacity to resolve the difference in the interests of a workable institutional order that offers enough if not all of what competing identities aspire to (Smelser and Alexander, 1999).

The recent increase in the incidence of nationalism in the contemporary period does not in fact indicate a return to nationalism as dominant in the organization of territories and identities. The return to nationalism is actually ambivalent about the future of nationalism in that it indicates that nationalism as an institutional principle must be radically relativized by other principles that respect difference within and without the nation. We would venture to say, therefore, that cosmopolitanism is in a less defensive position today than is nationalism, whose normative modes of legitimation are becoming more incompatible with the world in which it has to live.

This defence of cosmpolitanism does not mean the currently absurd idea that nations and nationalism might be somehow transcended and rendered irrelevant. Rather it is a call for balanced argumentation about the strengths and weaknesses of nationalism and competing cultural and territorial forms. This will affect both those within established and prosperous nation-states, who argue from strength, and those less fortunate who are excluded by virtue of their territorial status from possession of many of the collective goods of modernity or, worse still, are embroiled in the terrible destruction, dislocation and death caused by many contemporary nationalist conflicts. In this argument, nationalism, which for better or worse has done much to shape the modern world, must and will lose a great deal of its contemporary power.

NOTES

1 See Friese (2002).

2 For a fuller account see Delanty (2000b).

3 In Hobsbawm's review of Nairn's well-known book, *The Break-Up of Britain*, this assumption is made explicit (Hobsbawm, 1977).

4 For a full account of the relationship between internationalism and nationalism, see Mayall (1990).

5 On patriotism, see Dietz (1989) and Berns (2001).

6 For instance, Scruton (1990).

7 See Kymlicka (1989, 1995) and Kymlicka and Straehle (1999).

8 Originally an article in the *New York Times*, 13 February 1994.

9 See also Miller (1993, 1995).

10 Kedourie (1994), Minogue (1967), Gellner (1983).

11 See Archibugi and Held (1995), Archibugi et al. (1998), Beck (2000), Beitz (1999), Bohman and Lutz-Bachmann (1997), Held (1995), Hill (2000), Jones (1999), Pogge (1992).

12 For a contemporary interpretation, see Bohman and Lutz-Bachmann (1997).

13 Originally published in the *Boston Review*, October–November, 1994.

14 These contributions are all to be found in Nussbaum (1996).

15 See Habermas (1994, 1996, 1998).

16 For a critical study of Irish cultural nationalism, see O'Mahony and Delanty (1998).

17 A special session of the *Bundestag*, 29 March 2001. See also Brunssen (2001).

references

Acton, Lord (1907) 'Nationality', in J. N. Figgis (ed.) *The History of Freedom and Other Essays*, London: Macmillan.

Ahmed, A. (1995) '"Ethnic cleansing": a metaphor for our time', *Ethnic and Racial Studies*, 18 (1): 1–25.

Alexander, J. C. (1982) 'Differentiation theory: problems and prospects', in J. Alexander and P. Colomy (eds) *Differentiation Theory and Social Change,* New York: Columbia University Press.

Alexander, J. (1992) 'Durkheim's problem and differentiation theory today', in H. Haferkamp and N. Smelser (eds) *Social Change and Modernity*, Berkeley: University of California Press.

Alexander, J. (1995) *Fin de Siècle Social Theory*, London: Verso.

Allum, P. (1995) *State and Society in Western Europe*, Cambridge: Polity.

Alter, P. (1989) *Nationalism*, London: Edward Arnold.

Anderson, B. (1983) *Imaginary Communities: Reflections on the Origin and Spread of Nationalism*, London: Verso.

Anthias, F. and N. Yuval-Davis (eds) (1989) *Woman-Nation-State*, London: Macmillan.

Apel, K.-O. (2000) 'Globalisation and the need for a universalistic ethic', *European Journal of Social Theory*, 3 (2): 137–55.

Appadurai, A. (1993) 'Patriotism and its futures', *Public Culture*, 5 (3): 411–29.

Archibugi, D. and Held, D. (eds) (1995) *Cosmopolitan Democracy*, Cambridge: Polity.

Archibugi, D., Held, D. and Kogler, M. (eds) (1998) *Re-Imagining Political Community: Studies in Cosmopolitan Democracy*, Cambridge: Polity.

Arendt, H. (1969) *On Violence*, New York: Harcourt Brace Jovanovich.

Armstrong, J. (1982) *Nations Before Nationalism*, Chapel Hill: University of North Carolina Press.

Arnason, J. (1990) 'Nationalism, globalization and modernity', in M. Featherstone (ed.) *Global Culture*, London: Sage.

Arnason, J. (1993) *The Future that Failed: Origins and Destinies of the Soviet Model*, London: Routledge.

Arnason, J. (1997) *Social Theory and Japanese Experience: The Dual Civilization*, London: Kegan Paul International.

Aron, R. (1968) *Progress and Disillusion: The Dialectics of Modern Society*, London: Pall Mall.

Arrighi, G., Hopkins, T. and Wallerstein, I. (1989) *Antisystemic Movements*, London: Verso.

Badie, B. and Birnbaum, P. (1981) *Sociology of the State*, Chicago: University of Chicago Press.

Barber, B. (1996) *Jihad vs. McWorld*, New York: Ballantine Press.

Barkin, J. and Cronin, B. (1994) 'The state and the nation: changing norms and the rules of sovereignty in international relations,' *International Organization*, 48 (1): 107–30.

Barth, F. (1969) *Ethnic Groups and Boundaries*, Boston: Little Brown.

Baudelaire, C. (1964) 'The painter of modern life', in *The Painter of Modern Life and Other Essays*, London: Phaidon.

Bauman, Z. (1987) *Legislators and Interpreters: On Modernity, Postmodernity and Intellectuals*, Cambridge: Polity.

Bauman, Z. (1989) *Modernity and the Holocaust*, Cambridge: Polity.

Bauman, Z. (1992) 'Soil, blood and identity', *Sociological Review*, 40: 675–701.

Beck, U. (1994) *Ecological Enlightenment: Essays on the Politics of Risk*, New York: Humanities Press.

Beck, U. (2000) *What is Globalization?*, Cambridge: Polity.

Beissenger, M. R. (1996) 'How nationalisms spread: Eastern Europe adrift the tides and cycles of nationalist contention', *Social Research*, 63 (1): 97–147.

Beissenger, M. R. (1998) 'Nationalisms that bark and nationalisms that bite: Ernest Gellner and the substantiation of nations', in J. Hall (ed.) *The State of the Nation: Ernest Gellner and the Theory of Nationalism*, Cambridge: Cambridge University Press.

Beitz, C. (1999) 'Social and cosmopolitan liberalism', *International Affairs*, 75 (3): 515–29.

Berman, M. (1982) *All That is Solid Melts into Air*, New York: Simon & Schuster.

Berns, W. (2001) *Making Patriots*, Chicago: University of Chicago Press.

Bendix, R. (1964) *Nation-Building and Citizenship*, New York: John Wiley.

Benjamin, W. (1978) 'Critique of violence', *Reflections: Essays, Aphorisms, Autobiographical Writings*, New York: Harcourt Brace Jovanovich.

Bertilsson, M. (2000) 'From elite to mass education – what is next?', in C. Lindqvist and L.-L. Wallenius (eds) *Globalization and its Impact: On Chinese and Swedish Society*, Stockholm: Forskningradsnämnden.

Betz, H.-G. (1994) *Radical Right-Wing Populism in Western Europe*, London: Macmillan.

Bhabha, H. (1990) *Nation and Narration*, London: Routledge.

Billig, M. (1995) *Banal Nationalism*, London: Sage.

Bloch, M. (1964) *Feudal Society*, vol. 2, Chicago: Chicago University Press.

Blok, A. (1998) 'The narcissism of minor differences', *European Journal of Social Theory*, 1 (1): 33–56.

Bohman, J. and Lutz-Bachmann, M. (eds) (1997) *Perpetual Peace: Essays on Kant's Cosmopolitan Ideal*, Cambridge, MA: MIT Press.

Bourdieu, P. (1977) *Outline of a Theory of Practice*, Cambridge: Cambridge University Press.

Bourdieu, P. (1990) *The Logic of Practice*, Cambridge: Polity.

Bourdieu, P. and Passeron, J.-C. (1977) *Reproduction in Education, Society and Culture*, London: Sage.

Brand, K.-W. (1992) 'National movements in Europe and social movement theory'. Paper delivered to the first European Conference on Social Movements, East European Movements and Social Movement Theory, Berlin.

Brass, P. R. (1977) 'A reply to Francis Robinson', *Journal of Commonwealth and Comparative Politics*, 15 (3): 230–4.

Brass, P. R. (1979) 'Elite groups, symbol manipulation and ethnic identity among the Muslims of South-East Asia', in D. Taylor and M. Yapp (eds) *Political Identity in South Asia*, London: Curzon.

Brass, P. R. (ed.) (1985) *Ethnic Groups and the State*, London: Croom Held.

Brass, P. R. (1991) *Ethnicity and Nationalism: Theory and Comparison*, New Delhi: Sage.

Brennan, T. (1997) *At Home in the World: Cosmopolitanism Now*, Cambridge, MA: Harvard University Press.

Brennan, T. (2001) 'Cosmopolitanism and internationalism', *New Left Review*, 7, Jan/Feb: 75–84.

Breuilly, J. (1982) *Nationalism and the State*, Manchester: Manchester University Press.

Brint, S. (1994) 'Sociological analysis of political culture: an introduction and assessment', in F. Weil (ed.) *Research on Democracy and Society*, vol. 2, *Political Culture and Political Structure, Theoretical and Empirical Studies*, Greenwich, CT: JAI Press.

Brubaker, R. (1996) *Nationalism Reframed*, Cambridge: Cambridge University Press.

Brubaker, R. (1998) 'Myths and misconceptions in the study of nationalism', in J. Hall (ed.) *The State of the Nation: Ernest Gellner and the Theory of Nationalism*, Cambridge: Cambridge University Press.

Brunssen, F. (2001) 'Das neue Selbstverständnis der Berliner Republik', *Aus Politik und Zeitgeschichte*, 12 January.

Bull, H. (1977) *The Anarchical Society*, London: Macmillan.

Calhoun, C. (1995) *Critical Social Theory*, Oxford: Blackwell.

Calhoun, C. (1997) *Nationalism*, Buckingham: Open University Press.

Calhoun, C. (ed.) (1992) *Habermas and the Public Sphere*, Cambridge, MA: MIT Press.

Campbell, D. and Dillion, M. (eds) (1993) *The Political Subject of Violence*, Manchester: Manchester University Press.

Canovan, M. (1996) *Nationhood and Political Theory*, Cheltenham: Edward Elgar.

Castells, M. (1996) *The Rise of the Network Society*, vol. 2, *The Information Age*, Oxford: Blackwell.

Castells, M. (1997) *The Power of Identity*, vol. 2, *The Information Age*, Oxford: Blackwell.

Castoriadis, C. (1987) *The Imaginary Institution of Society*, Cambridge: Polity.

Cheah, P. and Robbins, B. (eds) (1998) *Cosmopolitics: Thinking and Feeling Beyond the Nation*, Minneapolis: Minnesota Press.

Chirot, D. (1991) *The Crisis of Leninism and the Decline of the Left: The Revolution of 1989*, Seattle: University of Washington Press.

Cohen, S. J. (1999) *Politics Without a Past: The Absence of History in Postcommunist Nationalism*, Durham, NJ: Duke University Press.

Cohen, S. (2001) *States of Denial: Knowing about Atrocities and Suffering*, Cambridge: Polity.

Colley, L. (1992) *Britons: Forging the Nation, 1707–1837*, New Haven: Yale University Press.

Connor, W. (1993) 'From tribe to nation', *History of European Ideas*, 13 (1/2): 5–18.

Corrigan, P. and Sayer, D. (1985) *The Great Arch: English State Formation as a Cultural Formation*, Oxford: Blackwell.

Coser, L. (1956) *The Functions of Social Conflict*, New York: Free Press.

Coulton, G. (1933) 'Nationalism in the Middle Ages', *Cambridge History Journal*, 5, 14–40.

Dahl, G. (1999) *Radical Conservatism and the Future of Politics*, London: Sage.

Dann, O. (ed.) (1986) *Nationalismus in vorindustrieller Zeit*, Munich: R. Oldenburg.

Delanty, G. (1995) *Inventing Europe: Idea, Identity, Reality*, London, Macmillan.

Delanty, G. (1999) *Social Theory in a Changing World: Conceptions of Modernity*, Cambridge: Polity.

Delanty, G. (2000a) *Modernity and Postmodernity: Knowledge, Power, and the Self*, London: Sage.

Delanty, G. (2000b) *Citizenship in a Global Age: Culture, Society and Politics*, Buckingham: Open University Press.

Delanty, G. (2000c) 'Nationalism', in G. Ritzer and B. Smart (eds) *Handbook of Social Theory*, London: Sage.

Delanty, G. (2000d) 'The resurgence of the city: the spaces of European integation', in E. Isin (ed.) *The Politics and the City*, London: Routledge.

Delanty, G. (2001a) *Challenging Knowledge: The University in the Knowledge Society*, Buckingham: Open University Press.

Delanty, G. (2001b) 'Cosmopolitanism and violence: the limits of global civil society', *European Journal of Social Theory*, 4 (1): 51–42.

Delanty, G. (2002b) 'The university and higher education', in C. Calhoun, C. Rojek and B. Turner (eds) *Handbook of International Sociology*, London: Sage.

Delanty, G. (2002c) 'Consumption, modernity and Japanese cultural identity: the limits of Americanization?' in U. Beck, N. Sznaider and R. Winter (eds) *Global America: The Cultural Consequences of Globalization*, Liverpool: Liverpool University Press.

Delanty, G. (2002d) 'The persistence of nationalism', in G. Delanty and E. Isin (eds) *Handbook of Historical Sociology*, London: Sage.

Delanty, G. (2002e) 'The university and modernity: a history of the present', in K. Robins and F. Webster (eds) *The Virtual University? Information, Markets and Management*, Oxford: Oxford University Press.

Delanty, G., Friese, H. and Wagner, P. (eds) (2001) 'War and social theory: reflections after Kosovo', special issue of *European Journal of Social Theory*, 4 (1).

Denitch, B. (1996) 'National identity, politics and democracy', *Social Science Information*, 35 (3): 459–83.

Derrida, J. (1990) 'Force of law: the "mystical foundations of authority"', *Carduzo Law Review*, 11 (919): 927–45.

Deutsch, K. (1953) *Nationalism and Social Communication*, Cambridge, MA: MIT Press.

Deutsch, K. (1969) *Nationalism and its Alternatives*, New York: Knopf.

Diaz-Andreu, M. and Champion, T. (eds) (1996) *Nationalism and Archaeology in Europe*, London: UCL Press.

Dietz, M. (1989) 'Patriotism', in T. Ball, J. Farr and R. Hanson (eds) *Political Innovation and Conceptual Change*, Cambridge: Cambridge University Press.

Dodd, N. (1999) *Social Theory and Modernity*, Cambridge: Polity.

Dominguez, J. M. (1999) 'Evolution, history and collective subjectivity', *Current Sociology*, 47 (3): 1–34.

Duara, P. (1995) *Rescuing History from the Nation: Questioning Narratives of Modern China*, Chicago: University of Chicago Press.

Durkheim, E. (1915) *The Elementary Forms of the Religious Life*, London: Routledge & Kegan Paul.

Eder, K. (1985) *Geschichte als Lernprozess? Zur Pathogenese politischer Modernität in Deutschland*, Frankfurt: Suhrkamp.

Eder, K. (1993) *The New Politics of Class: Social Movements and Cultural Dymamics in Advanced Industrial Societies*, London: Sage.

Eisenstadt, S. N. (ed.) (1986) *The Origins and Diversity of the Axial Age Civilizations*, New York: SUNY Press.

Eisenstadt, S. N. (1990) 'Modes of structural differentiation, elite structures and cultural vision', in J. Alexander and P. Colomy (eds) *Differentiation Theory and Social Change*, New York: Columbia University Press.

Eisenstadt, S. N. (1992) 'A re-appraisal of theories of social change and modernization', in H. Haferkamp and N. Smelser (eds) *Social Change and Modernity*, Berkeley: University of California Press.

Eisenstadt, S. N. (1995a) *Power, Trust and Meaning*, Chicago: University of Chicago Press.

Eisenstadt, S. N. (1995b) *Japanese Civilization: A Comparative View*, Chicago: University of Chicago Press.

Eisenstadt, S. N. (1998) 'The construction of collective identities', *European Journal of Social Theory*, 1 (2): 229–54.

Eisenstadt, S. N. (1999a) *Paradoxes of Modernity, Fragility, Continuity and Change*, Baltimore: Johns Hopkins University Press.

Eisenstadt, S. N. (1999b) *Fundamentalism, Sectarianism and Revolution: The Jacobin Dimension of Modernity*, Cambridge: Cambridge University Press.

Eisenstadt, S. N. (2000a) 'The civilizational dimension in sociological analysis', *Thesis Eleven*, 62, 1–21.

Eisenstadt, S. N. (2000b) *Die Vielfalt der Moderne*, Weilerswist: Velbrück Wissenschaft.

Eisenstadt, S. N. and Giesen, B. (1995) 'The construction of collective identity codes', *European Journal of Sociology*, 26 (1): 72–102.

Eisenstadt, S. N., Schluchter, W. and Wittrock, B. (eds) (2000) *Public Spheres and Collective Identities*, New Brunswick, NJ: Transaction Press.

Elias, N. (1978) *The Civilizing Process*, vol. 1, *The History of Manners*, New York: Pantheon.

Elias, N. (1982) *The Civilizing Process*, vol. 1, *State Formation and Civilization*, Oxford: Blackwell.

Elias, N. (1992) *Studien über die Deutschen*, Frankfurt: Suhrkamp.

Elshtain, J. (ed.) (1992) *Just War Theory*, Oxford: Blackwell.

Enzensberger, H. (1994) *Civil War*, London: Granta.

Evans, M. (1996) 'Languages of racism within contemporary Europe', in *Nation and Identity in Contemporary Europe*, London: Routledge.

Falter, J. and Klein, M. (1996) 'The mass basis of the extreme right in contemporary Europe in a comparative perspective', in *Research on Democracy and Society*, vol. 3: 41–61.

Fanon, F. (1966) *The Wretched of the Earth*, New York: Grove.

Featherstone, M., Lash, S. and Robertson, R. (eds) (1995) *Global Modernities*, London: Routledge.

Febrve, R. (2000) *The Demoralisation of Western Culture: Social Theory and the Dilemmas of Modern Living*, New York: Continuum.

Fichte, J. G. (1922) *Addresses to the German Nation*, Chicago: Open Court.

Flora, P., Kuhnle, S. and Urwin, D. (eds) (1999) *State Formation, Nation-Building and Mass Politics in Europe: The Theory of Stein Rokkan*, Oxford: Oxford University Press.

Forde, S. L. Johnson and Murray, A. (eds) (1995) *Concepts of National Identity in the Middle Ages*, Leeds: University of Leeds Press.

Foucault, M. (1979) 'Governmentality', *Ideology and Consciousness*, 6: 5–12.

Foucault, M. (1980) *Power/Knowledge: Collected Interviews and Other Essays, 1972–1977*, edited by Colin Gordon, Brighton: Harvester.

Freud, S. (1985) 'Why war?', *Sigmund Freud: Civilization, Society and Religion*, London: Penguin.

Friedman, J. (1994) *Cultural Identity and Global Process*, London: Sage.

Friese, H. (ed.) (2002) *Identities*, Providence, RI: Berghahn.

Frisby, D. (1986) *Fragments of Modernity: Theories of Modernity in the Work of Simmel, Kracauer and Benjamin*, Cambridge, MA: MIT Press.

Galtung, J. (1990) 'Cultural violence', *Journal of Peace Research*, 27 (3): 291–305.

Gamson, W. (1995) 'Hiroshima, the Holocaust, and the politics of exclusion', *American Sociological Review*, 60: 1–20.

Gellner, E. (1964) *Thought and Change*, London: Weidenfeld & Nicholson.

Gellner, E. (1983) *Nations and Nationalism*, Oxford: Blackwell.

Gellner, E. (1987) *Culture, Identity and Politics*, Cambridge: Cambridge University Press.

Gellner, E. (1994) *Encounters with Nationalism*, Oxford: Blackwell.

Gellner, E. (1998) *Language and Solitude: Wittgenstein, Malinowski and the Habsburg Dilemma*, Cambridge: Cambridge University Press.

Giddens, A. (1984) *The Constitution of Society: Outline of a Theory of Structuration*, Cambridge: Polity.

Giddens, A. (1985) *The Nation-State and Violence*, Cambridge: Polity.

Giesen, B. (1998) *Intellectuals and the Nation*, Cambridge: Cambridge University Press.

Gilroy, P. (1993) *The Black Atlantic: Modernity and its Double-Consciousness*, Cambridge, MA: Harvard University Press.

Girard, R. (1981) *Violence and the Sacred*, Baltimore: Johns Hopkins University Press.

Goody, J. (2001) 'Bitter icons', *New Left Review*, 7 Jan/Feb: 5–15.

Gorski, P. (2000) 'The mosaic moment: an early modernist critique of modernist theories of nationalism', *American Journal of Sociology*, 105 (5): 1428–68.

Greenfeld, L. (1992) *Nationalism: Five Roads to Modernity*, Cambridge, MA: Harvard University Press.

Greenfeld, L. (1996) 'Nationalism and modernity', *Social Research*, 63 (1): 3–41.

Greenfeld, L. and Chirot, D. (1994) 'Nationalism and aggression', *Theory and Society*, 23 (1): 79–130.

Gurr, T. R. (1993) 'Why minorities rebel: a global analysis of communal mobilization and conflict since 1945', *International Political Science Review,* 14: 161–201.

Habermas, J. (1984) *The Theory of Communicative Action,* vol. 1, *Reason and the Rationalization of Society,* London: Heinemann.

Habermas, J. (1987a) *The Theory of Communicative Action,* vol. 2, *Lifeworld and System: A Critique of Functionalist Reason,* Cambridge: Polity.

Habermas, J. (1987b) *The Philosophical Discourse of Modernity,* Cambridge, MA: MIT Press.

Habermas, J. (1989a) *The Structural Transformation of the Public Sphere,* Cambridge: Polity.

Habermas, J. (1989b) 'Modern and postmodern architecture', in *The New Conservatism: Cultural Criticism and the Historians' Debate,* Cambridge: Polity.

Habermas, J. (1989c) *The New Conservatism: Cultural Criticism and the Historians Debate,* Cambridge: Polity.

Habermas, J. (1991) 'Yet again, German identity – a unified nation of angry DM-Burghers', *New German Critique,* 12: 1–19.

Habermas, J. (1994) *The Past as Future,* Cambridge: Polity.

Habermas, J. (1996) *Between Facts and Norms: Contributions to a Discourse Theory of Law and Democracy,* Cambridge: Polity.

Habermas, J. (1998) *The Inclusion of the Other: Studies in Political Theory,* Cambridge, MA: MIT Press.

Habermas, J. (1999a) 'The European nation-state and the pressures of globalization', *New Left Review,* 235: 46–59.

Habermas, J. (1999b) 'The war in Kosovo: bestiality and humanity: a war on the border between legality and morality', *Constellations,* 6 (3): 263–72.

Habermas, J. (2001) *The Postnational Constellation,* Cambridge: Polity.

Hall, J. (1993) 'Nationalisms: classified and explained', *Daedalus,* 122 (3): 1–28.

Hall, J. (1998) *The State of the Nation: Ernst Gellner and the Theory of the Nation,* Cambridge: Cambridge University Press.

Hall, J. (2000) 'Globalization and nationalism', *Thesis Eleven,* 63, 63–79.

Hall, S. (1992) 'The question of cultural identity', in S. Hall, D. Held and T. McGrew (eds) *Modernity and its Futures,* Cambridge: Polity.

Hannan, M. (1979) 'The dynamics of ethnic boundaries in modern states', in M. Hannan and J. Mayer (eds) *National Development and the World System: Educational, Economic and Political Change 1950–1970,* Chicago: University of Chicago Press.

Hechter, M. (1975) *Internal Colonialism: The Celtic Fringe in British National Development, 1536–1966,* London: Routledge & Kegan Paul.

Hedetoft, U. (1995) *Signs of Nation: Studies in the Political Semiotics of Self and Other,* Aldershot: Dartmouth.

Hedetoft, U. (1999) 'The nation-state meets the world: national identities in the context of transnationality and cultural globalization', *European Journal of Social Theory,* 2 (1): 71–94.

Held, D. (1995) *Democracy and the Global Order: From the Modern State to Cosmopolitan Governance,* Cambridge: Polity.

Herder, J. G. (1969) *Herder and Social and Political Culture: A Selection of Texts,* Cambridge: Cambridge University Press.

Hill, J. (2000) *Becoming a Cosmopolitan,* New York: Rowman and Littlefield.

Hindess, B. (1998) 'Divide and rule: the international character of modern citizenship', *European Journal of Social Theory,* 1 (1): 57–70.

Hobsbawm, E. (1977) 'Reflections on "The break-up of Britain"', *New Left Review,* 105.

Hobsbawm, E. (1983a) 'Introduction: inventing traditions', in E. Hobsbawm and T. Ranger (eds) *The Invention of Tradition,* Cambridge: Cambridge University Press.

Hobsbawm, E. (1983b) 'Mass-producing traditions: Europe 1870–1914' in E. Hobsbawm and T. Ranger (eds) *The Invention of Tradition,* Cambridge: Cambridge University Press.

Hobsbawm, E. (1990) *Nations and Nationalism since 1780*, Cambridge: Cambridge University Press.

Hobsbawm, E. (1991) 'The perils of the new nationalism', *The Nation*, 4 November, pp. 555–6.

Hobsbawm, E. (1994) 'Barbarism: a user's guide', *New Left Review*, 206: 46–7.

Hobsbawm, E. (1996) 'Ethnicity and nationalism in Europe today', in G. Balakrishnan (ed.) *Mapping the Nation*, London: Verso.

Hobsbawm, E. and Ranger, T. (eds) (1983) *The Invention of Tradition*, Cambridge: Cambridge University Press.

Hockenos, P. (1993) *Free to Hate: The Right in Post-Communist Eastern Europe*, London: Routledge.

Holmes, D. (2000) *Integral Europe: Fast-Capitalism, Multiculturalism, Neofascism*, Princeton: Princeton University Press.

Hooson, D. (ed.) (1994) *Geography and National Identity*, Oxford: Blackwell.

Horkheimer, M. and Adorno, T. (1979) *Dialectic of Enlightenment*, London: Verso.

Horowitz, D. (1992) 'Irredentas and secessions: adjacent phenomena', *International Journal of Comparative Sociology*, 33 (1–2): 118–30.

Hroch, M. (1985) *Social Preconditions of National Revival in Europe*, Cambridge: Cambridge University Press.

Hroch, M. (1993) 'From national movement to the fully-formed nation', *New Left Review*, 198: 1–20.

Huizinga, J. (1959) *Men and Ideas: History, the Middle Ages, the Renaissance*, New York: Free Press.

Hunt, L. (1986) *Politics, Culture and Class in the French Revolution*, London: Methuen.

Huntington, S. (1996) *The Clash of Civilizations and the Remaking of World Order*, New York: Simon & Schuster.

Hutchinson, J. (1987) *The Dynamics of Cultural Nationalism: The Gaelic Revival and the Creation of the Irish Nation-State*, London: Allen & Unwin.

Hutchinson, J. (1994) *Modern Nationalism*, London: Fontana.

Ignatieff, M. (1994) *Blood and Belonging: Journeys into the New Nationalism*, London: Chatto & Windus.

Ignazi, P. (1997) 'New challenges: postmaterialism and the extreme right', in M. Rhodes, P. Heywood and V. Wright (eds) *Developments in West European Politics*, London: Macmillan.

Isin, E. and Wood, P. (1999) *Citizenship and Identity*, London: Sage.

James, P. (1996) *Nation Formation: Towards a Theory of Abstract Community*, London: Sage.

Jawardene, K. (1986) *Feminism and Nationalism in the Third World*, London: Zed.

Joas, H. (1996) *The Creativity of Action*, Cambridge: Polity.

Joas, H. (2000) *Kriege und Werte: Studien zur Gewaltgeschichte des 20. Jahrhunderts*, Weilerswist: Velbrück Wissenschaft.

Johnson, S. (1934) *Boswell's Life of Johnson*, vol. II, Oxford: Clarendon Press.

Johnston, H. (1994) 'New social movements and old regional nationalisms', in E. Larana, H. Johnson and J. Gusfield (eds) *New Social Movements: From Ideology to Identity*, Philadelphia: Temple University Press.

Jones, C. (1999) *Global Justice Defending Cosmopolitanism*, Oxford: Oxford University Press.

Joseph, M. (1999) *Nomadic Identities: The Performance of Citizenship*, Minneapolis: Minnesota University Press.

Jovic, D. (2001) 'The disintegration of Yugoslavia: a critical review of explanatory approaches', *European Journal of Social Theory*, 4 (1): 99–118.

Juergensmeyer, M. (1997) *New Cold War? Religious Nationalism Confronts the Secular State*, Berkeley: University of California Press.

Kahn, J. (2001) *Modernity and Exclusion*, London: Sage.

Kaldor, M. (1993) 'Yugoslavia and the new nationalism', *New Left Review*, 197: 96–112.

Kamenka, E. (1976) *Nationalism: The Nature and Evolution of an Idea*, London: Arnold.

Kamenka, E. (1993) 'Nationalism: ambigious legacies and contingent futures', *Political Studies*, XLI: 78–92.

Kant, I. (1970) 'Perpetual peace', in H. Reiss (ed.) *Kant: Political Writings*, Cambridge: Cambridge University Press.

Kaplan, R. (1992) *Balkan Ghosts: A Journey through History*, New York: St Martin's Press.

Kateb, G. (2000) 'Is patriotism a mistake?', *Social Research*, 67 (4): 901–24.

Kaya, I. (2000) 'Modernity and veiled women', *European Journal of Social Theory*, 3 (2): 195–214.

Keane, J. (1996) *Reflections on Violence*, London: Verso.

Kearney, R. (1997) *Postnationalist Ireland: Politics, Culture and Philosophy*, London: Routledge.

Kearney, R. (ed.) (1988) *The Irish Mind*, Dublin: Wolfhound Press.

Kedourie, E. (1994) *Nationalism*, 4th edn, Oxford: Blackwell.

Kepel, G. (1994) *The Revenge of God: The Resurgence of Islam, Christianity and Judaism in the Modern World*, Philadephia: Pennsylvania State University Press.

Kharkhordin, O. (2002) 'Nation, nature and natality: new dimensions of political action', *European Journal of Social Theory*, 5 (1): 459–78.

Kiberd, D. (1995) *Inventing Ireland*, London: Cape.

Kitschelt, H. (1986) 'Political opportunity structures and political protest', *British Journal of Sociology*, 16: 57–85.

Kitschelt, H. (1995) *The Radical Right in Western Europe: A Comparative Analysis*, Ann Arbor: University of Michigan Press.

Kohl, P. and Fawcett, C. (1995) *Nationalism, Politics, and the Practice of Archaeology*, Cambridge: Cambridge University Press.

Kohn, H. (1944) *The Idea of Nationalism*, New York: Macmillan.

Kohn, H. (1955) *Nationalism: Its Meaning and History*, Princeton: Van Nostrand.

Koopmans, R. (1996) 'Explaining the rise of racist and extremme right violence in Western Europe: grievances or opportunities?', *European Journal of Political Research*, 30: 185–216.

Koopmans, R. (1997) 'Dynamics of repression and mobilization: the German extreme right in the 1990s', *Mobilization*, 2: 149–64.

Kramer, M. (1993) 'Arab nationalism: mistaken identity', *Daedalus*, 122 (3): 171–206.

Kristeva, J. (1993) *Nations without Nationalism*, New York: Columbia University Press.

Kymlicka, W. (1989) *Liberalism, Community and Culture*, Oxford: Clarendon.

Kymlicka, W. (1995) *Multicultural Citizenship: A Liberal Theory of Minority Rights*, Oxford: Clarendon.

Kymlicka, W. and Straehle, C. (1999) 'Cosmopolitanism, nation-states, and minority nationalism: a critical review of recent literature', *European Journal of Philosophy*, 7 (1): 65–88.

Laitin, D. (1995) 'National revivals and violence', *European Journal of Sociology*, 36 (1): 3–43.

Law, J. (1994) *Organized Modernity*, Oxford: Blackwell.

Leach, N. (ed.) (1999) *Architecture and Revolution: Contemporary Perspectives on Central and Eastern Europe*, London: Routledge.

Lefort, C. (1986) *The Political Forms of Modern Society*, Cambridge: Polity.

Lefort, C. (1988) *Democracy and Political Theory*, Cambridge: Polity.

Lenin, V. I. (1970) 'The right of nations to self-determination', in V. I. Lenin, *Questions of National Policy and Proletarian Internationalism*, Moscow: Progress.

Levine, D. (1996) 'Sociology and the nation-state in an era of shifting boundaries', *Sociological Inquiry*, 66 (3): 253–66.

Lichbach, M. (1989) 'An evaluation of "does economic inequality breed political conflict" studies', *World Politics*, 41: 431–470.

Linklater, A. (1998) *The Transformation of Political Community*, Cambridge: Polity.

Lipset, S. and Rokkan, S. (1967) *Party Systems and Voter Alignments*, New York: Free Press.

List, F. (1909) *The National Systems of Political Economy*, London: Longmans, Green & Co.

Lowenthal, D. (1985) *The Past is a Foreign Country*, Cambridge: Cambridge University Press.

Luhmann, N. (1995) *Social Systems*, Stanford: Stanford University Press.

Luhmann, N. (1998) *Observations on Modernity*, Stanford: Stanford University Press.

Lyotard, J.-F. (1984) *The Postmodern Condition: A Report on Knowledge*, Manchester: Manchester University Press.

McAdam, D., McCarthy, J. D. and Zald, N. (eds) (1996) *Comparative Perspectives on Social Movements: Political Opportunities, Mobilising Structures and Cultural Framings*, Cambridge: Cambridge University Press.

McCrone, D. (1998) *The Sociology of Nationalism*, London: Routledge.

McNeil, W. (1986) *Poly-ethnicity in World History*, Toronto: University of Toronto Press.

Malcolm, N. (1994) *Bosnia: A Short History*, London: Macmillan.

Mann, M. (1987) 'Ruling class strategies and citizenship', *Sociology*, 21 (3): 339–54.

Mann, M. (1993) *The Sources of Social Power, Volume II: The Rule of Classes and Nation-States, 1760–1914*, Cambridge: Cambridge University Press.

Mann, M. (1999) 'The dark side of democracy', *New Left Review*, 235: 18–45.

Mannheim, K. (1952) 'Competition as a cultural phenomenon' in K. Mannheim (1952) *Essays in the Sociology of Knowledge*, London: Routledge and Kegan Paul.

Marcu, E. D. (1976) *Sixteenth Century Nationalism*, New York: Abaris.

Marshall, T. H. (1992) *Citizenship and Social Class*, London: Pluto.

Mayall, J. (1990) *Nationalism and International Society*, Cambridge: Cambridge University Press.

Meinecke, F. (1970) *Cosmopolitanism and the Nation State*, Princeton: Princeton University Press.

Melucci, A. (1995) 'The process of collective identity', in H. Johnson and B. Klandermans (eds) *Social Movements and Culture*, London: UCL Press.

Melucci, A. and Diani, M. (1983) *Nazioni Senza Stato*, Turin: Loescher Editore.

Mestrovic, S. (1994) *The Balkanization of the West: The Confluence of Postmodernism and Postcommunism*, London: Routledge.

Mill, J. S. (1971) *Considerations of Representative Government*, London: Dent.

Miller, D. (1993) 'The nation-state: a modest defense', in C. Brown (ed.) *Political Restucturing in Europe*, London: Routledge.

Miller, D. (1995) *On Nationality*, Oxford: Oxford University Press.

Miller, D. (2000) *Citizenship and National Identity*, Cambridge: Polity.

Minogue, K. (1967) *Nationalism*, London: Batsford.

Moore, B. (2000) *Moral Purity and Persecution in History*, New Haven: Princeton University Press.

Mosse, G. (1975) *The Nationalization of the Masses*, New York: Fertig.

Mosse, G. (1985) *Nationalism and Sexuality*, Madison: University of Wisconsin Press.

Münch, R. (1987) 'Interpretation in a complex institutional order', in J. Alexander, B. Giesen, R. Münch and N. Smelser (eds) *The Micro-Macro Link*, Berkeley: University of California Press.

Neal, A. G. (1998) *National Trauma and Collective Memory*, Armonk, NY: M.E. Sharpe.

Neilsen, F. (1985) 'Towards a theory of ethnic solidarity in modern societies', *American Sociological Review*, 50 (2): 133–149.

Nietzsche, F. (1996) *On the Genealogy of Morals*, Oxford: Oxford University Press.

Nussbaum, M. (1996) 'Patriotism and cosmopolitanism', in *For Love of Country*, Boston: Beacon.

O'Donnell, G. and Schmitter, P. (1986) *Transitions from Authoritarian Rule: Tentative Conclusions about Uncertain Democracies*, Baltimore: Johns Hopkins University Press.

O'Mahony, P. and Delanty, G. (1998; reissued 2001) *Rethinking Irish History: Nationalism, Identity and Ideology*, London: Macmillan.

Offe, C. (1996) *Varieties of Transition: The East European and East German Experience*, Cambridge: Polity.

Olson, M. (1965) *The Logic of Collective Action*, Cambridge, MA: Harvard University Press.

Olzak, Susan, (1992) *The Dynamics of Ethnic Competition and Conflict*, Stanford: Stanford University Press.

Ong, A. (1997) *Flexible Citizenship: The Cultural Logics of Transnationalism*, Durham, NJ: Duke University Press.

Ong, A. and Nonini, D. (1997) *Ungrounded Empires: The Cultural Politics of Modern Chinese Transationalism*, London: Routledge.

Oommen, T. (ed.) (1997) *Citizenship and National Identity: from Colonial to Globalization*, London: Sage.

Ozkirimli, U. (2000) *Theories of Nationalism*, London: Macmillan.

Pels, D. (2000) *The Intellectual as Stranger*, London: Routledge.

Pogge, T. (1992) 'Cosmopolitanism and sovereignty', *Ethics*, 103: 48–75.

Poole, R. (1995) *Morality and Modernity*, London: Routledge.

Ragin, C. (1979) 'Ethnic political mobilisation: the Welsh case', *American Sociological Review*, 44 (4): 619–35.

Ranum, O. (ed.) (1975) *National Consciousness, History and Political Culture in Early Modern Europe*, Baltimore: Johns Hopkins University Press.

Reicher, S. and Hopkins, N. (2001) *Identity, Mobilization and Nation: A Psychology of Mass Action*, London: Sage.

Renan, E. (1990) 'What is a nation?', in H. Bhabbi (ed.) *Nation and Narration*, London: Routledge.

Robertson, R. (1992) *Globalization: Social Theory and Global Culture*, London: Sage.

Robinson, F. (1977) 'Nation formation: the Brass thesis and Muslim separatism', *Journal of Commonwealth Studies*, 15 (3): 215–30.

Robinson, F. (1979) 'Islam and Muslim separatism', in D. Taylor and M. Yapp (eds) *Political Identity in South Asia*, London: Curzon.

Roche, M. (2000) *Mega-Events and Modernity: Olympics and Expos in the Growth of Modernity*, London: Routledge.

Roger, A. (2000) 'Expliquer le nationalisme: les contradictions d'Ernest Gellner', *Arch. Europ. Socio.*, XL1 (2): 189–224.

Rokkan, S. (1975) 'Dimensions of state formation and nation-building', in C. Tilly (ed.) *The Formation of National States in Western Europe*, Princeton: Princeton University Press.

Rorty, R. (1998) *Achieving Our Country: Leftist Thought in Twentieth-Century America*, Cambridge, MA: Harvard University Press.

Rose, N. (1989) *Governing the Soul: The Shaping of the Private Self*, London: Routledge.

Rothchild, D. and Groth, A. (1995) 'Pathological dimensions of domestic and international ethnicity', *Political Science Quarterly*, 110 (1): 69–82.

Roudometof, V. (1999) 'Nationalism, globalization, eastern orthodoxy: "unthinking" the "clash of civilizations" in southern Europe', *European Journal of Social Theory*, 2 (2): 233–47.

197

Rousseau, J.-J. (1968) *The Social Contract*, Harmondsworth: Penguin.

Rousseau, J.-J. (1972) *The Government of Poland*, Indianapolis: Bobbs-Merrill.

Salecl, R. (1993) 'The fantasy structure of nationalist discourse', *Praxis International*, 13: 213–23.

Sassen, S. (1992) *The Global City: New York, London, Tokyo*, Princeton: Princeton University Press.

Scheff, T. J. (1994a) *Bloody Revenge: Emotions, Nationalism and War*, Boulder, CO: Westview.

Scheff, T. J. (1994b) 'Emotions and identity: a theory of ethnic nationalism', in C. Calhoun (ed.) *Social Theory and the Politics of Identity*, Oxford: Blackwell.

Scheler, M. (1972) *Ressentiment*, New York: Schoken.

Schluchter, W. (1985) *The Rise of Western Rationalism: Max Weber's Developmental History*, Berkeley: University of California Press.

Schmitt, C. (1970) *Political Theology*, Cambridge, MA: MIT Press.

Scruton, R. (1990) 'In defense of the nation', in *The Philosopher on Dover Beach*, Manchester: Carcanet.

Sewell, W. (1987) 'Theory of action, dialectic and history: comment on Coleman', *American Journal of Sociology*, 93, 166–72.

Shannon, R. (1963) *Gladstone and the Bulgarian Agitation, 1876*, London: Nelson.

Sièyes, E. (1963) *What is the Third Estate?*, London: Pall Mall Press.

Silverman, M. (1991) *Deconstructing the Nation: Immigration, Racism and Citizenship*, London: Routledge.

Simmel, G. (1955) *Conflict*, Glencol, IL: The Free Press.

Smelser, N. and Alexander, N. (eds) (1999) *Diversity and its Discontents: Cultural Conflict and Common Ground in Contemporary American Society*, Princeton: Princeton University Press.

Smith, A. (1995) *Nations and Nationalism in a Global Era*, Cambridge: Polity.

Smith, A. D. (1986) *The Ethnic Origins of Nations*, Oxford: Blackwell.

Snow, D. and Benford, R. (1992) 'Master frames and cycles of protest', in A. D. Morris and C. McClurg Mueller (eds) *Frontiers in Social Movement Theory*, New Haven, CT: Yale University Press.

Sorel, G. (1950) *Reflections on Violence*, New York: Collier Books.

Soysal, Y. N. (1994) *Limits of Citizenship: Migrants and Postnational Membership in Europe*, Chicago: Chicago University Press.

Spivak, G. (1987) *In Other Words*, London: Routledge.

Stauth, G. and Turner, B. (1988) *Nietzsche's Dance: Resentment, Reciprocity and Resistance in Social Life*, Oxford: Blackwell.

Strydom, P. (1987) 'Collective learning: Habermas's concessions and their theoretical implications', *Philosophy and Social Criticism*, 13 (3): 265–81.

Strydom, P. (1999) 'Triple contingency – the theoretical problem of the public in communication societies', *Philosophy and Social Criticism*, 25 (2): 1–25.

Strydom, P. (2000) *Discourse and Knowledge: The Making of Enlightenment Sociology*, Liverpool: Liverpool University Press.

Sutton, M. (1982) *Nationalism, Positivism and Catholicism: The Politics of Charles Mauras and French Catholics, 1890–1914*, Cambridge: Cambridge University Press.

Szporluk, R. (1988) *Communism and Nationalism: Karl Marx and Friederich List*, Oxford: Oxford University Press.

Sztompka, P. (1994) *The Sociology of Social Change*, Oxford: Blackwell.

Sztompka, P. (2000) 'Cultural trauma: the other face of social change', *European Journal of Social Theory*, 3 (4): 449–66.

Taguieff, P.-A. (1994) *Sur la Nouvelle Droit*, Paris: Descartes & Cie.

Tambini, D. (1998) 'Nationalism: a literature review,' *European Journal of Social Theory*, 1 (1): 137–155.

Tamir, Y. (1993) *Liberal Nationalism*, Princeton: Princeton University Press.

Taylor, C. (1990) *Sources of the Self*, Cambridge, MA: Harvard University Press.

Taylor, C. (1994) 'The politics of recognition', in A. Gutman (ed.) *Multiculturalism: Examining the Politics of Recognition*, Princeton: Princeton University Press.

Taylor, C. (1998) 'Nationalism and modernity', in J. Hall (ed.) *The State of the Nation: Ernest Gellner and the Theory of Nationalism*, Cambridge: Cambridge University Press.

Theweleit, K. (1987) *Male Fantasies*, Cambridge: Polity.

Tilly, C. (1984) *Big Structures, Large Processes, Huge Comparisons*, Cambridge, MA: Blackwell.

Tilly, C. (1986) *The Contentious French*, Cambridge, MA: Harvard University Press.

Tilly, C. (1990) *Coercion, Capital and the European State*, Oxford: Blackwell.

Tilly, C. (1994) 'States and nationalism in Europe, 1492–1992', *Theory and Society*, 23 (1): 131–146.

Tilly, C., Tilly, L. and Tilly, R. (1975) *The Rebellious Century, 1830–1930*, London: Dent.

Tiryakian, E. (1992) 'Dialectics of modernity: reenchantment and dedifferentiation as counter processes', in H. Haferkamp and N. Smelser (eds) *Social Change and Modernity*, Berkeley: University of California Press.

Tiryakian, E. and Nevitte, N. (eds) (1985) *New Nationalisms of the Developed West*, London: Allen & Unwin.

Todorov, T. (1993) *On Human Diversity: Nationalism, Racism and Exoticism in French Thought*, Cambridge, MA: Harvard University Press.

Touraine, A. (1977) *The Self-Production of Society*, Chicago: University of Chicago Press.

Touraine, A. (1995) *Critique of Modernity*, Oxford: Blackwell.

Touraine, A. (1997) *What is Democracy?*, Oxford: Westview.

Trevor-Roper, H. (1983) 'The invention of tradition: the Highland tradition of Scotland', in E. Hobsbawm and T. Ranger (eds) *The Invention of Tradition*, Cambridge: Cambridge University Press.

Trotsky, L. (1931) *The Permanent Revolution*, London: Pathfinder.

Turner, B. S. (ed.) (1990) *Theories of Modernity and Postmodernity*, London: Sage.

Turner, B. S. (2000) 'Globalization, religion and cosmopolitan virtue', *European Journal of Social Theory* 3, 2.

Urry, J. (2000) *Sociology Beyond Societies: Mobilities for the Twenty-First Century*, London: Routledge.

Van Creveld, M. (1999) *The Rise and Decline of the State*, Cambridge: Cambridge University Press.

Van den Berghe, P. (1983) 'Class, race and ethnicity in Africa', *Ethnic and Racial Studies*, 6, 221–236.

Varshney, A. (1993) 'Contested meanings: India's national identity, Hindu nationalism, and the politics of anxiety', *Daedalus*, 122 (3): 227–261.

Viroli, M. (1995) *For Love of Country: An Essay on Patriotism and Nationalism*, Oxford: Claredon.

Vlastos, S. (ed.) (1998) *Mirror of Identity: Invented Traditions of Modern Japan*, Berkeley: University of California Press.

Vries, H. de and Weber, S. (1997) (eds) *Violence, Identity, and Self-Determination*, Stanford: Stanford University Press.

Vujacic, V. and Zaslavsky, V. (1991) 'The causes of disintegration in the USSR and Yugoslavia', *Telos*, 88: 120–40.

Wagner, P. (1994) *A Sociology of Modernity: Liberty and Discipline*, London: Routledge.

Wagner, P. (2001) *Theorizing Modernity*, London: Sage.

Walzer, M. (1977) *Just and Unjust Wars: A Moral Argument with Historical Illustrations*, New York: Basic Books.

199

Watkins, S. (1990) *From Provences into Nations*, Princeton, NJ: Princeton University Press.

Weber, E. (1976) *Peasants into Frenchmen: The Modernization of Rural France, 1877–1914*, Standford: Stanford University Press.

Weber, M. (1998) *Economy and Society*, vol. 1, Berkeley: University of California Press.

Wendt, A. (1994) 'Collective identity formation and the international state', *American Political Science Review*, 88 (2): 384–96.

Williams, R. M. (1994) 'The sociology of ethnic conflicts: comparative international perspectives', *Annual Review of Sociology*, 20: 49–79.

Wittrock, B. (1998) 'Early modernities: varieties and transitions', Daedalus, 127 (3): 19–40.

Wodak, R., de Cillia, R., Reisigl, M. and Liebhart, K. (1999) *The Discursive Construction of National Identity*, Edinburgh: Edinburgh University Press.

Wrong, D. (1994) *The Problem of Social Order: What Unites and Divides Social Society*, Cambridge, MA: Harvard University Press.

Yoshino, K. (1992) *Cultural Nationalism in Contemporary Japan: A Sociological Inquiry*, London: Routledge.

Yoshino, K. (1999) 'Rethinking theories of nationalism: market place perspectives', in K. Yoshino (ed.) *Consuming Ethics and Nationalism: Asian Explorations*, Richmond, Surrey: Curzon Books.

Yuval-Davis, N. (1997) *Gender and Nation*, London: Sage.

Zolo, D. (1997) *Cosmopolis: Prospects for World Government*, Cambridge: Polity.

Zubaida, S. (1989) 'Nations: old and new: comments on Anthony D. Smith's "The myth of the modern nation and the myths of nations"', *Ethnic and Racial Studies*, 12 (3): 329–339.

index

204

207